Human Resource Management in the Sport and Leisure Industry

The sport and leisure sectors possess unique characteristics that pose particular challenges for managers and human resource professionals. The age profile of workers, seasonality, the pressure to achieve short-term results, media intrusion, wide differences in pay between elite and community levels, and the importance of competition and consumer (fan) behaviour all combine to set sport and leisure apart from 'mainstream' business and management. *Human Resource Management in the Sport and Leisure Industry* is a comprehensive and accessible introduction to HRM in sport and leisure that examines these challenges in the context of organisational structure, systems, and individual and group behaviour, encouraging the reader to develop a strategic approach to HRM, and emphasising the importance of reflective professional practice.

The book explores the full range of key issues, themes and concepts in contemporary HRM, including:

- the labour market in sport and leisure
- personal skills in HRM
- recruitment and selection
- learning, training and development
- evaluation and performance appraisal
- change management
- coaching and mentorship.

Covering private, public and voluntary contexts, the book includes a wide range of examples and cases from the real world of sport and leisure management. Each chapter also includes highlighted definitions of key concepts, review questions, summaries and learning objectives, to guide student learning and help managers develop their professional skills. Effective human resource management and development is essential for business success, and therefore this book is important reading for any student or professional working in sport and leisure management.

Chris Wolsey is Principal Lecturer in the Carnegie Faculty of Leeds Metropolitan University. He has held several management and leadership positions including Carnegie Postgraduate Scheme Leader, Director of Undergraduate Studies, Leisure Studies Route Leader and various under/postgraduate course leaderships. In addition he has worked with both BTEC and SkillsActive on the development of national level sport and leisure related qualifications.

Sue Minten is Senior Lecturer in the School of Sport, Tourism and the Outdoors at the University of Central Lancashire. She has held management and leadership roles in both the sport industry and higher education.

Jeffrey Abrams is Subject Group Head for Sport Management and Development at Leeds Metropolitan University. Before becoming a full-time academic, he spent many years as a senior manager in the sport and leisure industry, both in community leisure and in facility management. He also taught physical education in the US.

Human Resource Management in the Sport and Leisure Industry

Chris Wolsey, Sue Minten and Jeffrey Abrams

Routledge
Taylor & Francis Group

LONDON AND NEW YORK

First published 2012
by Routledge
2 Park Square, Milton Park, Abingdon, Oxon OX14 4RN

Simultaneously published in the USA and Canada
by Routledge
711 Third Avenue, New York, NY 10017

Routledge is an imprint of the Taylor & Francis Group, an informa business

British Library Cataloguing in Publication Data
A catalogue record for this book is available from the British Library

Library of Congress Cataloging in Publication Data
Wolsey, Chris.
  Human resource management in the sport and leisure industry/Chris Wolsey, Jeff
  Abrams, Sue Minten.
    p. cm.
  Includes bibliographical references and index.
  1. Sports administration. 2. Sports–Management. 3. Leisure–Management. 4.
  Personnel management. I. Abrams, Jeff, 1956– II. Minten, Sue. III. Title.
  GV713.W65 2011
  796.0683–dc22

                                                                2011014010

ISBN: 978-0-415-42178-2 (hbk)
ISBN: 978-0-415-42179-9 (pbk)
ISBN: 978-0-203-88553-6 (ebk)

Typeset in Sabon and Frutiger
by Wearset Ltd, Boldon, Tyne and Wear

MIX
Paper from
responsible sources
FSC® C004839
www.fsc.org

Printed and bound in Great Britain by
TJ International Ltd, Padstow, Cornwall

Contents

Figures

Tables

Exhibits

Preface

Although there are an increasing number of textbooks dealing with general management issues within the sport and leisure industry, there are few that concentrate specifically on issues relating to human resource management (HRM). This textbook seeks to review a range of HRM issues, as they apply to management practices in both the UK and the wider international sport and leisure context. It seeks to do this by recognising the importance of people and the unique and complicated relationships that are created when an organisation seeks to fulfil its *raison d'être*.

In many ways sport and leisure organisations share several similarities with other industry sectors. However, in itself, the sport and leisure sector is far from homogeneous and represents unique challenges for the ongoing management of related resources; particularly of the human variety! This means that although generic management principles and concepts can be used to illuminate and improve upon current sport and leisure HRM practices, they must be adapted to reflect the unique context of any given situation at any moment in time. In any given set of circumstances there will be several viable options and rarely is there one best way to manage. It is incumbent upon sport and leisure managers, therefore, to understand both the main and all other related issues at play. The interrelatedness of structure, systems and associated people behaviours means that if both a deeper and a wider understanding is not achieved, attempts to solve one problem may generate several other issues down the line. For this reason, it is important for managers to consider the needs of staff, customers and other relevant stakeholders, in order to formulate more appropriate solutions.

Unsurprisingly, despite the range of examples used throughout the book, there are several common themes that emerge. Amongst others, these include the importance of 'learning how to learn' at all levels within the organisation and the fact that there is rarely one best way to manage. Given that the textbook is unlikely to be read in one sitting, it is important to permeate several related themes throughout the book. We do not see this as duplication, but as necessity, given how the book has been constructed and how the majority of its readers are likely to dip in and out of its contents.

Chapter 1 establishes the general context in which human resource (HR) practices take place and provides related links with the rest of the book. This is accomplished by first looking at the development of management theory and then applying this to the specific context of people management issues within sport and leisure organisations. The chapter emphasises the importance of a systems approach to understanding HR issues. This posits that organisations are constructed from a multiplicity of related parts, functions, communities and sub-communities. Of particular importance is the nature of such interrelationships and the way in which this is interpreted, in human terms, by different stakeholders on the ground. The consequence of this is that any decision and/or action is likely to have a ripple effect in other areas; although sometimes it may be an unexpected tsunami if the potential impacts are ill-considered! In some ways, sport and leisure organisations are no different from other organisations. However, in others, they have to respond to a unique set of characteristics not found in more mainstream areas of the economy. This is particularly true of the professional sports market where managers, officials and players are increasingly subjected to unprecedented levels of media scrutiny. This makes the job of working, productively, in this area all the more difficult!

Chapter 2 critically reviews the evidence relating to the UK's sport and leisure employment market. This particularly relates to the ability of the sector to recruit, retain and develop staff; although such areas are developed in more detail by other chapters. Overall, most areas have seen growth over the last two decades. Some issues are seen to be general to the overall labour market (e.g. economic, demographic, political/legal, geographic/globalisation), whilst others are seen to be specific to sport and leisure (e.g. flexibility of labour, volunteers, professionalisation). These are not mutually exclusive and interact to create a unique management context for this people dominated area of both the formal and informal economy. For example, many areas involve volunteers; whether referring to weekend amateur sport or the 70,000 volunteers needed for the 2012 London Olympics. Paradoxically, against this backdrop, there is a continual push to professionalise the industry. At the same time, despite the continued expansion of this area, there appears to be an oversupply of labour and sustained reports of a lack of suitably skilled and qualified staff. This presents unique strategic HRM challenges for this area. Perhaps the inauguration of the Chartered Institute for the Management of Sport and Physical Activity, in 2011, will provide fresh leadership and help resolve ongoing tensions for the industry.

Chapter 3 reflects upon the importance, significance and practical implications of organisational structure and culture for sport and leisure organisations. It takes a critical look at the relevant theories, models and concepts whilst providing an evaluation of their application and limitations. This is achieved by using examples from the world of sport and leisure to illustrate key ideas. The topic of structure can be a powerful and much underrated influence, both positive and negative, in terms of organisational performance. Structure often means an organisational chart on a wall with lines of accountability and responsibility. In practical, day-to-day dealings, structure is rarely associated with management issues such as strategy, customer needs and improving communication, staff motivation and overall performance levels. However, organisational structure has huge and often latent potential to positively move things forward in all of these important areas. It is the structure that places people in job related activities and provides the conduit for accountability, communication and resource allocation. In addition, it is likely to heavily influence the interpersonal relationships that form the lifeblood of all organisations and makes them tick. This relates to the concept of organisational culture, which represents the shared values that are at the heart of the organisation and are manifested in a number of ways that can either contribute or detract from both selective and overall measures of organisational effectiveness and performance.

Chapter 4 provides an overview of the factors affecting individual and group decision-making and behaviour. It does not set out to produce a detailed look at each theory, as this has been done many times before by various authors and textbooks. Instead, it seeks to provide a synthesis of related theory in order to produce a more coherent understanding of the issues as a whole. It begins by providing an historical context in which more contemporary theories have developed. What is interesting, however, is the extent to which the lessons of the past, whilst being mediated by the present, are still relevant to the current and, probably, future demands faced by sport and leisure managers. Unsurprisingly, what this means is that there is no easy prescription or one size fits all solution to such issues. What is clear, however, is that it is an understanding of the lived experiences both of staff and managers, combined with the influence of the prevailing context, that is likely to lead to better quality decisions, actions and subsequent performance. This makes it all the more important that managers are both reflective and reflexive in their approach both to their own individual development and to that of their co-workers.

Chapter 5 provides a summary of the historical development of the sport and leisure management profession and then progresses to explain some of the main areas of importance with respect to the personal skills required of its managers. Moreover, it seeks to review the tension between generic management skills and those required more specifically for the sport and leisure sector. Increasingly, managers from outside the sector are being headhunted to provide leadership in a number of related areas. For example, Paul Deighton, former chief operating officer with Goldman Sachs Europe, was recruited to the role of chief executive of the London 2012 Olympics. Where there is a large degree of agreement, however, is in relation to the perceived importance of the concept of 'self-awareness' and how this relates to the identification and subsequent development of appropriate personal skills in this area. This issue is located within a wider consideration of the evidence surrounding National Occupational Standards, competencies, emotional intelligence, learning styles, values, reflection and reflexivity. Such issues and concepts co-exist in a management context that can either be proactive or simply produces more of the same, failing to learn from ongoing mistakes and opportunities to promulgate performance improvements.

Chapter 6 looks at the issue of recruitment and selection practices within sport and leisure. Recruitment is regarded as being the identification of a relevant pool of applicants, whilst selection is the identification of the most appropriate candidate(s) from this pool. The evidence suggests that employment levels, in this area, appear to be on the increase. However, despite increasing levels of demand for such employment, there remain widespread reports of skill shortages (see also Chapter 2). Of course, whilst this also relates to many other HRM areas, such as training and development (see Chapter 7), it is incumbent upon organisations to ensure that recruitment practices are making a positive contribution to the overall HR processes and subsequent performance levels (see Chapter 8). Not just who, but the way staff are recruited may prove to be significant in the ongoing development of the psychological contract between employee and employer. Recruitment and selection should be seen as an integral component of an overarching approach to HRM and the overall achievement of organisational objectives. However, although evidence now suggests that more attention is being paid to such issues, many organisations still adopt an ad hoc approach that is unlikely to add planned value to overall performance levels. The chapter reviews the alternatives available and also highlights some innovative ways in which this HR function can be enhanced.

Chapter 7 provides a discussion of the evidence relating to learning, training and development initiatives within the sport and leisure sector. It starts by exploring related UK government strategies, such as 'Investors in People', with a specific focus upon industry upskilling. Given the complexity of the area, it is not surprising that moving forward from a relatively low paid, low skilled workforce is a complex issue. A key problem appears to be that sport organisations do not necessarily see a clear relationship between upskilling and improving the quality of the product. Likewise, they may also fail to make the links between investing in its employees and related HR functions, such as employee recruitment and retention. More importantly, perhaps, is the lack of evidence relating to the needs of the customer and attempts to directly link this with learning, training and overall development initiatives. Customer service is of crucial importance in this regard. However, particularly given the prevailing political and economic context, employers may be unwilling to invest in forms of development that fail to yield immediate and tangible added value. Overall, the evidence suggests that sport and leisure organisations adopt a lukewarm approach to learning, training and development initiatives, many failing to recognise the potential benefits and impact of embedding a learning culture into the overall performance of the organisation.

Chapter 8 considers evaluation and performance appraisal, primarily at the level of the individual and the group. Performance evaluation and rewards should take place within a strategic approach to HRM. This needs to take account of the open systems context in which most organisations operate. Managers must ensure that performance and reward systems are flexible enough to respond to such challenges. The chapter provides a review of the existing evidence and relates this to several examples from the public and private sectors of the sport and leisure industry. What is clear is that there is no one best way of organising this and that there are, often, a number of different stakeholders to account for within this process. As a consequence, each organisation, each team and each individual represents a unique set of motivations and associated implications; both positive and negative. It is only when all such factors are combined do the inputs both of capital and of human resources transform into outputs that can be measured against overarching organisational objectives. It is only by better understanding such interrelationships and developing complementary systems, procedures, training and personal skills that the performance appraisal process can be more effectively used both for appraisal and developmental purposes.

Chapter 9 provides an overview of the area of organisational development (OD) and how it may be relevant to the process of managing change within sport organisations. In addition, it examines the related concept of organisational change and the key theories that have been used to manage change within sport organisations; including selected approaches to managing resistance to change. OD has been traditionally associated with planned approaches to change. However, as this area of study has developed, the dynamism and complexity of related issues have been better recognised by the literature. This has led to OD and change management approaches that are termed emergent, rather than wholly planned. A key feature of OD continues to be its underpinning humanistic values. This is important to sport and leisure organisations who should respond to the impetus to change by thinking through the consequences with respect both to the internal staff and to external stakeholders. Several examples from the sporting world are used to illustrate such issues including Sport England's approach to organisational restructuring, Phil Jackson's approach to team development within professional basketball and the approach taken by the Amateur Athletic Association, in the UK, to strategy development and the resistance to change.

Chapter 10 concludes the book by picking up and running with one of its main themes, i.e. how to encourage ongoing learning within individuals, teams and the wider organisation. In this context, the chapter begins by arguing the case for coaching and mentoring within sport and leisure organisations and concludes by locating this within the wider concept of the learning organisation. There is a growing body of evidence that suggests that embedding appropriate coaching and mentoring systems can yield benefits in terms of individual, group and organisational learning/development. However, this is not just about well-resourced talent development programmes and the executive coaching of senior managers. In order to have a discernible impact, it must also have a much greater reach. This relates as much to part-time, casual and voluntary staff as it does to full-time employees; arguably more so dependent upon the sport or leisure sector under consideration. HR thinking and initiatives should seek to get the very best out of all staff, particularly those on the front line of service delivery who are much more likely to understand the needs of the customer.

Overall, the book seeks to utilise the lessons from both the generic and related HR management literature. These have then been applied to the unique context and practice of sport and leisure organisations. Given the sports psychology origins of business coaching, reviewed in the concluding chapter, it is interesting that wider business organisations are now seeking to transfer the lessons from sport to the business context … it's good to see it's not all just one way traffic!

Chapter 1

Human resource management in the sport and leisure industry

Learning outcomes

By the end of this chapter you will be able to:

- define human resource management and associated models;
- locate human resource management within a wider systems and strategic management framework;
- identify the unique nature of sport and leisure management in the context of this textbook.

1.1 Introduction

> For us, our employees matter most. It just seems common sense to me that if you start off with a happy well-motivated workforce, you're much more likely to have happy customers. And in due course the resulting profits will make your shareholders happy.
>
> (Richard Branson, 2009:410)

Richard Branson operates a number of businesses in the broad area of sport and leisure and highlights the critical role of people in their successful operations. This opening chapter will both define and explain the origins of human resource management (HRM) and its ongoing relationship with wider management issues such as organisational strategy and performance. Moreover, it will locate such discussions within the specific context of the market for sport and leisure, in all of its various guises. In doing this, it will provide a 'systems' context in which all the following chapters can be located. This requires a discussion of the functional elements of HRM, such as recruitment and training, but also an understanding of the interrelationships between each area and the wider organisation environment.

Concept check

Systems context

Slack and Parent (2006) argue that a 'systems' approach dominates organisational theory as applied to sports management research. Within related management literature 'systems thinking' and 'systems theory' refers to the contention that an organisation is made up of many interrelated parts. To change one is likely to affect the workings of another. It is, therefore, necessary both to understand and to extrapolate the effects both of decisions and of subsequent actions upon all areas within the organisational system.

Although there are both practical and conceptual challenges involved in this endeavour, a deeper understanding of workplace complexities is more likely to lead to better strategic and operational decision-making. This, in turn, allows for a much more considered approach to the implementation of decisions through enhanced individual, group and organisational performance.

1.2 Sport and leisure

It is important to identify what is meant by sport and leisure in order to set out the scope of what will be included in this text and the specific context in which pertinent examples will be applied, developed and/or understood.

Sport and leisure refers to an extremely wide range of activities delivered by a wide range of providers in a wide number of different settings (also see Chapter 2: The market for labour in leisure and sport). With regard to sport, there has been much debate over its definition and, as a consequence, there is 'no universal agreement about the meaning, purpose, and organisation of sports' Coakley (2003:25). Furthermore, Horne *et al.* (1999:xv) argue that sport 'has different meanings in different societies and refers to different activities at different historical moments'. This view is acknowledged by Coakley (2003:25), who states that any definition of sport 'reflects the structure and organisation of relationships and social life in a particular society at a particular point in time'. This establishes the importance of context when considering management issues and their likely positive and negative affects upon a variety of stakeholders.

> ### Concept check
>
> ## Stakeholders
>
> This refers to all parties who can either yield a tangible effect upon and/or can be affected by the decisions and actions of any given organisation or industry.

Given the potential complexities associated with defining 'sport' and wider notions of 'leisure', the book will utilise the more restricted typology provided by SkillsActive, the UK's Sector Skills Council for Active Leisure and Learning (refer to Table 1.1).

Broadly speaking, 'SkillsActive' defines the area in terms of facility and institutional provision. As a consequence, the book will tend to concentrate upon sport and 'active' leisure. We will use this typology, but will also extend this to wider notions of related commercial provision, such as sports retailing, as appropriate.

1.3 Management

The generic term of management has been explained in a number of ways. Lussier and Kimbal (2009:12) posit that there are four main management functions; namely planning, organising, leading and controlling. These are overlaid with the management roles of dealing with interpersonal, informational and decisional issues. All act concurrently to produce a performance outcome that, typically, is measured against the prevailing objectives of the organisation.

In many ways, such contemporary notions of management represent little change from the early 'classical management' theorists such as Henri Fayol's (1916) and Frederick

Table 1.1 Categories of organisational settings in sport

Sport and recreation	Sport and leisure facilities, sports clubs, stadia/arena facilities, sports services, sports administrators, sports development, national governing bodies of sport, community/youth centre, coaching, activity leadership.
Health and fitness	Private fitness clubs, hotel-based clubs, multi-group clubs, workplace clubs, public leisure centres, residential clubs.

Source: SkillsActive (2005).

Taylor's (1911) related concepts of 'classical' and 'scientific' management, respectively. Fayol argued that there were six basic functions of management:

1 forecasting
2 planning
3 organising
4 commanding
5 coordinating
6 controlling.

Although, contemporary notions of management have tended to conflate the terms planning, forecasting and commanding under a more generic 'leadership' banner, there has been surprisingly little movement over the last 100 years in this regard.

Where Fayol advocated a general theory of management, Taylor was much more concerned with the efficient use of available resources to produce the most advantageous and productive outcomes for the organisation. By identifying the best way to achieve defined outcomes (typically with regard to manufactured products), it should then be possible to incentivise the workforce based upon the production systems in place.

However, although both approaches have to be placed within the prevailing socio-political and economic context of the time, what neither factored into their thinking was the pivotal role that 'people' can play in securing organisational performance. Under such early notions of management, workers were merely a cog in the wheel; an important cog, but a cog nevertheless. It was the managers' role to 'command' and then 'control' specified actions in order to maximise production and thus profit.

In 1945 the social psychologist, Elton Mayo, moved the thinking forward by attempting to better understand the motivation of individuals within groups and thus, management 'systems' of organising, commanding and controlling. Mayo 'argued that managers would only succeed if these groups accepted their authority and leadership. He concluded that it was a major role of the manager to organise teamwork and so sustain co-operation' (Stacey, 2003:27) ... rather like the role of the coach in team based sports (also see Chapter 10). As a consequence, a 'Human Relations' school of thought developed, based loosely upon behaviourist principles and the notion that understanding people's motivations and influences is critical to ensuring business success (see Chapter 4). Interestingly, what was beginning to emerge was a realisation that there needed to be an alignment between the values and goals of the worker(s), the manager(s) and, by implication, the wider organisation. Such symbiotic behaviour necessitates management recognition of the unique importance of workers and requires an ongoing confidence and trust between both parties.

Concept check

Behaviourism

Behaviourism is founded on the study of observable behaviours. The major flaw in this learning theory is that it does not seek to consider the reasons for action, merely the consequences. This can be related to classical and scientific notions of management by providing information on the behavioural effect(s) of external stimuli, e.g. the effect of working conditions on productivity.

Hence, early notions of management were dominated by a preoccupation with production. Although certain aspects of the sport and leisure industry fit with such ideas, e.g. sports retailing, a significant proportion of sport and leisure provision is dominated by more intangible notions of 'experience' and 'customer service'.

1.4 Sport and management

In the world of contemporary sport it is commonly claimed that, at its elite end at least, sport's management is complex because the product it delivers to participants and fans are so idiosyncratic. This claim is accompanied by the view that while professional sport is in large part just another form of business, it has a range of special features that demand a customized set of practices to ensure its effective operation.

(Smith and Stewart, 2010:1)

Exhibit 1.1

The impact of the external environment on English rugby

Adcroft and Teckman (2008) looked to develop a conceptual model that applies performance and competitiveness to the Rugby World Cup. Unsurprisingly, they conclude that it is a complex area reflecting the interplay of the internal characteristics of the teams and the external conditions. This is a feature of all organisations and can be demonstrated by the evolution of rugby union during the period 1995–2010.

In 1995 the International Rugby Board ushered in a new era of professionalism to the game. This represents a common theme in many sports where popularity raises the possibility of a more commercial focus. In rugby, this resulted in non-sanctioned rebel tours and an increasing number of 'stars' moving code to rugby league, where the perception was that their talents would be better remunerated. Under such external pressures, governing bodies, in an attempt to retain some degree of control, are often forced to acquiesce to the pervasive tide of profit and professionalism.

Fast forward to 2010 and we can see the difficulties of attempting to balance the competitive 'on-pitch' pressures of rugby union, with those relating more directly to its management off the pitch. This continues to be problematic for a number of high profile clubs who continue to struggle to pay costs, particularly player wages, from insufficient revenue streams. This reflects a common theme within many professional sports. This has also attracted an influx of several overseas investors into the UK game who are not heavily influenced by the prevailing amateur rugby culture. In 2008, South African businessman Johann Rupert invested £7 million into Saracens and appointed fellow South Africans Brendan Ventera as Director of Rugby and Edwards Griffiths as Chief Executive. Griffiths argues: 'I think some people still haven't grasped the full overall reality of English rugby which is that many of the clubs rely for survival on what amounts to charitable donations by individuals. That's not sustainable' (in Kitson, 2009:11). Griffiths is currently overseeing a significant organisational change at Saracens who, according to Kitson (2009), are reported to be losing around £2 million per season. This is designed to inject a much more commercial focus which has also entailed cost controls resulting in an unprecedented 15 players being released by the club. Despite the bad feeling and discontent generated by such moves, Saracens won the Guinness Premiership in 2009 and continue to push on with their business plans, for example, a revenue generating match at Wembley Stadium with South Africa in November 2009 which Saracens won 23–22.

Whilst South African Rugby players are moving to England, several of England's rugby stars are moving to France and farther afield; largely influenced by the external pull of higher wages and a different lifestyle. This has important implications for the English game. Ian McGeechan was the former Director of Rugby at Wasps before leading the British Lions tour to South Africa in the summer of 2009. He argues:

> If a player wants to play for the money, that is his decision ... It's a bigger problem that maybe the RFU are facing. With the Euro and the pound as it is, the majority of money is in France and I think the concern must be that we'll end up with players who are probably still having an ambition of playing for England not playing as part of the Premiership and I don't think that is a good thing for English rugby.
>
> *Source*: Stafford (2009:9)

In France, many professional rugby clubs are owned and subsidised by the local authority (Stafford, 2009). In many ways this gives them an advantage over English clubs who survive purely upon commercial criteria. In economic terms, France is attractive because of the poor value of the pound against the euro and the more favourable tax treatment for professional sports performers in France, although this is currently under review. Combine this with the fact that, from April 2010, in the UK, those earning more than £150,000 will have to pay a further 10 per cent in tax. It is clear, therefore, that sport does not exist in its own vacuum and will be subject a variety of external influences and pressures. This has consequences for both club and international rugby as the RFU does not have the same 'release' agreements with French clubs as they have negotiated with their English counterparts. This will continue to cause issues until resolved to the mutual satisfaction of players, agents, clubs, coaches and governing bodies.

When applying generic management principles to the sport and leisure context, it is necessary to understand the fragmented nature of the industry. Such heterogeneity, in both the internal and external environment, often leads to unique challenges. For example, when thinking about a typical sports manager, many people would think about the management of local, public sector, sport and leisure centres. However, over the last 10–15 years there has been an explosion in similar private sector provision and a concomitant increase in customer expectations and, thus, standards. This presents differing challenges both to staff and managers, who are tasked with delivering a service that is measured against a variety of public, commercial and voluntary sectors' strategic objectives. Increasingly, such areas are operating in the same marketplace; the local golf club vs the Marriot or De vere Country Club concept; the public swimming baths vs the latest state of the art leisure and fitness complex provided by the self-proclaimed UK's premier health charity 'Nuffield Health' or the commercial operator 'Virgin Active'. This makes managing, within such areas, all the more challenging and interesting!

Chapter 2, 'The market for labour in leisure and sport' looks more specifically at the voluntary sector, which has been subject to significant change during the past 20 years and still relies heavily upon non-paid staff. Indeed, Cuskelly *et al.* (2006, quoted in Doherty 2006:105) note that sports volunteering accounts for approximately one-quarter of all volunteers in Australia, Canada, New Zealand and England. Similarly, Hoye *et al.* (2006) presents a typology of sports organisations based upon three sectors:

1 state or public (and specialist agencies);
2 non-profit or voluntary (e.g. clubs, voluntary associations, government bodies);
3 professional or commercial sport organisations (professional leagues and teams).

Concept check

The internal and external environment

The internal (or micro) environment refers to all the operations and management issues found within the control of the organisations. Typically, these would include operational issues such as the organisational culture and the internal politics that exist within all organisations. It would also include many of the functional issues that are traditionally dealt with by personnel departments.

The external (or macro) environment includes all the issues that are located outside the boundaries of the organisation. Such issues are subject to either limited (in)direct control or no control whatsoever. Typically, these would include political, economic, social, technological, environmental and legal (PESTEL). As such, these include wider issues to do with the local, national and/or world economy.

What is important, however, is that there is an appropriate strategic and operational fit between the idiosyncrasies exhibited by both the internal and external environment.

However, in reality, the above represents at least six areas all with differing functions and agendas. In addition, it would be inappropriate to ignore the role that sport/leisure activities play within the overall approach to employee well-being and general organisational health in non-sport/leisure companies, through initiatives such as corporate fitness programmes (Lillian *et al.*, 2009).

Clearly, the purpose and context of the organisation will impact upon all management decisions and, in particular, those relating to its workers. This is further complicated by a multiplicity of agendas, from both internal and external stakeholders. This can lead to conflict, apathy or cooperation, dependent upon how this is handled by management. In this context Checkland and Holwell (2004:51) argue: 'that multiple conflicting objectives from multiple stakeholders are the norm in human situations. Rational intervention in such situations requires that to be accepted.' They go on to give the examples of the Olympic Games where the agendas of the International Olympic Committee, host city, athletes, coaches, officials, hot dog sellers, sponsors, television companies, television viewers or even potential terrorist groups, are all operating simultaneously.

As with all organisations, one must also differentiate between the different types and levels of management. Lussier and Kimball (2009), in a sporting context, make the distinction between Top, Middle, First-Line managers and operatives. Moreover, they argue it is possible to further specify managers as being 'general', 'functional' or 'project' oriented, as below:

● **general:** deal with all aspects of management, but tend not to specialise;
● **functional:** typically, specialise in one aspect of management such as marketing, operations, finance, HRM, but may not have a general overview;
● **project:** deal with a specific aspect of management or case study such as event management or new product development. This, usually, requires a general range of skills and knowledge but applied to a specific issue.

In addition, there are several other factors that both individually and collectively contribute to the uniqueness of this area, particularly when applied specifically to sport.

1.5 The unique characteristics of sport

Hoye *et al.* (2006:4–5), based on the earlier work of Smith and Stewart (1999), offer a useful synopsis of how sport varies from other areas of the economy. It is incumbent upon sport managers to recognise this when dealing with both general and people management issues. These are both reviewed and added to in the remainder of this section.

Product vs service. Whilst the majority of early management literature was concerned with productivity and 'products', much of the sport and leisure market relates to more intangible notions of 'service' and 'experience'. This makes the management of such provision, potentially, more problematic.

Social capital. The literature surrounding sport and leisure highlights the externalities that sport and leisure can bestow upon its participants and society as a whole. This forms the agenda of many public and voluntary sector bodies. However, Sam (2009) argues that this may result in 'wicked problems' for public sector sport providers due to the multiplicity of competing agendas. For example, the need to be increasingly professional and commercially oriented whilst ensuring that important, but non-profit-making aspects of provision are protected. This is also true of many voluntary, public and quasi public sector bodies. Often such issues are not mutually exclusive and may promote the possibility of partnership working as each organisation looks to tap into the expertise of the other.

Professionalisation. Houlihan and Green (2009:678), in a case study of Sport England and UK Sport 'suggest that modernisation has resulted in a narrowing of the two organizations' objectives, the adoption of business-like principles and a "command and control" regime in relationships with key frontline delivery partners'. Whilst this may also mirror a similar need for other, related, sporting bodies to become more professional in their approach, there are potential consequences for those, on a regional and more local level, who are asked to deliver a more substantive management function whilst still operating on a largely voluntary basis. Indeed, as a result of a change of government and differing economic and political agendas, both organisations (Sport England and UK Sport) are now set to merge resulting in a new variety of both strategic and HR issues to resolve.

Stakeholders. Sport and leisure provision typically attracts an increased number of stakeholders. Potentially, this makes the management of such provision more complex.

Brand loyalty and passion of customers/fans. Often sport, in particular, attracts a very passionate and loyal following which is difficult to replicate with other non-sport products/ services. Customers are 'fans' and regard themselves as de facto owners of the organisation with a strong emotional attachment to something that plays a very important part of their lives. However, this view is not universally supported. Smith and Stewart (2010) argue that this claim is difficult to empirically support.

Competitive balance. Sport and related competitive leisure activities are predicated on the unpredictability of the outcome. In order to maintain the currency of the activity it is necessary to have a business and/or management model that ensures that there is competitive balance when in most other areas of business/management the aim is to dominate the competition in order to maximise profits over the longer term. This means that professional sports leagues try to equalise the power that exists between the teams. In the US, the business model is predicated upon the draft pick system where the weakest teams are able to recruit the best new players. Similarly, the English Rugby Football Union operates a 'revenue smoothing scheme' where each Premiership team supplying a player to the Elite Player Squad (EPS) generates approximately £150,000 to be paid to the Premier Rugby League. This is then distributed equally amongst all 12 teams. However, this is by no means the case in all sports. In the UK, the English Football Premiership is predicated upon a less inclusive revenue distribution model. This makes it extremely difficult, in the absence of a rich bene-factor, for other teams to challenge the top four 'Premiership' teams of Manchester United, Chelsea, Liverpool and Arsenal. Arguably, this inequity also extends to the European con-text where UEFA, the governing body for football in Europe, are currently looking to intro-duce a 'Fair Play' policy to all clubs who play in European competition. This limits the impact of external money in football, by providing disincentives for clubs to spend more than they legitimately earn; particularly in the player transfer market. Interestingly, this does not include investment in areas such as youth player development and therefore pro-vides a further incentive for clubs to promote from within.

Accountability and media intrusion. From public sector leisure providers (councillors, users, non-users, voters, government agencies) to professional sports clubs (government, fans, media) there is more likely to be an increased accountability for performance. Often within the highly visible world of professional sports this can lead to accountability both on and off the field of play, as individuals are expected, by some, to be role models for wider societal standards of behaviour. John Terry, the England football captain, lost this honour due to a number of alleged 'off-pitch' difficulties, whilst Wayne Rooney, the Manchester United star, has endured similar personal difficulties and media intrusion. However, Rooney and his agent managed to negotiate a healthy pay rise around the same time, whilst Terry has now been given back the captain's armband. In such instances, context is extremely important and judgements must often be made very quickly and in the full introspective spotlight of the omnipresent and all pervasive sports media. However, abstention may often be viewed a less risky alternative; although in some cases this could be viewed an abroga-tion of responsibility. For example, whilst the England football manager, Fabio Capello, may have been right to remove the armband from Terry, in the first instance, reinstating this honour will have inevitable consequences. As Winter (2011) argues:

> Let's get this right. Fabio Capello took the armband off John Terry because the England manager worried about how his off-field exploits could impact on the dressing-room dynamic. Now Capello intends handing it back without worrying about the dressing-room dynamic ... Capello's action is naive, bemusing and poten-tially very damaging. Let's face it: England are stuck with Capello, team and manager locked in a loveless marriage. Usual Football Association paralysis ensured he survived the World Cup fiasco despite a catalogue of errors before and during the tournament, on and off the pitch. Some poor form and results have not prompted the FA to inter-vene to rescue the team.

Lack of strategic view. The scrutiny and pressure to achieve success provides unique challenges for those operating in such areas, particularly in relation to professional sport, where success is often measured in very narrow and short-term ways. This may lead to quick fixes that belie a more strategic and long-term view. For example, Queens Park Rangers Football club, on paper, represent one of the richest clubs in world football. However, they have had 12 managers during the preceding four years to January 2010. It doesn't take a genius to observe that a period of stability and joined up strategic thinking may well lead to more success here for owners, managers, players and fans.

Size of organisation. There is often a misconception that sports clubs represent major employers when the reality is that many represent very small business operations; both at professional, commercial and voluntary sector level. This results in operational restrictions and, often, a very limited organisational structure that cannot support elaborate strategic aspirations/plans; particularly in relation to small or non-existent HR departments.

Pay. In the voluntary sector, monetary gain is rarely a motivator and plays a much more limited role in the psychological contract that draws participants to such sport and/or leisure organisations. The application of early management theories would advocate the critical role that pay has to play in the psychological contract between workers and the organisation. Conversely, in professional sports organisations, traditional notions of pay are turned upside as it is the producers of the 'experience' on the field (equivalent of shop floor), that are the main financial beneficiaries (Hoye *et al.*, 2006).

Seasonality and variability of demand. The very nature of many sporting and leisure pursuits dictates that demand will vary throughout the year. Golf courses and other outdoor activities may well be poorly attended during the winter, whilst health clubs will be relatively empty on a hot summer's day. This leads to a need to have a flexible labour force that can respond to such fluctuations in demand. This is reviewed further during Chapter 2.

The age profile of workers. Wolsey and Abrams (2010) argue that young people make up an important proportion of the UK workforce in the area of sport. Although there is a paucity of information in this area, Primault (2006) also alludes to similar trends across Europe. However, despite this, as we enter a new decade, UK unemployment rates amongst the 16–24 age band are at record levels. This has several consequences; for example, employers in this area may become complacent in their recruitment strategies, which may then lead to future retention difficulties (also see Chapter 6). In addition, there is a burgeoning literature dealing with the employment of Generation X vs Generation Y sectors of the population. Broadly, younger segments of the population are categorised as Generation Y, whilst those middle age 'baby boomers' are categorised as Generation X. Overall, the Generation Y section of the population are looking to feel challenged and engaged by their work, whilst also looking for flexibility and a better work life balance. It is important to recognise the needs of both groups when developing HR strategies designed to extract maximum value from such employees.

1.6 The psychological contract

Clearly, the successful performance of sport and leisure organisations is dependent upon a number of important and interrelated variables. Management must balance such factors in order to create long-term vision and strategic direction whilst simultaneously ensuring that day-to-day operational imperatives are adhered to and reviewed, as appropriate.

By its very service nature, the sport and leisure sectors are very staff intensive, making HRM essential to understanding successful business practice in this area. Many of the factors reviewed above, demonstrate the importance of human performance, both at individual and at group level. This, in turn, is mediated by individual differences in attitudes and related behaviours (see Chapter 4). It is the role of management to understand and implement appropriate organisational responses both to internal and external factors that affect such performance. Within this performance rubric, the psychological contract between the individual and the organisation is key to future successes.

Concept check

The psychological contract

The **psychological contract** represents a tacit series of role expectations between the individual and the organisation. To some extent, particularly on initial recruitment, a substantive proportion of this may be covered by the original job description and employment contract. However, roles have a habit of changing during the tenure of employment and, therefore, the 'psychological contract' is likely to vary, through time, being governed largely by individual perceptions of the trade-off between context, effort and reward.

The English female cricket team represents one of the best female sporting teams in the world, when measured against their competitive results. Their success is predicated upon a number of variables; chief amongst these is their professional approach to the sport. Whilst their international competitors are still restricted by their amateur status and lack of investment, the English team are backed by the England and Wales Cricket Board (ECB) who, from April 2008, have provided funding for five full-time and three part-time coaching contracts. This level of player support is unprecedented in the female game and gives England a clear advantage. Paradoxically, Claire Taylor, who is acknowledged as one of the best female cricketers in the world, has chosen to maintain her developing career as a management consultant, alongside her cricketing commitments, in order to maintain a greater work–life flexibility; a 'Generation Y' decision if ever there was one! (see reference to the age profile of workers earlier in the chapter). According to Booth (2009:13)

> the amateurism of the opposition is doing England's cause no harm at all, and Taylor believes that the structure put in place by the England hierarchy is maintaining their edge. 'There are now higher expectations as to how much work the team puts in', she says. 'We're a well-drilled squad and there's plenty of time to practice … it's an advantage.'

In other words, the psychological contract is evolving and in return for the increased resources of the ECB, the English players are now subject to a more professional ethos and a more demanding series of expectations.

1.7 The management of human resources in sport and leisure

Although there are those that point out that there is little consensus around the meaning of HRM (Boselie et al., 2005; Edgar and Geare, 2009), it is useful to develop an overview of this area in order to then construct a better understanding of how this can be applied to a variety of sporting and leisure contexts.

Writing in connection with professional rugby clubs, Darcy et al. (2008:414) argue that 'the fundamental issues of how to recruit, develop and motivate key people are central to all HRM. HRM encompasses seven discrete HRM practices, namely: planning, recruitment, screening, orientation, training and support, performance management and recognition'. Similarly, Hoye et al. (2006:112–113) adds retention to the mix by arguing that: 'Human Resource Management refers to the design, development, implementation, management and evaluation of systems and practices used by employers to recruit, select, develop, reward, retain and evaluate their workforce.'

Given the increasingly short-term and transient nature of paid employment in this area (Ravenscroft and Gilchrist, 2005), combined with a seemingly declining number of volunteers (Cuskelley et al., 2006), it is not surprising that the issue of retention finds its way into the list of functional tasks to be undertaken under the generic HR heading. Similarly, it is not surprising that both definitions are reflective of earlier notions of classical and scientific management. However, whilst such definitions are also reminiscent of the traditional role of the 'personnel' officer, the missing and critical HRM ingredient is the management link between these functions and the strategic objectives of the sport or leisure organisation (Wendell Braithwaite, 2004).

Similarly, Robinson (2008) argues that strategic HR is important with respect to the performance of the organisation, when measured against its objectives. A Chartered Institute of Personnel and Development survey (2007, quoted in Robinson, 2008:42) found that nine out of ten HR professionals regarded being 'more strategic' to be very important over the medium term. What is interesting, however, is that this should already be an important and integral part of HR. This may imply that the realities of business practice mean that it is difficult to move from a micro perspective, based on the traditional personnel function, to one that is more strategic in its orientation. In this context, Brown *et al.* (2009) argue that HR managers still tend to retain the employee centredness of the personnel function but are then challenged to put this in a management context.

One of the main ways of achieving a more strategic outlook is through integration with business partners (Robinson, 2008). This is particularly relevant to sport and leisure organisations, who are more likely to have a range of disparate stakeholders. However, whilst partnership working may force a number of strategic questions to be asked, it also adds a further layer of complexity to the general management process, particularly in relation to an agreed set of shared objectives and, also, their subsequent implementation through related HR initiatives.

Hoye *et al.* (2006:109) argue that 'There are, however, significant differences between business and sport organizations, which result in modifications to generic human resource practices.' Given earlier discussions about the unique nature of sports this is hardly surprising. However, this does prove to be problematic as 'Rarely before has sport been taken seriously in a management research context' (Adcroft, 2009:5). Similarly, Slack and Parent (2006) argue that there is a paucity of research in this area with limited theoretical approaches and narrow research methodologies. As with much generic management research, this results in a relatively narrow and restrictive understanding of issues affecting such HR practices.

What is clear is that generic prescriptions are of limited use and strategic initiatives are highly context dependent. However, whilst evidence appears to indicate this is true in general business terms (Harney and Dundon, 2006; Robinson, 2008; Antonio *et al.*, 2008) there is a paucity of evidence with respect to sporting performance (Adcroft and Teckman, 2008; Böhlke and Robinson, 2009).

Moreover, HRM should be viewed as an holistic series of management functions designed to elicit maximum performance from its employees. This requires an integrative approach to the HR systems employed by the organisation.

1.8 Systems theory

Slack and Parent (2006) argue that a 'systems' approach dominates organisational theory as applied to sports management research. Systems theory posits that organisations turn inputs into desirable outputs as efficiently and effectively as possible. In other words organisational objectives are achieved for the lowest cost and, therefore, highest return. This could be measured in a number of ways. For example, in terms of profit for cinema operators, or league titles for sports teams, or numbers returned to education/work for community leisure outreach programmes. However, Slack and Parent (2006:13) view such studies as

> overly deterministic, ignoring the role of strategic choice in the construction of organisations.... Such an emphasis also presents a view of organizations as functionally unified with all the component parts working together to a common end. Consequently, as with mechanistic approaches, issues of power and politics are ignored and conflict is dismissed as being 'dysfunctional'.

In other words, human beings are deemed impartial and unimportant within such 'mechanistic' processes founded upon earlier positivistic principles of scientific management. This is a central issue for the philosopher Kant, who 'held that human individuals are autonomous and so can choose the goals of their actions and they can choose the actions required to release them ... made possible because of the human capacity for reason' (Stacey 2003:23). Clearly, the power of the individual and/or group to mediate HR processes is central to developing a better understanding of a particular management context and performance outcome (see Chapter 4).

Exhibit 1.2

John Amaechi

John Amaechi is a former NBA basketball player. Whilst there is nothing extraordinary about this, he is one of the few British players to make it in the US and is just as well known for his views and campaigning on a variety of issues. In 2007 he was the first NBA player to 'come out' and publicly acknowledge his sexuality. In addition, he is Amnesty International's first sporting ambassador. Organisations such as the International Olympic Committee and FIFA are very careful to avoid mixing sport with politics; at least overtly! The Olympic Charter makes it clear that athletes should not use their status and the Olympic platform to promote third party causes. Similarly, FIFA have been vocal in their opposition to politics influencing the administration of football throughout the world. However, in practice, it is sometimes very difficult to avoid views that may be inconsistent with overall organisational policy. For example, following the in-fighting of the French football team and their early exit from the 2010 World Cup in South Africa, FIFA warned that any attempt of the French government to influence the internal issues of the French Football Federation may lead to their suspension and the subsequent banning of all sides from international competition. However, Amaechi's sense of conscience makes it difficult for him to tow the party line where his views are in clear opposition to the prevailing orthodoxy. In 2008, he became a sports commentator for the BBC in Beijing. In his own words:

> I doubt very much whether human rights is going to come up on air at tip-off but I am an individual not defined by the parameters of the BBC and as a person of good conscience I will speak when the opportunities are appropriate.... Let's see how long I last.
>
> *Source*: Kelso (2008:9)

This illustrates the fact that people are motivated by a number of factors and it is rarely a straightforward task to harness such passions in a way that is consistent with the internal and external processes impacting upon the organisation. Moreover, it demonstrates the influential power that some sports stars hold. This can be used both positively and negatively and the increasing levels of media scrutiny can be both a blessing and a curse for those who find themselves in the celebrity spotlight.

In a critical review of related articles Boselie *et al.* (2005) argue that most studies offer a 'hard' look at the relationship between inputs and outputs; between HRM actions and concomitant performance improvements. This implies a positivistic and scientific management approach in order to identify innate 'regulative ideas' that can bring order to organisational processes (Stacey, 2003). However, what are generally ignored are the transformative processes that happen within the 'black box' in the middle.

Regulative ideas

Regulative ideas are those that bring order to a situation. They are fundamental truths or laws that explain general phenomena by establishing a causal link between HR inputs and both positive and negative performance outputs.

Furthermore, is clear that each situation is unique and, therefore, creative responses must be grounded in a solid understanding of the context. Moreover, it is felt that there is a need to adopt more 'soft' approaches to understanding such processes, particularly in relation to the perceptions of a wider range of staff outside management/senior management (Baptiste, 2008; Boselie *et al.*, 2005). With this in mind, existing research appears to suggest that HR practices and performance are positively related where there are stronger management–employee relationships based upon support and trust (Baptiste, 2008). Similarly, Françoise *et al.* (2008) suggest that HR specialists need to play a more hands on role in daily operations instead of delegating this function to 'line' managers who have a more general and non-specialised outlook. In particular, it is suggested that it's better to ask 'who' rather than 'what' when attempting to understand the mediating variables in overall performance (see Chapters 4 and 8). This implies the central importance of leadership and worker engagement within modern HR practice. It also explains the importance attached to this process by the UK government of the time, through the Macleod and Clarke (2009:1) report:

> This timely Report sets out for the first time the evidence that underpins what we all know intuitively, which is that only organisations that truly engage and inspire their employees produce world class levels of innovation, productivity and performance.
> The lessons that flow from that evidence can and should shape the way leaders and managers in both the private and public sectors think about the people who work for them. They should also shape the way employees approach their jobs and careers.
> (Lord Mandelson, 2009)

Hard and soft issues

Hard HR issues are those traditionally associated with formal planning and represent the functional aspects of managing people. Hard HR issues are typically associated with more classical and scientific notions of management through monitoring, planning and control, e.g. recruitment and selection practices. They refer to the more deterministic and transactional processes that convert inputs to outputs.

Soft HR issues represent the more informal and qualitative forms of management. They are more closely associated with the human relations approach to management and refer to the transformative and developmental black box processes that help convert inputs, often through a circuitous and indirect route, into outputs.

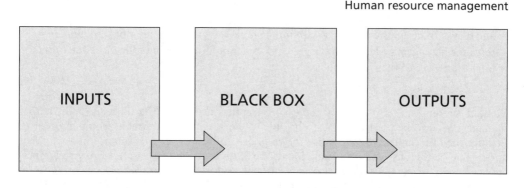

Figure 1.1 The 'black box' of organisational processes.

In a study of 5,000 employees from across a wide variety of organisations containing at least 50 employees, 'soft' HR issues such as retention, effort, advocacy and passion for the job were highly correlated with individual performance. Notably:

- Fortune 500 companies in the lowest quartile with regard to company profits had 50 percent fewer engaged employees than those in the top quartile.

- When it comes to individual performance, high performing employees were twice as engaged as their low performing counterparts.

(Feather, 2008:29)

1.9 Towards a more integrative approach

The evidence reviewed in this chapter appears to suggest that one of the main mediating factors affecting individual, group and organisational performance is the ability of the manager to engender a sense of belonging, purpose, enthusiasm and team spirit consistent with organisational values and strategic objectives. Lussier and Kimball (2009) build on the work of Katz (1974, quoted p. 4) to suggest that good managers need to have well-developed technical, people, communication, decision-making and conceptual skills. All are important and are covered within this book. However, it is not just the acquisition of knowledge that is important here. It is the refinement of conceptual skills that helps individuals to develop their own conceptual models or 'regulative ideas'. As Lussier and Kimball (2009:9) argue:

> Conceptual skills are the ability to understand abstract ideas. Another term for conceptual skills is systems thinking, or the ability to understand an organization or department as a whole and the relationships among its part. Managers need to be equipped with conceptual skills to think outside the box and come up with creative ways to improve performance.

Furthermore, Wendell Braithwaite argues that psychological motivation is critical to understanding the impact of HR upon performance, which is influenced by three interrelating factors:

1 a system of **interaction** – that is, the basic nature of any interpersonal relations;
2 a system of **influence** – in other words, a system of reciprocal impact between a sports organisation's situational factors, the human resource manager or leader (coach), and the subordinates (employees, athletes or team) upon each other;

3 and a system of **empowerment** – within the employer–employee relationship, human resource managers or leaders have a greater potential for exerting influence, due to the intrinsic power of their position.

(2004:94)

Wendell prefers the term 'intelligence' to 'conceptual skills' but the unifying point is that managers need to be proactive and to be able to work with and through people in order to identify the HR challenge, rationalise the response and improve performance in a way that adds value to the customer, the individual, the team and the organisation. A systems perspective seeks to compare desired organisational performance with actual performance in order to improve practice. Similarly, in relation to individual managers, Edwards (1999) advocates the central importance of 'reflection' in the professional toolkit of sport managers. With this in mind there is a need to establish a dialectic between 'hard' mechanistic notions of 'systems' practice and those associated with a more 'critical' look at the more overtly qualititative 'black box' processes involved in generating performance improvements.

Janssens and Steyaert (2009) use the term R(econstructive)-reflexivity to signify the need to establish a personal understanding of the work context(s) in which we operate. They argue that this 'stimulates scholars and practitioners to reflect upon their own relationship with "performance" in their daily lives and to fully engage with the discussion on reflexivity and how it can redirect the field of HRM' (p. 153). In other words, it is hoped that you, the reader, will be able to develop a better appreciation of the unique nature of working within a variety of sport and leisure organisations and the impact this may have upon related HR practices. In order to accomplish this it is important that you develop your own mental (or systems) maps of each of the many areas addressed both within and between the various book chapters. Try putting 'systems maps' into an Internet search engine and you will find an array of software, often available free, that will help you identify the many interrelationships that exist. It is incumbent upon you, as an existing or future advocate of this area of work, to be able to continually refine the ways in which you understand today's practice as a prelude to positively influencing the future context in which you and others operate. Good luck!

Chapter 2

The market for labour in leisure and sport

Learning outcomes

By the end of this chapter you will be able to:

- define and explain the concept of the labour market;
- identify the importance of understanding the labour market for sport and leisure managers;
- critically examine the factors that impact on sport and leisure labour markets.

2.1 Introduction

The aim of this chapter is to provide an overview of the labour market and how it impacts on human resource management (HRM) within sport and leisure organisations. An understanding of the labour market is crucial for managers in sport and leisure organisations. It is a dynamic entity that is influenced by a wide range of factors that affect the ability to recruit, retain and develop staff (see Chapters 6 and 7).

The labour market is based on the concepts of labour demand and supply. Labour demand consists of the demand, by employers, for people to undertake work. Considerations include the number of people in work, the hours they work and the number of vacancies. Labour supply, also known as the labour force, is the number of people over 16 who are either in employment or potentially could supply their labour. Also referred to in this chapter is the sport and leisure workforce, which refers to those specifically employed in sport and leisure. However, as will be seen, the size and scope of the sport and leisure workforce is extremely difficult to measure.

> ### Concept check
>
> **The labour market**
>
> The pool of available talent in which employers compete to recruit and subsequently retain staff (Torrington *et al.,* 2005).

Despite the recent economic downturn key sectors in sport and leisure, such as health and fitness, sport and recreation, and the outdoors, have continued to experience growth (SkillsActive, 2009a). Over at least the last five years, a major labour market issue for these sectors has been the difficulty in attracting appropriately skilled people. Consequently within UK sport and leisure organisations there are a number of hard to fill job vacancies (SkillsActive, 2006a). Moreover, this is not just a problem for sport and leisure but is also found within the UK economy as a whole.

The Chartered Institute of Personnel and Development (CIPD) undertake an annual survey of recruitment, retention and turnover in December each year. The 2008 survey found that despite a dramatic decrease in the number of vacancies compared to 2007, 81 per cent of organisations surveyed still experienced difficulties in recruiting people with appropriate skills (CIPD, 2009a). This issue illustrates that although the labour market is related to the balance of demand for and supply of people, there are a number of intervening factors that affect whether an organisation is able to fulfil its workforce needs. This chapter will explore those in relation to sport and leisure.

In order to analyse the labour market for sport and leisure the chapter will briefly outline the employment structure of the sport and leisure industry in order to set the context for the demand and supply for labour. It will then explore key influences on the sport and leisure labour market and the issues that these create.

2.2 The sport and leisure industry

The sport and leisure industry is pluralist and fragmented in nature meaning that, although there are generic labour market factors that are likely to impact on all sport organisations, there are also factors that are more likely to affect specific parts of the sport and leisure industry. This fragmentation makes it extremely difficult to estimate the actual size of the sport and leisure workforce due to the problems of defining the scope of the industry.

At a basic level, the sport and leisure industry is made up of the public, commercial and voluntary sector. Table 2.1 provides an indication of the balance of employment within those sectors in England for sport related organisations and indicates the overall growth over the last two decades. The only sector that has shown a decline over recent years is commercial non-sport which includes the production of sport-related goods and services by non-sport organisations. The companies within this sector are not providing a sport product themselves but they provide inputs or revenue that assist in the production of a sport product (SIRC 2007). The illustration provided by SIRC is the sponsorship revenue received by a football club from a beer company. Interestingly, this is the only area where there was a decline in employment although the value of the sector increased during that time.

Table 2.1 demonstrates that the commercial sector dominates the industry in terms of paid employment, but it also includes sports goods manufacturers, retailers, professional and participant sport. SIRC (2007) identified that the increase in jobs in this sector, since 2000, can partly be attributed to the expansion in sport retail, which increased by 25 per cent between 2000 and 2005. However, this is also subject to variability, particularly during times of economic downturn. Some retailers, such as JJB sports, struggle to avoid administration, whilst others, such as Sports Direct International, owned by Newcastle United owner Mike Ashley, capitalise on such weaknesses by increasing profits in the same area (Fletcher, 2011).

The public and voluntary sectors are both focused on participant sport and represented approximately 12 per cent of sport jobs in 2005 (SIRC, 2007). More recent figures from SkillsActive (2009), which provides a lead for skills development and training in the active leisure sector in the UK, indicates a continued growth in sport and leisure employment. Their calculation of the size of the workforce and job opportunities and the sectors they are responsible for can be seen in Table 2.2.

The difficulties of filling posts within sport and leisure are due to a combination of issues; some are more specific to sport and leisure and others are more generic influences that are likely to affect all organisational labour markets. The next section will discuss the generic influences; this is followed by a discussion of issues that are more specific to sport.

2.3 Generic influences on the labour market for sport and leisure

There are a number of influences on the labour market that are likely to affect all organisations' labour markets, but these effects may be different depending on the organisation.

Table 2.1 Sport-related employment in England 1985–2005 (in thousands)

	1985	2000	2003	2004	2005
Commercial sport	97	115	116	133	134
Commercial non-sport	144	175	192	202	197
Voluntary sector	31	38	46	47	52
Public sector	32	37	48	49	51
Total	304	365	401	431	434

Source: Sport Industry Research Centre (SIRC) (2007:9).

Table 2.2 Active leisure workforce size and job opportunities

	Workforce	Job opportunities*
Health and fitness Includes: independent clubs, hotel based clubs, public leisure centres, residential clubs	49,500	9,218
Sport and recreation Includes: sport and leisure facilities, sports clubs, stadia/arena, sports services, sports development, national governing bodies of sport, community/youth centres	371,200	73,086
The outdoors Includes: outdoor recreation, outdoor development training, outdoor sport development, outdoor education, exploration and expeditioning	26,200	4,734

Source: compiled using data adapted from SkillsActive (2009).

Note

* Sector Skills Agreement forecasted jobs 2004–2014.

2.3.1 Economic

The state of the economy has major implications for the labour market as it determines overall demand for an organisation's products and services. Consequently it will determine the number of staff an organisation needs to recruit, retain and develop in order to meet market demand. As staff are recruited from the labour market, the economic conditions will affect their availability and rates of pay, depending on the number of people available for work.

Labour markets are categorised into 'tight' and 'loose'. A labour market is loose where organisations have little problem in finding the appropriate staff and is usually found during periods of high unemployment. Tight labour markets exist where organisations find it hard to recruit and retain staff because of the high demand for labour. However, in some occupational areas the labour market may be constantly tight, whatever the economic conditions, purely because there are insufficient numbers of people who have the skills or are willing to undertake the job. The wide variety of employment possibilities in sport and leisure exhibits results in a labour market that exhibits both characteristics. For example, in sport coaching there are shortages of appropriately qualified people in the UK (Loughborough University, 2008) whilst in the Health and Fitness Sector Dundjerovic and Robinson (2001: 25) report that

> the health and fitness industry exploits this passion for working in the industry in terms of pay and working conditions. While this is not a major concern as long as the large labour pool continues to exist, it will cause difficulties with staff recruitment should alternative industries create this passion.
>
> (cited in Wolsey and Whitrod Brown 2003:166)

Tight and loose labour markets

Tight labour market: demand for labour is higher than supply.

Loose labour market: supply of labour is higher than demand.

2.3.2 Demographic trends

Within the labour market there needs to be an understanding of demographic trends and how these will affect the supply of labour. In the UK, and many other Western countries, the following trends are affecting national labour markets:

- falling birth rates;
- increased number of women within the workforce;
- ageing population;
- increasing number of young people remaining in education and the growth in the number of graduates;
- increasing diversity within the workforce;
- growth in immigrant workers.

Exhibit 2.1 provides an illustration of the benefits of a mixed-age workforce with regard to leisure.

Exhibit 2.1

Jobcentre: mixed-age workforce is important

A quarter of older workers in the leisure industry believe their younger colleagues teach them skills they previously did not have, according to recent research.

The study, commissioned by Jobcentre Plus, also found that working in a mixed-age workforce is important both for older (29 per cent) and younger (66 per cent) UK workers in the leisure industry.

Chief executive of Jobcentre Plus, Lesley Strathie, said: 'The research shows that having the right balance of age and skills can bring numerous benefits to establishing a complete workforce for both employers and individuals.'

The survey shows that the qualities that younger workers think their older colleagues bring is experience (88 per cent), while reliability (65 per cent) and knowledge (82 per cent) also featured highly.

Jobcentre Plus carried out the research as part of its ongoing work to offer support to older workers looking for employment. Details: www.jobcentreplus.gov.uk

Source: Tuchscherer (2007)

2.3.3 Political

Price (2007:119) identifies that governments have a powerful influence on the labour market as they 'set the legislative, regulatory and economic contexts in which people work'. Legislation and regulations that affect the labour market in the UK include:

- Disability Discrimination Act
- Sex Discrimination Act
- Equal Pay Act
- Race Relations (Amendment) Act
- Parental rights at work (maternity and paternity leave and pay)
- Part-Time Workers (Prevention of Less Favourable Treatment) Regulations
- Transfer of Undertakings (Protection of Employment) Regulations
- Age discrimination legislation
- Working Time Regulations
- Employment Equality (Sexual Orientation) Regulations
- Employment Equality (Religion or Belief) Regulations
- Fixed-Term Employees (Prevention of Less Favourable Treatment) Regulations
- Right to request flexible working.

As a member of the European Union (EU) the UK is also influenced by European legislation and the EU's pursuit of a single market has led to the standardisation of employment regulation and protection measures (Price, 2006). This also includes measures that allow free circulation of employees and freedom of residence in any EU country.

An example of a legal influence on the sport labour market is the impact of the 1995 Bosman Ruling made by the European Court of Justice on the professional sport labour market. Prior to the ruling, player mobility in association football was controlled by the 'retain and transfer' system. Only players registered with the Football Association were allowed to play professional football; this registration is held by the club therefore the club had control over the player's movements. Also a club could retain a player's registration even if it did not renew their contract (Downward and Dawson, 2000). This retention and transfer system was overturned by the case of Jean Marc Bosman, who was a player for RC Liege in Belgium. His two-year contract was due to expire in 1990 and RC Liege offered him a new one-year contract on a much reduced salary. Bosman refused these terms and was transfer listed, but due to the high transfer fee set by Liege no other clubs made an approach. Bosman then agreed terms with a French club, US Dunkerque, at a much reduced fee; however the two clubs failed to agree terms and the contract lapsed. Bosman took the clubs to the European Court of Justice under article 177 of the Treaty of Rome, which enshrines the free mobility of land, labour and capital in the EU, for damaging his employment opportunities by fixing a transfer fee. The court declared that, in the absence of pressing reasons of public interest, the transfer rules did not constitute an obstacle to the free movement of workers. Consequently the key outcome of the Bosman ruling was that no fee could be expected by clubs on the transfer of an out-of-contract player.

Pearson (2009) observes that the Bosman case has had a major effect on football clubs in that they now have to sign players for longer contracts or risk losing players on free transfers. He argues that it has increased 'player power' as those with the highest skill levels have more control over their own career; those players who are out of contract or nearing the end of their contract have increased bargaining power, leading to higher wages. Wayne Rooney represents a good example of this, holding Manchester United to ransom, in 2010, over his career and monetary ambitions. This resulted in assurances that Manchester United would seek to strengthen the team, whilst also agreeing to a significant increase in Rooney's wages (Draper, 2010).

Other key government influences on the labour market are education and skills policies. Price (2007) argues that economic growth partly depends on skilled human resources – a country's human capital. Arguably, a key feature of the UK economy is that firms are predominantly competing in relatively low quality, low value-added markets, therefore skill levels remain persistently behind that of its main competitors (Lloyd, 2005a). The government's skills strategy aims to address this by shifting firms up-market to enable them to compete on the basis of quality. In order to facilitate upskilling the previous Labour government set up Sector Skills Councils across a number of occupational areas; SkillsActive is the council for active leisure, which includes sport. A major part of its work has been assessing skill needs in the sector and developing regional level sector skills agreements in order to drive workforce development for active leisure.

Concept check

Human capital

Human capital refers to the collective skills, knowledge, attitudes, experiences and potential of people.

The issues affecting the supply of labour for sport organisations reflect the wider labour force issue of the need to develop a more highly skilled sport workforce (Department for Culture, Media and Sport, 2003; Sport England, 2004; SkillsActive, 2006a). At the lower levels, as with many other occupations, there has been criticism of the standards of school leavers in terms of poor literacy and numeracy (SkillsActive, 2006a). However the key issue is with recruiting and developing staff with higher level skills. For example SkillsActive (2005) identified that only 26 per cent of sports staff had a level 4/5 qualification (the level equivalent to a degree).

An issue that is impacting on the labour market in general is the increasing number of graduates. In relation to sport, a key aspect is the integration of graduates into sports organisations. Low numbers of sports graduates entering the sports industry have been seen as a major problem by SkillsActive (2005) and over the years issues have been raised about oversupply and the appropriateness of sports graduates to the sport industry. There is some evidence that graduates may lack practical, vocational skills (SkillsActive, 2006a:24); however, there is also evidence that sports graduates do not perceive the sports industry as an attractive place to work (Hanson *et al.*, 1998; Minten, 2010). Graduates have high expectations of where they will enter the sport workforce but in contrast the sport industry has a culture of working up from the bottom. This means that when graduates enter the sport workforce they are not fully utilising their graduate attributes and many become so frustrated with the outcome that they leave (Minten, 2010). Moreover, the Leitch Review (2006:67) suggested that as younger people within the workforce gain degrees and enter into occupations where employers may not be educated to the same level, 'it increases the likelihood of poor deployment of higher-level skills with relatively under-skilled owners, managers and leaders unable to find the best uses for new graduate recruits'. Again government is directly impacting on the workforce for sport through its policy of mass higher education; however, this creates two interrelated issues: are there enough sport related jobs that are appropriate for graduates and are employers in the industry able to manage graduates to enable utilisation of their attributes?

2.3.4 Geographic variations

Labour markets will vary geographically depending on the nature of the organisation and also the nature of a particular job. For example, does the organisation normally recruit locally, regionally, nationally or transnationally? It is likely that the more senior the level of the job or the higher the skills required, the wider the geographical area. Consequently, it is crucial that managers define their organisation's labour market area and then identify the underlying trends and workforce characteristics that may impact on their ability to recruit and retain appropriate staff.

SkillsActive have undertaken research to identify the labour market issues for sport and leisure organisations in all the UK regions. From this research regional Sector Skills Agreements have been developed that summarise these issues. They can be found at the SkillsActive website.

Review question

Visit the SkillsActive website and find the Sector Skills Agreement for your region – http://www.skillsactive.com/resources/publications. What are the key issues that it identifies? If you are studying outside the UK choose one of the regional Sector Skills Agreements. How do the issues it identifies compare with the labour market issues affecting the region you are studying in?

An example of where geographical location has a major impact on the workforce is Aviemore in Scotland. Outdoor activity providers in the area have had problems recruiting and retaining local young people who tend to move to urban areas to work or study. In order to address this providers such as Badaguish Outdoor Centre have been central to setting up work experience programmes with local schools and colleges to enable the young people to gain an appreciation of the career opportunities available in the outdoors industry (SkillsActive, 2009a).

2.3.5 Globalisation

The two key effects of globalisation on the sport labour market is the movement of labour and the movement of capital and technology to locations that utilise cheaper labour. Football has been described as the most globalised of all sports and so provides a good case in which to explore the movement of labour (Milanovic, 2005) (see Exhibit 2.2).

Exhibit 2.2

Globalisation of football

Thirty years ago, when Tottenham Hotspur, a London football club, signed two members of Argentina's World-Cup-winning squad, English fans marvelled at such boldness. Now imports are so common that FIFA and UEFA, the governing body in Europe, would like to cap them, but under European Union labour law players must be able to move freely between member states. The transformation in England, with the richest television contracts in the sport, has been remarkable. More than half the players in the Premier League are from outside Britain, up from one-quarter ten years ago. English clubs employed almost one-eighth of the players in the Euro 2008 tournament this June, even though the national team failed to qualify. Only German clubs were better represented.

The supply side of football's labour market has shifted too. Brazil has long been a big exporter. Most of the clubs in this year's Asian Champions League, for instance, have at least one Brazilian. Over the past decade or so there has been a scramble for Africans. French and Belgian clubs had been using Africa as a cheap source of talent for years, but lately the English have been keen buyers, often via Belgium or France, of such talents as Ghana's Michael Essien and Togo's Emmanuel Adebayor.

Ten years ago just under half the players at the African national championships played in their own leagues and two-fifths were with clubs in Europe. Of the 146 men involved, 41 worked in France and only three in England. At this January's tournament, less than one-third were with domestic teams, mainly in north Africa. Well over half were working in Europe: 202 in all, 57 of them in France and 41 in England.

It is not surprising that sport's labour markets are globalising. The most talented people are gravitating towards the richest employers, whose ability to pay has been enhanced further by juicy television contracts. In turn, the best players make the sport more enjoyable to watch, bringing in more fans and more revenue.

Source: Lane (2008)

The migration of players from underdeveloped to developed nations, described in Exhibit 2.2, has been termed 'feet drain' (Walters and Rossi, 2009). Many European clubs have set up global networks, academies and training camps in order to recruit young talent rather than paying for already formed players (Milanovic, 2005; Walters and Rossi, 2009). This practice has had negative outcomes with Andreff (2009: 16) reporting that, in 2000, 15 young African players won a case in the Belgian court against professional clubs and players agents relating to 'trade and trafficking' of human beings. In a reaction to other reports of players who were unsuccessful in trials with European football clubs being left without labour contracts or return tickets home, UEFA introduced regulations in 2001 that international transfer is only allowed for players over 21 (Andreff, 2009).

Interestingly, the Lisbon Treaty, which came into operation during December 2009, gives the Court of Justice of the European Union jurisdiction over sport for the first time. As a result, in March 2010, it issued a judgment on the 'Bernard' case. Oliver Bernard was an apprentice with the French club Olympic Lyonnais but decided to sign, instead, with Newcastle United, in England. The case ruling effectively allows clubs to seek compensation for players who are poached in this way (Zylberstei, 2010). However, for the right players, it remains to be seen if the levels of compensation will prove to be much of a disincentive to clubs tempted to buy in talented young players in this way. No doubt UEFA's Fair Play initiative will further influence such areas as the biggest football clubs in Europe may be encouraged to look again at the ability of their player development programmes as a means of strengthening their first team squad.

With regard to the free movement of capital and technology, globalisation has facilitated the development of 'transnational' or 'multinational' companies. These companies operate in more than one country, so they are able to switch resources and production from one country to another to maximise the benefit to the organisation of greater skills availability and lower employment costs (Price, 2007). Silk *et al.* (2005:3) describe them as nomadic economic institutions 'that scour the globe for the ever cheaper labour costs and underexploited markets'. An example in sport is Nike: almost all of its footwear and apparel is manufactured outside the USA. In 2008, contract suppliers in China, Vietnam, Indonesia and Thailand manufactured 36 percent, 33 percent, 21 percent and 9 percent respectively of Nike brand footwear. Furthermore its apparel production occurred in China, Thailand, Indonesia, Malaysia, Vietnam, Turkey, Sri Lanka, Honduras, Mexico, Taiwan, Israel, Cambodia, India and Bangladesh (Nike, 2008).

Slack (2004:269) argues that companies such as Nike locate in countries such as China because they offer investments and 'refine' labour laws in order to attract them, whilst also avoiding Western regulatory systems. This has meant that Nike along with adidas and Reebok have come in for criticism of the allegedly low wages paid to workers in the factories producing their goods (Stonehouse *et al.*, 2004), although Nike has attempted to address this with a code of conduct that sets out its expectations of its global contractors. Nike's (2007) Code of Practice can be found at http://www.nikebiz.com/responsibility/documents/Nike_Code_of_Conduct.pdf.

This section has provided an overview of a range of generic factors that influence organisational labour markets in general and has highlighted examples specific to sport and leisure. The next section will explore the factors that are more specific to sport and leisure labour markets.

> **Review question**
>
> Choose a professional sports team that you are familiar with and examine the extent to which it has been affected by globalisation of the labour market.

2.4 Labour market issues specific to sport and leisure

2.4.1 Flexibility of labour demand

A major feature of the sport and leisure industry is the fluctuation in demand both seasonally and over a typical week and day. Consequently, this has a major effect on an organisation's demand for labour which means that there is a need for a flexible workforce. Two different strategies commonly used within leisure labour markets, which can be applied to participant sport organisations, events and sports retail are functional flexibility and numerical flexibility (Baum, 2006; Ogden and MacVicar, 2001). Functional flexibility relates to extending the range of tasks that individuals can perform so that they are using multiple skills, undertaking jobs at different skill levels or moving between different functions (Lockstone *et al.*, 2010). Numerical flexibility is the organisation's ability to increase and decrease staffing in accordance with fluctuations in business demand (Baum, 2006).

Baum (2006) identified that numerical flexibility can be achieved in four different ways.

1 Contractual working time flexibility – in sport this is obtained through the use of short-term and part-time contracts. This is reflected in SkillsActive's (2008) Working in Fitness survey where 15 per cent of respondents were permanent part-time staff and 4 per cent were seasonal/casual workers.

2 Numerical flexibility is achieved through distancing flexibility where an organisation will use outside employees who have commercial contracts. This is a particular feature of health and fitness – 36 per cent of respondents were self-employed/freelance workers, such as personal trainers, aerobics, yoga, group exercise and aqua instructors (SkillsActive, 2008). It is also a feature of the coaching labour market where the demand for coaches has led to commercial and publicly funded coach recruitment agencies being set up in recent years. Major events will also use outsourced personnel, employed by other organisations that are contracted in for the event (Hanlon and Stewart, 2006). In addition, this is also becoming more prevalent in professional sports; although this is not without its controversy. For example, Carlos Tevez, the Argentinian football player, has played for West Ham United, Manchester United and Manchester City. However, he is effectively 'owned' by a third-party management company and leased to a club for a contracted period with options built in. This complicates employment issues, but does increase overall levels of flexibility both for the player and for the football club.

3 | Exit flexibility, which is achieved by using self-employed/freelance staff, means that administrative procedures and dismissal costs are reduced when there is a decrease in demand.
4 | Internal flexibility or time flexibility is fundamental to the sport industry and relates to the scheduling of work time such as the use of shift working and contracts based on annual hours worked.

In major events, the numbers of staff may expand by over 1,000 per cent for an event and then reduce back to their original size in a short period of time (Hanlon and Jago, 2004). This is termed the pulsating effect, which means that human resource practices have to be adapted to meet the specific characteristics of event organisations (Hanlon and Stewart, 2006).

Flexibility in the sport and leisure labour market has both advantages and disadvantages. The benefits are that employees can make a choice to work flexibly in order to manage work and childcare responsibilities (Bach, 2005; Ogden and MacVicar, 2001). Baum (2006) also recognises this and that it may also be beneficial for those with caring responsibilities, undertaking further education or training, approaching retirement or with health issues or disabilities.

There are two main disadvantages with flexible working. First, managers may be tempted not to provide appropriate induction and training to outsourced or seasonal staff, which could lead to a poorer quality of service. Second, if work schedules are not managed appropriately organisations may fall foul of the UK Working Time Regulation, which sets out the following basic rights and protections (CIPD, 2008):

- a limit of an average of 48 hours a week over a 17-week period which a worker can be required to work;
- a limit of an average of eight hours work in 24 hours which night workers can work;
- a right to 11 hours rest a day;
- a right to a day off each week;
- a right to an in work rest break if the working day is longer than six hours;
- a right to 28 days paid leave per year for full-time workers.

2.4.2 Volunteers

A labour supply feature of participant sport organisations and events organisations is their reliance on volunteers (Madella, 2003). The Leisure Industries Research Centre (LIRC, 2003) identified that in the UK there were 5,821,400 volunteers in sport, which they estimate is the equivalent to 720,000 full-time jobs. When this is compared to Table 2.1 showing employment in sport, it dwarfs the other sectors. This dependence on volunteers means that recruitment and retention are critical issues (Cuskelly, 2006; Taylor *et al.*, 2006). In the UK, 74 per cent of sport clubs identified that there were not enough people willing to volunteer and in 65 per cent of clubs increasingly work is being left to fewer people (Nichols *et al.*, 2005). This is further highlighted by the Sport England (2002) findings that there is one 'lapsed' volunteer for every two active volunteers. There are two interrelated reasons for this: pressures from other commitments are squeezing the time available for volunteering and at the same time the workload on volunteers is growing. This has been due to the introduction of new rules and regulations, particularly linked to child protection and health and safety obligations (Nichols *et al.*, 2005). Furthermore, voluntary sporting organisations have had to modernise and improve the quality of their management (Cuskelly *et al.*, 2006, Houlihan and White, 2002). An example is Sport England's Running Sports Programme, which has identified the need for the introduction of HRM systems into voluntary sports clubs that model work organisations.

However, a study by Cuskelly *et al.* (2006) of Australian rugby union clubs found that the relationships between volunteers and the individual club are complex. They observe that volunteers are not like human resources in the public and commercial sector as they are also the constituent body, co-workers, managers and clients. Consequently, it is difficult to introduce systems that have been based on paid work organisations.

The attempt to modernise has led to an influx of paid professional staff into voluntary sport organisations. This may create tensions between paid employees and volunteers as the employees are likely to want the organisation to be run professionally as its success will impact on their own livelihoods (Roberts, 2004). These issues and the importance of volunteers mean that many regional workforce development plans for sport in the UK have identified key priorities of increasing the number and quality of volunteers (Greater Manchester Sport, 2007) This will be a particular issue with the lead up to the London Olympics in 2012 which will require 70,000 volunteers (London 2012, 2009b).

2.4.3 Professionalisation

Professionalism is an issue that has preoccupied the sport and leisure workforce over a number of years. Initially it was mainly the concern of sport and leisure managers but in more recent years it has been an aspiration for sports development, coaching and the health and fitness sector. It is argued that the focus on professionalisation came from the previous Labour government which, in line with its upskilling policies, attempted to establish minimum training standards for sports workers in the UK (Lloyd, 2005a).

A major reason why the sport and leisure workforce strives for professionalisation is to raise its status and authority (Henry and Spink, 1990; Bacon, 1996). This is important in terms of attracting more highly skilled workers, enhancing training and education of the workforce and clarifying career pathways. In addition, Bacon (1996:2) argues that professionalisation enhances 'the value of their member's human capital within the labour market' and enables the professional body to regulate access to the occupational area. Moreover, Baum (2006) suggests there may be an impact on the remuneration of employees. Thus, if professionalisation of the sport labour force were to be achieved it could have a fundamental impact on the sport labour market.

Fleming (1996:248) has argued that the terms 'profession and professionalism are often used in a loose and inexact sense'. Furthermore, Smith and Stewart (1999) suggest that in relation to the sport labour market there are two key aspects to professionalisation: the development of a strong professional body and the development of expert competence in sport workers to improve management practices. Taylor and Garrett (2008) identify that most professional occupations have the following characteristics:

- professional education
- a distinct and specialised body of knowledge
- career structures and pathways
- explicit ethical and value systems
- an independent professional membership body
- professional practice
- clarity and definition with regard to their role and remit.

Despite the overall push towards professionalisation in the sport industry and an attempt to fulfil the characteristics identified by Taylor and Garrett (2008), different sectors have taken different approaches. Consequently, sports management/development, coaching and health and fitness will be considered separately.

With regard to sport management/sport development, the first sport related professional bodies in the UK can be traced back to the Institute of Baths and Recreation Management (IBRM) formed in 1921, and the Institute of Parks and Recreation Management formed in 1926 which concentrated on technical qualifications such as swimming pool technology and horticulture.

However, sport and leisure have been unable to achieve professionalisation as defined by Taylor and Garrett's characteristics (Bacon, 1990; Fleming, 1996). A fundamental problem is that there has never been one professional body. The two main professional bodies for sport and leisure are the Institute of Sport, Parks, Amenities and Leisure (ISPAL) and the Institute of Sport and Recreation Management (ISRM). There have been several attempts to merge the bodies; the 2006/2007 aborted attempt combining the Institute of Leisure and Amenity Management (ILAM) with the smaller National Association of Sports Development (NASD) to create ISPAL. Unfortunately, this still left two competing professional bodies and no one authoritative voice for the sector. However, the importance of professionalisation and the encouragement of the government via the Department for Culture, Media and Sport (DCMS) means that from early 2011 a new unified body, under Royal Charter, will come into existence. The Institute for the Management of Sport and Physical Activity (IMSPA) represents an exiting opportunity, just before the 2012 London Olympics, to move several steps closer to the holy grail of true professional status for the sector.

Coaching's aspirations of professionalisation are more recent than sport management and really began in the 1990s. However, it was not until 2001 that the Coaching Task Force was established to review coaching and coach education. Its main conclusions were that there was too much reliance on volunteers and there was a need for more paid opportunities, a clear career structure was required, and nationally recognised qualifications needed to be developed (DCMS, 2002). The Vision for coaching as set out by Sports Coach UK is provided in Exhibit 2.3.

Exhibit 2.3

The Vision

By 2012 the practice of coaching in the UK will be elevated to a profession acknowledged as central to the development of sport and the fulfilment of individual potential.

Coaching will have:

- professional and ethical values and inclusive and equitable practice;
- agreed national standards of competence as a benchmark at all levels;
- a regulated and licensed structure;
- recognition, value and appropriate funding and reward;
- a culture and structure of innovation, constant renewal and continuous development standards.

Source: Sports Coach UK (2009)

As with sport managers, a fundamental reason for professionalisation is to strengthen coaches' position in influencing and shaping their occupation so that the professional body must be seen as a key institution in the 'protection, promotion and governance of coaches by coaches' (Taylor and Garret, 2008:14).

In Taylor and Garrett's (2008) review of the professionalisation of coaching they identified, as a fundamental concern, the degree of transformation required from what has historically been a sector founded on volunteers. They also noted that in some aspects of sport the transition will be less problematic than others; for example, the professional/elite sector of sport coaching where additional support and funding streams already exist. Different sports are also further down the road of modernisation and professionalisation; an example being swimming which is identified for Sports Coach UK as a trail blazing sport. It has already produced a workforce development plan and an extract is shown in Exhibit 2.4.

Exhibit 2.4

Workforce development: people make the difference

For swimming to ac hieve its vision and objectives it relies profoundly on the skills, knowledge and commitment of its workforce, which comprises of a vast number of volunteers working in partnership with a vocational workforce.

Swimming will:

- Provide a comprehensive teacher/coach education and development programme through implementation of the UK Coaching Framework.
- Continue to pursue and implement new opportunities with sport, youth and volunteering organisations to progress policies that ensure the continued development of an effective, knowledgeable and valued workforce.
- Development of an effective, knowledgeable and valued workforce.
- Continue to support and educate clubs about good practice that will ensure they can successfully recruit and retain their workforce whilst supporting them to fulfil their ambitions.
- Continue to support the recruitment, training and deployment of volunteers ensuring there is a new generation of volunteers that have the skills, knowledge and commitment to allow our sport to continue to grow.

Source: British Swimming (2007:5)

An aspiration of coaching is the introduction of a licence to practise where the possession of a qualification is required to enter the occupation. The health and fitness sector has already introduced this on a voluntary basis with the Register of Exercise Professionals (REPs). The reason for introducing the REPs was, as with other areas of sport, to improve the image of the industry, reduce turnover and increase levels of pay (Lloyd, 2005). This was again partly influenced by the incumbent Labour government's determination to upskill industries and encourage labour market regulation. A basic outline of REPs is provided in Exhibit 2.5.

Exhibit 2.5

Register of Exercise Professionals

The REPs' Mission Statement is: 'To ensure that all exercise professionals are suitably knowledgeable and qualified to help safeguard and to promote the health and interests of the people who use their services.' The REPs is a system of self-regulation for all instructors, coaches, trainers and teachers involved in the exercise and fitness industry. The REPs creates a framework within which individual instructors can achieve the highest standards of professionalism, linked to best practice in the exercise and fitness industry. Registration is achieved and maintained through the gaining of qualifications and training which are nationally recognised and which are linked to the National Occupational Standards for exercise and fitness.

The REPs exists because it is the only way to independently demonstrate that fitness professionals are competent and qualified to do their job. The register is a central feature of the professionalism of the industry that is essential to giving customers, users, the public and partners in the medical professions, the necessary level of confidence in the quality of services provided by fitness professionals.

Registration signifies that an exercise and fitness professional has met certain standards of good practice. The REPs encourages a properly qualified base of exercise professionals who:

- have gained recognised and approved qualifications;
- can demonstrate competence in their working environment;
- are committed to Continuing Professional Development (CPD);
- have appropriate public liability insurance for the level at which they are working;
- demonstrate commitment to the industry Code of Ethical Practice.

Source: Register of Exercise Professionals (2009)

Lloyd (2005) undertook an analysis of the impact of REPs and concluded that the self-regulated approach to training standards had done little to improve the position of employees in the health and fitness industry, it had had minimal impact on training levels and there was little evidence that pay in the industry was rising. She suggested that a key factor was that the industry appeared to be a highly popular option for young people and that there was a ready flow of new entrants into the labour market. She also warned that pay and conditions for workers could deteriorate further if companies shifted to directly employing personal trainers, as one company had done, rather than using self-employed. This concurs with the earlier assessment by Dundjerovic and Robinson (2001) (cited by Wolsey and Whitrod Brown, 2003), and points to this sector having a relatively loose labour market structure for new entrants.

Lloyd's last concern does not appear to have materialised as yet as the 2008 Working in Fitness survey indicated that 76 per cent of personal trainers are self-employed, perhaps linking back to the need for flexibility discussed earlier in the chapter. However, the survey did support her view regarding a lack of impact on pay and training. It reported that low pay was cited as the main factor for employees intending to leave, along with there being better career prospects and paths elsewhere. In terms of training, it identified that 19 per cent felt that they had not received enough training – but when this is broken down into freelance and employed, 23 per cent of employed said they had not received enough compared to 12 per cent of self-employed. This is reflected in the fact that 45 per cent of the respondents paid for their own training.

However, the survey did identify that there is a good level of education amongst those responding, with 39 per cent holding a degree qualification or higher and 12 per cent with a level 3 NVQ/SVQ qualification. Although Lloyd's suggestion that there are a ready flow of young entrants is supported by the high level of turnover in the industry, with 42 per cent of fitness workers having less than four years' experience and those in management roles being in the industry the longest. These two findings may be reflecting Minten's (2010) suggestion that a significant number of graduates are obtaining low level jobs in the industry. Furthermore, the inability of related organisations to effectively utilise and harness their talents, combined with a lack of genuine career development opportunities, lead sport and leisure graduates to look for jobs which make better use of such attributes. Indeed, if the figures presented by the joint ISPAL and ISRM working party into the Chartered Institute of Sport (CIS) are accurate, it is not surprising that graduates of this area will need to start with lower aspirations and/or look elsewhere to apply their graduate level skills. They argue that there are 250,000 sport related professionals and yet there are 50,000 graduates per annum in this area alone (CIS Project Working Group, 2009). Even if we assume that this is an error and should, instead, read a more realistic 5,000, this still means that the sector would need to grow by 2 per cent per annum in order to accommodate the graduates produced by the UK's higher education sector. Whilst this is more realistic and sustainable, it further indicates the relatively loose labour structure that exists in this area of employment.

Lloyd's view on the apparent lack of impact of REPs is further supported in the conclusion of the survey which states that 'there are still the same messages coming through about low pay, inequalities in pay between the sexes, poor career progression and not getting the right training' (SkillsActive, 2008:3).

The difference between professionalisation of the health and fitness industry compared to sports management and coaching is that in the former the process has been firmly controlled by employers who have a different set of priorities (Lloyd, 2005). Within the latter, the emphasis has been on the professionals themselves controlling and directing their profession. Thus, even though there is a move to professionalisation throughout the sport workforce there is likely to be different outcomes for the labour market of each occupation depending on whether the employers or employees have control.

Review question

The figures below show the pattern of usage at a university sports centre. Identify the labour demand issues that they have and how those issues could be addressed.

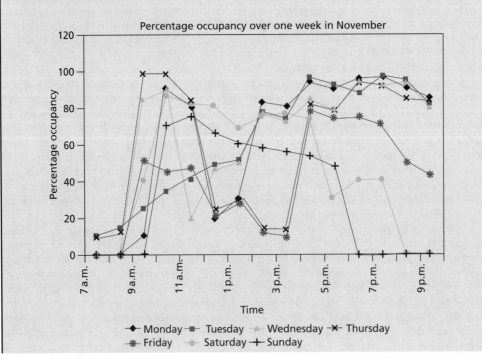

Percentage occupancy over one week in November

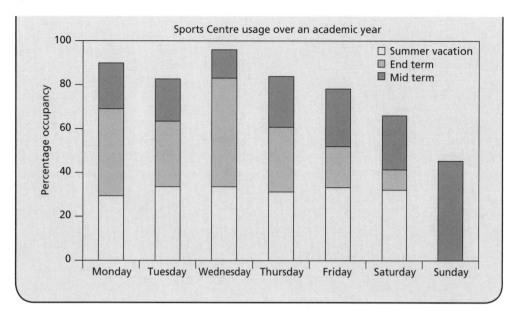

2.5 Summary and conclusion

The review of the sport and leisure labour market illustrates that it is influenced by many of the same factors that affect organisations within other industries. However, it has also shown that there are specific issues, particularly around voluntary workers and profession-alisation. These are likely to have a major effect on the labour market for sport in the future.

Organisational structure and culture

3.1 Introduction

The purpose of this chapter is to define and reflect upon the importance, significance and practical implications of organisational structure and culture for sport and leisure organisations. In order to do this effectively we need to have a critical look at the relevant theories, models and concepts and provide an evaluation of their relevance, application and limitations.

The topic of structure can be a powerful and much underrated influence, both positive and negative, in terms of organisational performance. Structure often means an organisational chart on a wall with lines of accountability and responsibility. In practical, day-to-day dealings, structure is rarely associated with management issues such as strategy and improving communication, morale and overall performance. However, organisational structure has huge and often latent potential to positively move things forward in all of these important areas. It is the structure that places people in job related activities and provides the conduit for accountability, communication and resource allocation. In addition, it is likely to heavily influence the interpersonal relationships that form the life-blood of all organisations. That said, according to Blumstein and Kollock (1988, in Berscheid 1994:81) earlier psychological studies, attempting to identify related themes, are limited in the sense that 'there is scant recognition that the behavior in a close relationship is shaped by the structural circumstances and cultural definitions of that relationship'.

The concept, models and theories of organisational structure and culture are well rehearsed in the management literature. The term 'organisational structure' often elicits notions of rigidity, rules, procedures, hierarchy and discipline. Whilst, for some, this is not the most exciting of management issues, it is often pivotal in the establishment of both formal and informal relationships. Relationships make the world go around and this is no less true within sport and leisure organisations. Indeed, when one considers the idiosyncrasies of such organisations (refer to Chapter 1), the issue of interpersonal relationships can be of particular significance for sport and leisure organisations who often exist in partnership with a number of stakeholders. Structural arrangements should not, therefore, be underestimated as a determinant of organisational performance. They need to be carefully constructed and 'fit for purpose' in order to mould an appropriate and 'can do' organisational culture with a strong emphasis on performance and human satisfaction. These two factors are far from mutually exclusive (see Chapter 4).

Sport and leisure organisations need to be careful that when designing structures there is clarity about the purpose of the organisation. Without this the mission of the organisation can become easily distorted in an organisational context in which processes become more important than the overall outcomes; the tail wagging the dog if you will! In the management literature this is termed the classic dysfunction of bureaucracy. Chandler's (1962) seminal research into this area concluded that structure should follow organisational strategy, not the other way around. However, in common with much of management theory, whilst this appears an obvious point to make, the reality of organisational life means that this is frequently difficult to achieve in practice.

Sport and leisure organisations can be more effective if the formulation of strategy and associated structural arrangements is clearly linked to the external competitive context, customer requirements and the internal needs of the various types of workers. However, it does not immediately follow that such strategic thinking is easily translated into structural arrangements and associated operational activities. This requires that the development, design and implementation of strategy is clearly linked with the formal structural arrangements and operational imperatives of the organisation. It is necessary to gain consensus with respect to the overall mission of the organisation and the customers it is seeking to serve. As Wolsey and Abrams (2010:349–350) argue:

Of course, whilst there are many 'structural' models that help us to understand such fundamental organisational building blocks, their 'effective' operationalisation is always subject to a range of tensions. These include the developing needs of the customer in relation to constantly changing levels of competition. Such issues act collectively and cumulatively to either create a positive organisational culture or one that subverts the original intention of the initial structural arrangements. In other words, it is rarely as simple as merely delegating the roles and responsibilities needed for the organisation to fulfil its overall mission and underlying business objectives. In the real world, the ability to understand and respond positively to such challenges is critical to the role of the manager.

3.2 Control and trust

Clearly, the type of structure is likely to influence the development of cultural and interpersonal behaviour patterns for some time to come. As a rule of thumb, the more structure or managerial layers found within an organisation the more potential control it will have upon its employees. In turn, there is a real danger that more control has a negative impact upon fundamental issues such as trust and autonomy. This has the potential to both positively and negatively affect the dynamism, productivity and future growth of the organisation, as demonstrated by Exhibit 3.1.

Exhibit 3.1

UK Football Association structural review: Lord Burns Report (August 2005:2–4)

The goal of the Burns report was to examine the external environment affecting football in general and the UK's football governing body in particular. Its aim was to make recommendations with regard to potential structural changes within the Football Association (FA), that are considered to be acceptable to those both leading and administering the game. The report was compiled after receiving in excess of 200 responses to an initial consultation paper. Perhaps surprisingly, given the number of stakeholders involved in administering football in the UK, there was broad agreement about the purpose of the FA, i.e. 'governance with integrity; the promotion of participation, standards, and financial well-being of the game; the fostering of development at all levels; and effective representation of the game abroad'.

With specific reference to structural issues, there were several important issues that emerged, as below:

● …the huge growth in revenues from television rights and sponsorship of professional football has provided a substantial increase in financial resources for both the professional game and, indirectly, the National Game. In turn, this has created the need for the arrangements that worked well in the past to be modified and to evolve in order to accommodate the needs of modern football. However, some of these changes have not worked in the way that was hoped, and instead have led to a lack of clarity as to who is responsible for what, which has inhibited the organisation's ability to make decisions. This has led to some frustration and tension, which has undermined the authority and the effectiveness of the organisation.

- . . . six major elements of my proposals, namely: the role and composition of the Board, the role and composition of Council, the proposed Regulation and Compliance Unit, the creation of a new Community Football Alliance, the interaction between what I have called the 'core FA' and the professional game, and the way in which FA surpluses are distributed.

- the Council of The FA should evolve so as to become more representative of the diverse interests in the game, including supporters, players, managers, coaches, referees, and so on. In addition, the weight of representation given to the professional and semi-professional games should be expanded. However, the clear majority on Council held by representatives of the National Game should be retained. Transitional arrangements should be put in place to ensure that individuals currently serving on Council are not disadvantaged by the changes.

- The FA's own direct 'delivery' functions, essentially the FA Cup and the senior national team (including the generation of revenues from their activities), should continue to be carried out by the core FA, as should oversight of the activities of The FA's Wembley subsidiary. Similarly, the Board and the executive team should continue to be responsible for the high level policy and strategy functions of The FA as governing body: it should prove much easier to concentrate upon these core 'governing body functions' once the simplifying and streamlining effects of the new structure begin to show.

The review clearly illustrates several of the issues already covered during this chapter. Namely, that the starting point of any structural changes should be an agreed organisational mission. However, whilst Burn's alludes to a consensual clarity of purpose, it is clear that the way to achieve this has to be cognisant of a range of competing opinions and stakeholders. Burns is clear that whilst these should be more adequately represented, the ultimate control of several central functions of the FA should reside with a much smaller executive committee. This enables all views to be taken into consideration, but also allows decisions to then be taken quickly and decisively. However, some five years after the publication of the report, the resignation of the FA's Chief Executive, Ian Watmore, in 2010, serves to illustrate how logical thinking and recommendations are very difficult to operate in practice. Indeed, Lord Burns (2011), commenting for the first time upon the lack of progress on such issues, offers the following observation: 'My perspective is that the FA have struggled to come to terms with the changes in the game and therefore they have operated a subsidiary model with the management of the leagues' (in Scott, 2011). In other words, organisations such as the 'Premier League' still hold a disproportionate amount of power with respect to the overall governance of football. Clearly, despite the general consensus surrounding the issues and recommendations identified by the report, the lack of its effective implementation still raises questions with respect to whether, structurally, as a governing body of twenty-first century sport, the FA can be considered 'fit for purpose'.

The concepts of span of control and chain of command are relevant to any consideration of organisational structure and culture. The span of control is the number of subordinates reporting to a supervisor. The chain of command represents the lines of authority to be found in an organisation from the top to the bottom. As a rule of thumb, it is generally thought that it is better to have a wide span of control and a narrow chain of command. This provides a more direct link to the top of the organisation and gives greater freedom and autonomy throughout the structure. However, this is not always thought to be the most productive way to organise, depending on the culture and level of maturity within the organisation. For example, to operate a wide span of control in an operational context in which subordinates need support, training and supervision, is likely to lead to dissatisfaction and poor job performance. Moreover, the wider the span of control the more difficult it is for managers to control the type and quality of work produced.

Concept check

Span of control and chain of command

Span of control: this represents the number of subordinates (staff) reporting to a supervisor or manager.

Chain of command: this represents the lines of authority to be found in an organisation, from the top to the bottom.

A wide span of control does require that subordinates are up for the challenge of autonomy and that senior managers are ready to delegate power in a way that provides them with less control. Of course, the empowerment of staff in this way should not simply mean delegating roles and responsibilities without ongoing training and support to more effectively facilitate this. There are certainly advantages and disadvantages of such an approach. On balance the advantages of a decentralised organisational structure tend to outweigh the disadvantages, particularly in large organisations where this is almost a necessity.

Review questions

What is meant by a narrow span of control?

Under what circumstances is this likely to be effective in terms of overall performance?

If, under this scenario, performance is relatively poor, what issues could be contributing to this?

Much of the literature, on the topic of human motivation, signposts the need for self-development, reflection and autonomy as a conduit to individual satisfaction and personal growth (see Chapters 4, 7, 9 and 10). The literature clearly shows that there is no one best way to organise, support and motivate employees within sport and leisure organisations. Instead, there is a judgement call to be made with regard to how much and what type of structure is needed. Such decisions will impact upon all aspects of the organisation including inter-group behaviour, resourcing, flexibility, decision-making, organisation development and, ultimately, individual and group satisfaction and performance. As always, consideration needs to be carefully given to the impact that any organisational structure may have on the informal aspects of organisational life. In other words the behaviours, feelings and attitudes that cannot be identified on the organisational chart but manifest themselves in informal behaviour both at the group and individual level. This can both be very positive and support the organisations objectives but equally the informal dynamics may also work against the best interest of the organisation if not carefully considered and respected. There are several possible structural alternatives.

Concept check

Structural types

Centralised structures. Centralised structures are those that place the control at the centre of the organisation. Charles Handy (1986) has described such structural arrangements as 'power cultures' where the power and control is wielded from the centre of the organisation. Elements of this type of structural arrangement will be found in most sport and leisure organisations. Under this web-like structural framework, power and control is centrally maintained and key decisions radiate out to the wider organisation. However, the larger the organisation, the more difficult this becomes in practice. In reality, some form of decentralisation is almost inevitable; particularly with respect to today's large multi-functional organisations who may operate on a local level (e.g. local authority provision), regional level (e.g. county cricket), national level (e.g. national health and fitness chains) or global level (e.g. Nike/International Olympic Committee).

Decentralised structures. Conversely, decentralised organisations will spread responsibility for specific decisions across various levels within the organisation. In doing so, responsibility, power and accountability are shared. Decisions are made locally, in line with the increased responsibility and accountability. In Handy's terms this could be described as a 'task culture' where the focus is on the achievement of locally agreed goals and objectives. Unit managers of sporting or leisure facilities would fit this structural type. They would have overall responsibility for setting budgets, agreeing targets and managing their staff.

Departmental structures. Departmental structures organise work according to departments, for example, marketing, finance, human resources, events, recreation programming, catering and hospitality, front of house. This is a combination of role and task cultures in Handy's typology of cultural types.

Matrix structures. Matrix structures are attempts to work across both line and function. In other words, functional departments work across their areas of responsibility in order to achieve organisational aims. This is often the case when teams need to work on special projects requiring expertise from across functional areas. This is most commonly found, for example, during major sporting or leisure events where marketing, finance, events and programme teams have to work across their traditional areas of responsibility to ensure a coordinated effort is achieved.

Hybrid structures. Hybrid structures are a combination of the above structural types.

The above structural types are not an exhaustive list but merely an indicative range of possible organisational arrangements that contribute to the working environment, or 'culture' of the organisation.

3.3 Organisational culture

Culture can be defined as a pattern of shared attitudes, beliefs, expectations and assumptions, which shape the way people act and interact within an organisation. Broadly speaking, it underpins the way things are and the way things get done!

The corporate culture, as it is known, revolves around norm and core values. These manifest themselves in management style and the overall organisational climate. The culture of an organisation is often considered a key component in the achievement of the organisation's strategies and mission.

When analysing the culture of the organisation, there are a number of issues that should be considered, as below:

● *How managers treat subordinates and how, in turn, subordinates relate to their managers.*

This relationship is pivotal in many ways. It will determine how and, indeed, if, organisational objectives are achieved, having a significant impact upon individual levels of employee motivation. It will also determine the balance between control and trust, as outlined in previous sections of this chapter. There are many aspects to this relationship including the measurement of individual performance through staff appraisal and employee development programmes.

In traditional organisations, such as local authorities and large private sector sport and leisure providers, the balance of power will almost always be with the senior managers of those organisations. It is clear, in these cases that the responsibilities and actions of senior managers will help to shape the organisational culture. This will also have an impact on the relationship between the managers and the managed.

However, in less traditional sporting organisations, for example professional sports teams, the balance of power can sometimes be with the highly paid sport performers rather than the managers and coaches. We have seen this during the 2010 Football World Cup, in South Africa, where both the French and English teams were vocal in their opinions about the strategies and general approach being adopted by management. This, in turn, will have an impact on the internal dynamics within the team and may also impact team performance and culture. Indeed, the power of athletes may even extend to dictating terms to management. Nathan Robertson is a powerful figure within English badminton and appears to have an effective influence over the way things are done (see Chapter 4, Exhibit 4.1). He also happens to be an athlete, not an administrator. His influence may even extend to the recruitment and selection of the next head coach. Robertson argues:

> People often think we should appoint somebody from Asia, because Asian countries are the best in the world. But I would prefer a British or European coach. Asian coaches do not always understand the lifestyle of the British player and it can be difficult when they try to apply their own way of doing things.
>
> (in Dineen, 2010:63)

● *The work ethic. Is there a 'work hard, play hard' attitude to work? Do people come in early, stay late? Are staff conscious that they need to look busy at all times?*

How work is allocated, achieved and rewarded is also a good barometer of organisational culture. For example, if an employee has a lot of control of the work that they carry out this will signpost a cultural dynamic based on autonomy and employee control. On the other hand if work is tightly controlled and allocated on this basis the opposite would be true. Clearly, these examples are at polar ends of a continuum and illustrate how the allocation of work can send important messages to employees about the way things are done. Each case could be effective depending on the nature of the work carried out and the expectations of employees with regard to their relationship with their line managers. What is important here, in relation to shaping organisational culture, is how these managerial behaviours influence employee actions and how these actions in turn are interpreted by the wider organisation.

- *Status. How much importance is attached to it? How is this communicated within the organisation? Do commonly recognised status symbols exist and what are these?*

Status is also considered an important aspect in shaping organisational culture. Employees will watch each other very carefully and learn through what is rewarded and what is considered to be most important to the organisation. This can be symbolised through the status differentials achieved through reward and promotion; for example, being given a bigger office space or being recognised in organisational publications and through perceptions of enhanced promotional prospects. In professional team sports, this may relate to those players who are consulted by coaches before an important decision; the captain often being critical here. However, this varies between sports and situations, with some overestimating their position and abilities in this regard (see Chapter 10, Exhibit 10.2). This requires management who are sensitive to such dynamics and can assess situations quickly and make the right calls under pressure.

Status differentials can have a positive impact on those who know how to play the game, but a very different impact on those who find it difficult to navigate the promotion and status pathway. In practical terms, areas such as succession planning, carefully constructed talent identification and employee development programmes, coupled with regular employee review discussions can help to reduce the negative aspects of status differentials; particularly if they are seen to be unfairly allocated and lacking in clarity and/or equity.

- *Ambitions. How explicit are the ambitions of the organisation? Are these aggressively pursued and how does this manifest itself within day-to-day operations?*

The concept of ambition at individual, group and organisational level is multifaceted and can also help to shape organisational culture. It would be a truism to say that all organisations strive to be ambitious and that all employees will also have ambition. How this manifests itself, in the reality of the organisation, is the important consideration here. For example, is it the leadership of the organisation that drives ambition and, if so, how far can this ambition spread across the organisation?

The larger the organisation, the more difficult it is for leadership ambition to drive individual and group ambition. In fact leadership ambition can be a source of conflict within the organisation if the wider culture is not in tune with the drive of its leaders. In these cases you will be inevitably left with a model of coercive managerial practice followed by employee resistance, compliance or distance. Ambition, as with all aspects of managerial practice, has to be carefully managed and considered, in the round, rather than just from the top. This is also true in professional team sports where the players hold a considerable degree of power. For example, in October 2010, Wayne Rooney, the Manchester United and England striker publicly questioned the ambition of Manchester United as he negotiated with them over the future of his career and pay packet. This led to assurances from senior management and a healthy pay increase for Rooney.

- *Performance. How is this measured, monitored and rewarded? To what extent is short-term performance encouraged at the expense of more strategic approaches?*

Performance is clearly a key concern for all sport and leisure organisations. The culture of the organisation should be closely aligned to the approaches taken to achieve improved performance. This also works at individual, group, inter-group and organisational levels. The ideal situation is for all levels within an organisation to be in tune with the overall organisational goals and with a clear view of how their individual contributions can help achieve such objectives.

Sports teams provide a useful example of how this might work in practice. The goals of sports teams are clearer than most other types of sporting organisation. Sports teams want to win, want to improve and want to learn from their experiences. The coaches and managers are there to facilitate and lead in these endeavours. Performance can be measured in a variety of ways and, with technological advances, reviewed again and again. But even here this is not as simple as it sounds. Individual sports performers will have their own individual goals that may or may not match the needs of the team. This issue would be amplified in more traditional sport and leisure organisations where you will find multiple constituencies, sometimes with competing rather than consistent goals. The approach taken by managers and leaders, in this context, will be pivotal in terms of creating the appropriate culture to succeed and at the same time motivating and involving subordinates.

Available approaches include top down approaches through to approaches that are more inclusive and developmental. In each case the approach taken to improving performance will depend on the circumstances of the organisation, the external environment and the people involved in the process of improving and developing performance. Unfortunately, there are no quick fix solutions to improving performance, but we do know when things go wrong and it is thought that culture will play a part in how effective organisations are at achieving their objectives.

Etizioni's (1959) seminal work on authority and structure in organisational effectiveness provides a useful framework to help to understand how culture can impact organisational performance and the relationships between managers and subordinates. Etizioni identified three types of relationships between workers and managers. The first is based on coercion, where workers will do the minimum amount of work and will respond and indeed expect coercive managerial behaviour and will only do what they are told. The next is based on a utilitarian relationship, or in other words workers will do a day's work, but no more, and the relationship is a calculative one. The final relationship is a normative relationship where workers are committed to doing the job for its own sake. It is in this last relationship where there is a greater chance for the needs of both workers and managers to be aligned.

The key to Etizioni's theory is that there is a need for congruence between worker expectations and managerial actions. So if workers are normative in their outlook, then a coercive managerial stance would be incongruent and could lead to conflict and motivational issues. Conversely, if there is an expectation that workers need to be told what to do and managers neglect to approach the work in this way, then work may not be done and again this would be incongruent. The key is to create congruence between worker expectation and managerial actions.

- *Power and politics. How is this expressed and distributed throughout the organisation? To what extent is promotion based on ability or relationships? To what extent do managers largely control work? To what extent is there genuine delegation of authority and power (empowerment) throughout the organisation? To what extent is political behaviour overt or hidden? To what extent is it perceived to be punished, admonished, tolerated or even rewarded?*

The issue of power and politics also needs to be carefully considered when attempting to assess and evaluate the culture of a sport or leisure organisation. The difficulty here is that managers do not go into work every day to discuss the power and politics within the organisation and yet are influenced in much of what they do by such dynamics. Again this is not as straightforward as it may appear, with such Machiavellian tendencies exacerbated under the media spotlight and pressure of professional team sports.

Much of the popular literature on management tends to suggest that management is a linear process. In other words senior managers create the vision, identify the strategic position of the organisation, align it to the external environment and then implement organisational policy with everyone moving in the same direction. Unfortunately sport and leisure organisations can be more complex than is suggested by this simplistic prescription. Often organisations are made up of competing interest groups looking to protect their interests. If this were not the case then there would be no need for trade unions for example. The managerial challenge here is how to successfully align organisational goals with group and individual needs when these may be different. The simple answer is that this is not simple!

Often there is a need to compromise and before such compromise is possible, there is a need for all parties to recognise this. Herbert Simon's (1982) work on bounded rationality would help to explain this situation and subsequent actions. Simon postulated that it is difficult for organisations to maximise performance due to the types of limitations identified above. In addition, organisations are limited in terms of their ability to collect, interpret and act on complex and extensive sources of information. As a consequence of these factors organisations often come to satisfactory rather than optimal outcomes, particularly where there is a need to satisfy a number of related stakeholders, as with many sport and leisure organisations. There is a danger here that the organisation pursues the line of least resistance and produces, at best, average levels of performance, finding it difficult to move beyond the lowest common denominator. Under such circumstances, skilful and positive leadership is required; although this will be mediated by the position and legitimate power afforded to the leader. Alex Ferguson, the manager of Manchester United, has this in abundance, influenced heavily by his previous successes and length of tenure. Few football managers have this luxury, however, and even this cannot always provide appropriate levels of insulation from the power, influence and politicking of star players and their agents, as with the previously cited Wayne Rooney example.

● *Behaviour and accountability. How do people behave in different situations? Who do staff report to? What individual, team and organisational performance targets exist? To what extent are targets considered fair and equitable? What types of rewards are available? Are individuals encouraged to think creatively and take risks? What happens when mistakes are made or targets are not met?*

Behaviour is another key component in determining the practical aspects of organisational culture. People in organisations watch each other very carefully to determine what is acceptable and what is not acceptable behaviour. This has an impact on who is rewarded, who is promoted, who is disciplined and the amount of effort that each individual puts into a day's work. Behaviour, as we know, can be shaped by how senior managers lead, how groups work within and across organisations and how individuals behave from day to day.

All of these behaviours will have an impact on performance and outcomes. Festinger's (1957) concept of 'cognitive dissonance' is relevant here. This is the mismatch between what individuals or groups are asked to do and their psychological set. This causes anxiety and stress in the individual or group and could be the source of conflict or poor performance if not managed appropriately. The alternative view has been termed 'cognitive consistency'. Cognitive consistency refers to situations where there is a match between individual and group needs and work requirements, i.e. what they are being asked to do. This is clearly the better position to be in and is consistent with Etizoni's normative model of power dynamics discussed earlier.

More often than not, however, people working in the sport and leisure industry have to deal with the pressures of doing more with less and, at the same time, maintaining or enhancing flexibility and performance; a breeding ground for cognitive dissonance if ever there was one! This will need to be understood and carefully managed.

● *Loyalty. To what extent are managers considered to be loyal to their staff? To what extent are staff considered to be loyal to their team, managers and/or organisation? How does this manifest itself in day-to-day behaviour? To what extent do the staff feel looked after? What level of staff turnover exists? Is there a clear and readily identified career path within the organisation?*

Loyalty is an important feature in any organisation but in recent times has been put under strain due to the nature of labour markets and the increasing focus on career mobility; a factor of particular importance to professional athletes who are likely to have a relatively short period of time to maximise individual personal and/or monetary ambitions. This is further compounded by the flexible nature of the sport and leisure industry and the transient nature of some work patterns; not least professional athletes, but also a tendency for sport and leisure labour markets to require part-time casual labour (see Chapter 2). Nonetheless, employees at all levels need to feel secure and valued in order for loyalty to be present. This requires a conscious effort, on the part of senior management, to create the environment and culture where this is possible. Human resource strategies, during periods of organisational change and realignment, have encouraged staff mobility rather than staff loyalty through exercises in downsizing (reducing the number of staff) and delayering (reducing the number of layers in the organisation's structure). This too will create tensions when it comes to developing loyalty within the organisation.

- *Approachability. To what extent are decisions made behind closed doors? Do managers have time for their staff? Are managers considered empathetic and knowledgeable about day-to-day operational issues?*

Approachability is one of the easier managerial practices to develop, if thought to be important. It will also send messages to employees about how things are done within the organisation. Open door policies and providing genuine opportunities for people in organisations to raise concerns is a common sense approach to management. This could also release the creative potential in individuals by creating opportunities to also share ideas and better ways of achieving organisational goals. This is consistent with much of the literature available to us on human motivation in the workplace, which tends to suggest that a focus on higher order developmental needs is the key to individual motivation.

- *Formality. Is there a formal or more informal approach to the typical way in which business is done? How does this influence staff attitudes, motivation, behaviour and performance?*

Formality and the degree of informality can also provide a useful insight into the nature of the organisation and its culture. Formal aspects of an organisation relate to the organisation's structure and nature of rules and procedures governing actions. The extent to which the formal organisation is fit for purpose and linked to key organisational goals is the important feature here. This will also impact the degree of control or trust that an organisation creates through its formal systems. Clearly, the more structure, rules and procedures, the less likely it is that trust and autonomy will exist. This will be closely aligned to very traditional scientific and classical approaches to management discussed in earlier chapters.

What sport and leisure managers need to be careful about is not allowing systems and procedures to become more important than performance and outcomes. This is, once again, easier said than done. In the management literature such situations have been described as goal displacement; when the ends and means become confused. Goal displacement is also tied into the power and political aspects of organisational life, as there is often more than one goal and multiple stakeholders, who may have competing or different goals.

Informal aspects of organisations are also important features in determining an organisation's culture. Alongside the formal aspects of an organisation there will always be informal behaviours that help to shape the organisation's culture. Informal aspects of the organisation can either sit quite nicely alongside the formal aspects of the organisation or it can be in conflict with the main aims of the organisation. Both situations will need to be managed; but it is the latter situation that has the potential to create conflict and reduce the potential for goal achievement. For example, the ex-Liverpool football manager Rafa Benitez, speaking on the BBC about the strained relationship between him and Liverpool's two American owners, has said:

> They didn't understand the game, they didn't understand the mentality, the philosophy, the fans, the culture. I think that they thought that Liverpool Football Club was a business, a company, a franchise and it's more than this. You can see the fans, you can see the feeling, you can see the stadium ... it's different.
>
> (*Football Focus*, 26 February 2011)

In the worst-case scenarios, the informal organisation can restrict work outputs and may even lead to strike action. Sometimes this is inevitable, given the pressures of modern organisations, but a conscious recognition of the power of the informal organisation may help to reduce the potential for such conflict. The England football team, during the 2010 World Cup in South Africa, provide a good example of this. They qualified in impressive form, galvanised by a new authoritarian coach, following a period where player power appeared to rule the roost. As McIlvanney (2008:24) argues:

> Where Sven-Göran Eriksson and Steve McClaren sought to lead with matey persuasion, Capello leaves no doubt that he is the master and commander. The players know where they are with him and they know where they will be if they underperform, which is out of the team.

However, whilst this proved to be a positive influence, in small doses, during the qualifying campaign the longer-term consequences of such an approach appeared very different. The team's World Cup base and training camp was isolated, amidst reports of strict rules and boredom amongst the millionaire players, used to their own way and an infinite number of amusement options. This may have contributed to team solidarity, cohesion and, ultimately, performance during the tournament.

Concept check

Organisational culture

Organisational culture is characterised by the attitudes, beliefs, expectations and assumptions that are shared within an organisation. This underpins the way things are and the way things get done.

There are several constituents of organisational culture, as below:

Norms. These are unwritten rules of behaviour that strongly influence the organisation climate, management style and how people work together. Norms, as with most things, are not absolute but exist on a continuum between:

1 relaxed and friendly atmosphere, lots of informal chat, drifting in and out of offices, ad hoc meetings that appear inconclusive, but still things get done;

2 relationships are formalised, distances are maintained between levels, meetings are structured and everything is recorded on paper with clear reporting mechanisms and levels of accountability for specific actions.

Core values. These represent the way in which basic beliefs about what is good for the organisation are manifested throughout the organisation;

in other words, what managers think is important. These values may or may not be expressed formally in a value statement and may or may not be accepted by members of the organisation. An organisation's core values may include some or all of the following:

● care and consideration for people
● care for customers
● competitiveness
● enterprise
● equity in the treatment of employees
● excellence
● innovation
● market/customer orientation
● priority to organisational rather than people's needs
● performance orientation
● provision of equality of opportunity
● social responsibility
● teamwork.

Organisation climate. This represents the working atmosphere as perceived by its members; the norms, values and behaviour of the hierarchy, which sets the 'tone' of the organisation. The organisational climate could be:

● flexible or bureaucratic
● formal or informal
● hierarchical or loosely structured
● friendly or distant
● cooperative or individualistic
● status-conscious or free and easy
● relaxed or stressful
● reactive or proactive
● innovative or stick in the mud
● political or apolitical
● profit-conscious or cost-conscious
● action-oriented or laissez-faire
● result or process-oriented.

Management style. This describes how managers set about achieving results through people. It describes how managers behave as leaders and how they exercise authority. How they behave will depend partly on their natural inclinations, their own experiences and on the norms, values and climate of the organisation.

Organisation behaviour. This is the way in which people act in the organisation as individuals or as in groups. It also includes various processes in the organisation such as planning, innovation, coping with change, delegating, rewarding. These processes will critically affect the way things get done and the results achieved. Organisational behaviour is strongly influence by the norms, corporate culture, values and climate and management style.

> *A power culture.* This typically depends upon a central power source as an entrepreneurial organisation. It is tough and abrasive but morale is often low and it can easily fall apart.
>
> *A role culture.* This represents a bureaucratic organisation working by logic and rationality. It offers security and predictability but can be frustrating to individuals who want results quickly.
>
> *A task culture.* This tends to be job- or project-oriented. It is adaptable and flourishes where flexibility and sensitivity to the market or environment are important.
>
> *A person culture.* Is where the organisation exists to serve the people in it – as in professional partnerships.

3.4 How is culture achieved?

Schein (1987) suggested that the most powerful primary mechanisms for culture reinforcement are:

- what leaders pay attention to, measure and control;
- leaders' reactions to critical incidents and crises;
- deliberate role modelling, teaching and coaching by leaders;
- criteria for allocation of rewards and status;
- criteria for recruitment, selection, promotion and retirement.

Cultures are usually difficult to change as they evolve over a number of years. Changes in culture usually occur under traumatic circumstances such as a change in ownership or reorganisation. However, there is very limited definitive evidence about the importance of culture during periods of significant change. This is probably due to the difficulty in defining and measuring organisational culture in any meaningful way. We are then left with the practical realities of dealing with individual and group behaviours and shifting these through the use of power; either through coercion or reason, or both.

According to Armstrong (1992) behaviour can be changed by:

- leadership setting an example;
- the issue of mission and vision statements (they must be realistic and followed up by workshops, training sessions and discussions);
- discussion workshops involving staff to facilitate change;
- education and training programmes to extend knowledge and teach people new skills;
- performance management programmes such as appraisal schemes;
- reward management systems.

These programmes can be used not only to change, but also to reinforce culture. Sport and leisure organisations need to consider many interrelated variables in order to ensure that the full potential of the organisation is achieved. As you might expect this is not an easy task and involves not just human resource issues but a consideration of the wider organisational contexts, including externalities. Abrams (2001) identified a model, which has been adapted below, that can help to begin to address some of these wider considerations. The model maps out some of the key considerations, both internal and external, that can help a sport or leisure organisation to develop an appropriate framework to address such issues. These wider issues will help to dictate the culture and structural arrangements that the organisation puts in place. It is the interface between the external factors and the internal dynamics of the organisation that is the key here.

Outer context: the external environment

- **Socio-political considerations.** This includes changing consumer tastes and experiences as well as macro political interventions in the form of government intervention. Examples of this are the implementation of Compulsory Competitive Tendering and Best Value in the UK public sector and the successful bidding for the 2012 Olympics in London.
- **Legal considerations.** The legal responsibilities of leisure and sport providers are continually assessed. The regulatory framework within which sport and leisure managers operate will often shape the decision-making process. Increasingly sport and leisure managers are required to do more with less and to a higher level of quality. This can put a strain on staff workloads and as such there is legal protection in the form of health and safety legislation that requires employers to have a duty of care towards their employees. This will include workload considerations.
- **Technological considerations.** The pace of work is often dictated by the innovations and the speed of technological change. This also has an impact on consumer tastes and expectations and does create real challenges for sport and leisure managers. Information flow is faster than ever and as a consequence the pace of work has increased. This brings with it expectations for improved customer service in all of its facets.
- **Competitive business environment of the organisations.** Structural and cultural considerations should be shaped by the competitive environment in which the organisation finds itself. This is a truism, to an extent, and is much easier said than done. Defining the competitive environment is not an easy task. There are tools available such as SWOT (strength, weaknesses, opportunities and threats) analysis and PESTLE (political, economic, social, technological and environmental) analysis that can help. The limitations of time and expertise in the use of these tools is a major limiting factor in the implementation of such approaches (see Whittington, 1993; Gilligan and Wilson, 2003; Baraldi *et al.*, 2007; Chermack and Kasshanna, 2007, for further explanations and discussion of these theoretical and practical issues).

The next part of the model deals with the internal dynamics of the organisation. These are real human elements that are impacted by external forces. It is easy if everyone in the organisation is 'on the same page' when it comes to dealing with these externalities. This is often not the case and it is here that sport and leisure managers have their greatest challenges in aligning individual, group and inter-group needs with that of the external realities. It is this interface that will make the difference between success and failure.

Inner context: the internal organisation dynamics

- **Leadership.** It almost goes without saying that leadership is a central factor in the success of any organisation (see Chapters 4 and 9). It is often the leaders in the organisation who initiate structural and cultural change. This could be in the form of reorganisation, or in identifying the core values for the organisation and the subsequent behavioural consequences of such actions. The approach to leadership adopted (e.g. consultative, authoritarian, pseudo-democratic), will significantly influence how groups and individuals perceive and react to their work environment. This requires careful navigation on the part of leaders as their actions are carefully watched by peers, superiors and subordinates.
- **Organisation structure.** Structures are often the first thing that senior managers look to change in organisations when faced with significant challenges posed by the external environment. As stated above, this often results in downsizing organisations as a way to reduce costs but also improve efficiency. Sport and leisure managers are now required to

do more with less and at the same time maintain or improve quality. This is clearly a tall order providing significant challenges for all managers. In addition, flexibility in working practice is also now required. Multi-skilling allows fewer people more opportunity to provide the necessary expertise.

- **Organisational culture.** As previously reviewed within this chapter, organisational culture relates to the values and beliefs held by the majority of the people working in a sport and leisure organisation. This is shaped by the history of the organisation, its people and, primarily, its leaders. It is thought that the leader's role is to articulate the values required in the sport and leisure organisation and to reinforce what is acceptable behaviour. As in all issues of human dynamics, this is not as easy as it may first appear. In most sport and leisure organisations there will be sub-cultures working alongside the formal organisational structures and accepted cultures. These sub-cultures will have their set of values and behavioural patterns which may, or may not, be consistent with that of the more dominant cultural norms or that of senior executives. This can have a significant impact on organisational success and will influence the power dynamics, the degree of resistance and control required with the organisation.
- **Personalities and people.** This issue is very closely aligned to the issue of culture, behaviour and control. Being sensitive to the needs, skills and informal networks is also important. It is thought that change is now becoming a way of life in most sport and leisure organisations, generating a range of responses including enthusiasm, neutrality, hostility, resistance and compliance.
- **Political processes.** Ideas for change must proceed through political processes. The timing, pace and historical context for change is also relevant. Given the importance of this factor, it is necessary to become both knowledgeable and skilful in this area. This helps to ensure that future ideas and actions become reality. Unfortunately, it may also mean that the best ideas may not prevail as they are consumed by the political machinations of the ruling hegemony (see Exhibit 3.1).

The important feature of the above model is the extent to which the internal organisation is in fit with external drivers. A health warning is needed here as this is notoriously dangerous territory (see Wilson 1992 for a critical explanation of the limitations of strategy as this relates to defining the external environment during periods of change). For example, how do you first define and then evaluate the external environment when a multitude of inter-related variables are in a constant state of flux?

So far we have been outlining the problems and challenges of structure and culture within sport and leisure organisations, without really identifying appropriate solutions. That said, there is never one solution to such complex problems. It would depend on the context, the nature of the problem and the people involved in trying to identify and solve these complex and interrelated issues. One model that may help to rationalise such issues is provided by the McKinsey 7S Framework.

3.5 The McKinsey 7S Framework

The 7S Framework was developed in the late 1970s at McKinsey and Company and popularised by two of its consultants Tom Peters and Robert Waterman (Peters and Waterman, 1982). It can be used in a variety of circumstances, from a major restructure of large multinational corporations, to the realignment of a much smaller work team.

Fundamentally, it is based on identifying, understanding and aligning seven different factors; the key point for organisational effectiveness being how they are aligned with each other, rather than any preoccupation with things like organisational structure in isolation. It is still widely used today as a means of rationalising the way that organisations are positioned in relation to their mission and a variety of related operational imperatives.

The Framework is made up of three 'hard' elements (Strategy, Structure, Systems) and four 'soft' elements (Shared Values, Skills, Style and Staff). Whilst the former are characterised as being relatively easy to define, via structural charts etc., the latter are considered more elusive and, as such, are more aligned with the much more ephemeral concept of organisational culture. Chapter 1 identified the need to consider the interdependence of all variables affecting performance; this is certainly true of this framework, with no one element assuming dominance. In this sense, the understanding and subsequent application of the model is more about the coordination and synthesis of 'hard' structural and 'soft' cultural issues. As Kaplan (2005:43) explains: 'Often, senior executives pay insufficient attention to adapting and aligning their systems even while they are introducing new strategies and structures.'

Concept check

McKinsey's hard and soft elements

Hard elements: Strategy, Structure, Systems

Soft elements: Shared Values, Skills, Style, Staff

Kaplan (2005:41) characterises the 7S model as below:

1. Strategy. The positioning and actions taken by an enterprise, in response to or anticipation of changes in the external environment, intended to achieve competitive advantage.

2. Structure. The way in which tasks and people are specialized and divided, and authority is distributed; how activities and reporting relationships are grouped; the mechanisms by which activities in the organization are coordinated.

3. Systems. The formal and informal procedures used to manage the organization, including management control systems, performance measurement and reward systems, planning, budgeting and resource allocation systems, and management information systems.

4. Staff. The people, their background and competencies; how the organization recruits, selects, trains, socializes, manages the careers, and promotes employees.

5. Skills. The distinctive competencies of the organization; what it does best along dimensions such as people, management practices, processes, systems, technology and customer relationships.

6. Style/culture. The leadership style of managers – how they spend their time, what they focus attention on, what questions they ask of employees, how they make decisions; also the organizational culture (the dominant values and beliefs, the norms, the conscious and unconscious symbolic acts taken by leaders, job titles, dress codes, executive dining rooms, corporate jets, informal meetings with employees.)

7. Shared Values. The core or fundamental set of values that are widely shared in the organization and serve as guiding principles of what is important; vision, mission, and values statements that provide a broad sense of purpose for all its employees.

Furthermore, Kaplan asserts commonalities between this and his balanced scorecard approach (Kaplan and Norton, 1992, 1996), which is also used by many organisations for a similar purpose and is particularly well suited to sport and leisure organisations who have to manage a range of competing priorities and stakeholders. He argues: 'They both articulate that effective strategy implementation requires a multi-dimensional approach. They both stress interconnectiveness.... Both models help managers align their organization for effective strategy execution' (Kaplan, 2005:42).

Shared Values (represented by the organisation's culture and sub-cultures) is at the heart of the model and should serve as a centre point and source of coherence that glues the rest together. In using the model, it is important to reconcile each of the seven elements, until a degree of consistency and balance is achieved. In order to do this, it is important to have knowledge of how the hard and soft elements manifest themselves within the organisation. However, analysing the evidence by asking appropriate questions is only half the story. It is also of critical importance to have understanding of how the seven elements are interrelated. To attempt to change just one element is likely to have some effect on all the others. Once knowledge and understanding of the starting position is achieved, this can then be mapped against a more desirable target position, thinking through and making adjustments within an iterative process that attempts to return the overall system to a degree of balance, normality and consolidation (see Chapter 9, which deals with the related issues of organisational change and development).

3.6 Summary and conclusion

The chapter has provided a critical overview of the theories and concepts of organisational structure and culture. In attempting to accomplish this, the chapter has also looked at ways of relating these two important aspects of organisational life to each other and, also, to the HRM context of sport and leisure organisations. What seems clear is that structure should be reflective of the purpose and mission of the organisation that, in turn, should be directly influenced by the needs of managers, workers, consumers and customers. In addition, the chapter reveals a recurring theme of complexity and the importance of understanding the interrelationships between a number of contributing variables. This relates not only to the content of this chapter, but also the issues discussed within many of the other chapters of this book. This implies that in order to understand organisational structure and culture, one also needs to develop a more informed understanding of a systems approach to organisational efficiency and effectiveness. This is a topic which was discussed during Chapter 1 and will be returned to at numerous other points within the overall approach taken by this book. The McKinsey 7S model was presented as one vehicle for achieving this complex aim. However, in order to unpack its true potential, there is a need to master the way in which related themes and concepts are experienced, over time, within sport and leisure organisations. This requires managers to be both reflective and reflexive in their approach to managing both systems and people.

Individual and group behaviour

> **Learning outcomes**
>
> By the end of this chapter you will be able to:
>
> - appreciate the history and development of individual and group performance as this applies to the sport and leisure management environment;
> - understand the impact of individual differences both on personal and group performance;
> - appreciate the nature of group dynamics and the impact that this can have on individual and group goals;
> - identify the relationship between decision-making and behaviour.

4.1 Introduction

There are three basic rules when considering managing people. These are:

1 People are different.
2 People are different.
3 People are different.

The literature surrounding behaviour, decision-making, motivation and personality reflects an endless array of 'individual differences'. For example, Young-Kil's (2005:72) literature search revealed '572 psychological elements which influence football performance' alone. As a consequence, the chapter does not set out to discuss all variables and associated theories in detail, as this can be better accomplished by referring to more general textbooks (for example, see Leary and Hoyle 2009). Instead the chapter seeks to provide a more general overview of the variables affecting motivation, decision-making and behaviour. Unsurprisingly, it reveals a complex interplay of interrelated factors that, collectively, dictate that there can be no quick fixes or one size fits all solutions to such issues. People seldom work in a vacuum; whether this is a cleaner within a leisure facility, a personal trainer in a health club, the manager of a local amateur sports team or a professional athlete engaged in an individual sport. Most individuals have people who they are accountable to, people upon whom they depend and people who, in turn, may depend upon them. This represents a complex series of relationships between individual personalities, experiences, ambitions, intellects, priorities, perceptions and skill sets. This, in turn, is set within the prevailing organisational context of personal and group decision-making and performance. Broadly, the chapter will consider these issues from a social psychological perspective.

Exhibit 4.1

Robertson's jam

The future success of Great Britain's badminton team could all hinge upon the relationships that exist between a handful of key individuals and how the sport's governing body, Badminton England, subsequently manages these. Nathan Robertson is an Olympic badminton silver medallist and is considered to be extremely important to Great Britain's preparation for the London 2012 Olympics.

Until December 2010 Andy Wood was head coach and had a strong and long lasting professional relationship with Robertson. However, Wood left the role when he was overruled by Badminton England's decision to invite another player, Robert Blair, to continue his training at their Milton Keynes headquarters. According to Dineen (2010:63): 'Robertson is widely thought to have refused to play in the same team as Blair because of an apparently irreparable personality clash and the former accused his Scottish team-mate of lacking commitment.'

Blair had been controversially excluded from the team for the 2010 Commonwealth Games in India. It's likely that this decision had something to do with the perception, held by some, that such individual differences and conflict had a negative influence upon the whole team dynamic. Commenting upon the situation, Robertson asserts:

> It's an issue for the new management to address when it comes in. It's like in football when players on the same team don't get on. You always get personalities that don't go together in sport.... It is very disappointing. Andy has had great success over the past 16 years or so and I have had a lot of success working with him, both as part of the team and on an individual level.
>
> *Source*: (2010:63)

Review questions

In both sport and business who is the most important ... the individual or the team?

Should personal relationships be allowed to negatively affect professional relationships?

In what ways can sports organisations, such as Badminton England, seek to better reconcile the two?

Repeat these questions after you have completed the chapter and compare your responses in the light of how your understanding of the central issues has developed.

The chapter will begin by discussing the historical aspects of individual and group performance as this applies to the sport and leisure management environment. In such organisations it is inevitable that individual performance will be largely dependent upon how individuals interface with a multiplicity of both internal (staff) and external (third party) stakeholders. These, in turn, can be positively or negatively related to decision-making and performance over a period of time. The second part of the chapter will move on to discuss the nature and development of groups and their importance with respect to effective organisational performance. Finally, the chapter will conclude with a discussion of individual motivation and performance.

4.2 Historical context of individual and group performance

The study of management has its roots in the developments around the time of the industrial revolution. Underpinning much of the thinking was the need to address the question, 'what leads to effective performance both at individual and group levels?' Rules of thumb based upon unassailable assumptions were used to address such questions. Most notably was the classical management movement with its emphasis on command and control and the need to have a formal organisational design that closely aligned management control with output and performance enhancement. The rule of thumb here was that workers were fundamentally concerned with individual well-being and that work was primarily a means to an end. Therefore workers needed to be controlled and policed carefully to ensure work was carried out efficiently (also see Chapter 1).

Fredrick Taylor's belief in 'scientific management' (1911) is central to this thinking. Taylor believed that workers were motivated by pay and that managers should focus on providing workers with the best opportunity to gain as much pay as possible. The responsibility of management was to ensure that the best work methods were identified and that workers were trained in these methods. Broadly, this necessitated an autocratic method of management in order to direct, supervise and control work productivity. What this creates, according to Taylor's view, was a virtuous cycle of improved performance and motivation. Everybody wins! If management methods were seen to be successful, the workers would achieve increased pay directly linked to their effort, whilst the organisation benefits from improved efficiency, productivity and performance. Under this scenario Taylor did not see the need for trade unions, as everyone's needs would be met. On the flip side, however, such thinking was predicated upon a wholly different historical and cultural context, which impacted upon individual motivations and the relationships that existed between workers and managers at the time. In many ways this represented a much simpler cultural dynamic which made it easier to impose management methods based upon unassailable assumptions about how best to do this. For example, it was predicated that success could be clearly measured through productivity measures and that third party interests were entirely secondary to this process. However, as reviewed in Chapter 1, much of sport and leisure has substantial 'service' components that do not always lend themselves to such ideas and management style. As we shall see later in the chapter, management approaches, whilst being cognisant of such fundamental ideas, must become more refined in order to accommodate the nuances of working in the sport and leisure field in the twenty-first century.

Much of the early classical management thinking and practice was based on such rules of thumb (or heuristics). It revolved around a systematic approach to planning, coordinating, controlling, commanding, rewarding and organising both people and resources, providing the foundation for what we now call work-study and management science. It is clear that Taylor's influence has left a long lasting impact on the way organisations manage themselves and both the people and processes within them. Issues of organisational efficiency and effectiveness will always be relevant, particularly for capitalist societies in which production and profitability issues tend to dominate. As Hamel and Breen (2007:12) contend:

> We are prisoners of our paradigms. And as managers, we are captives of a paradigm that places the pursuit of efficiency ahead of every other goal. This is hardly surprising, since modern management was invented to solve the problem of inefficiency.

Hence, the enduring related paradigms of both classical and scientific management still have their place in modern management practice. In the UK we can see examples of this through such initiatives as competitive tendering and best value within public sector leisure and sport provision. The roots of these ideas are that the public sector would benefit from competition in order to improve efficiency. This leads to a productivity led model of management that is very much about process control, measurement, evaluation and performance improvement. In addition, it has been argued that competition has an inherently relational component. Kilduff *et al.* (2010), in an investigation of American college basketball, argue that this has management implications with respect both to motivation and performance issues. This must be placed in an historical context of increasingly competitive markets and differentiated consumer demand. As a consequence of this, we can see the impetus for the development of professional management during the twentieth and twenty-first centuries. This is inextricably linked with concomitant changes in management thinking, in general, and people management thinking, in particular, over this time period.

Review questions

Using what you know about the context of managing people in sport, to what extent are such classical management principles still relevant today?

Think of a sport or leisure organisation with which you are familiar. How would you seek to apply Frederick Taylor's ideas to your example? What additional issues would you need to address?

The traditional criticisms of Taylor revolve around the lack of appreciation of individual difference and, as a consequence of this, a lack of understanding of individual psychological impact. Under this paradigm, it was logical for work to be fragmented, measured and, therefore, rewarded accordingly. In an early application of such literature to the sport arena

Ulrich and Parkhouse (1979) point out that rewards have to be congruent with desired performance and that it is important to learn the contemporary lessons of management science as they apply to the sports context. However, such early theories do little to consider the psychological development of individuals and the group(s). Potentially, this extremely narrow and instrumental approach to both management and productivity could lead to boredom and psychological alienation. We know that change is fast paced and that sport/leisure organisations have to respond to such changes in order to survive and prosper. However, to what extent have we fundamentally moved on from the traditional models of 'command and control' espoused in early managerial thinking? The answer(s) to this question is at the root of many contemporary management challenges.

What is clear is that sport and leisure managers have to do more with less and be creative with how they use scarce resources. As a consequence of this, there will be a need to fall back upon traditional managerial paradigms that value measurement and productivity above all other things. Given this possibility, the question then becomes ... 'to what extent can we recognise such practices in contemporary management behaviour specifically applied to the sport and leisure sector?' The honest answers to such questions are fundamental to how we approach HRM and development in the twenty-first century.

The work of Chris Argyris has a valuable contribution to make to this discussion. His work describes two types of behaviour in organisations. He calls the first behaviour 'espoused theory' and the second 'theory in use'. Simply put, this is the difference between what people say they do (espoused theory) compared to what they actually do (theory in use). The important feature of this set of ideas is that individuals don't often recognise that there is incongruence (mis-match) between what they say and what they do. So, for example, you may find that senior managers say that they involve subordinates in decision-making but in reality this does not happen. Instead, decisions are, all too often, perceived by staff to be very top down in their orientation. Similarly, managers often claim their fundamental focus is on individual and group development but in reality the focus is on efficiency and productivity improvement; much like the approach taken in scientific management. This is particularly problematic in sport where outside investors are impatient for success. For example, Harman (2010:63), commenting on the expense involved in developing Britain's tennis potential, explains: 'In austere times any potential sponsor will probably demand instant gratification for its investment and that's not what tennis is about. It is about staying loyal to young players when things get tough, about the long haul.' Moreover, this should also be balanced by a dose of realism on both sides with respect to performance indicators. Individuals, whether in a traditional work or professional sporting environment, may be overly optimistic about their contribution and potential. In some ways this is even more difficult to recognise and manage, as individuals (or their representatives) may truly believe in their espoused theory. However, when the evidence is more objectively reviewed, it is often easier, based on the metrics available, to make the opposite case, i.e. they are not performing at a level commensurate with their view of their own performance and/or potential. Of course, all things are relative and individual perspectives are important. As too are the quality of metrics used to measure individual and group performance (see Chapter 8). Typically, there are arguments on both sides. It is the role of managers to understand and rationalise such potential incongruence and establish a supportive and productive way of working against the sometimes ill-defined needs of the individual(s), group(s) and organisation(s).

The prevalence of classical and scientific approaches to efficiency and production was also synonymous with the related development of bureaucratic models of management. The work of the German academic Max Weber is significant here. Weber believed that the best way to organise large complex organisations was through a form of bureaucratic organisation based on formal systems and administration. There needed to be a formal link between systems, tasks and relationships. In addition, there needed to be a formal hierarchy of authority with clear lines of command and control. In order for this to be effective the approach needed to be both impersonal and rational, with work standardised and workers closely controlled.

Traditional critiques of this approach suggest that, by becoming too formalised, organisations do not account for the prevalent, pervasive and important informal aspects such as organisational cultures and individual/group behaviours (see Chapter 3). In addition, bureaucracy is often tied to the problem of 'red tape' and an inability for organisations to act quickly and decisively when required to do so. There is also the problem of goal displacement where process becomes more important than the outcome. In these circumstances, there is a real danger that the rules become more important than the actual performance.

Each of the above models of management have limitations but can also be seen to be applied to today's sport and leisure organisations in one form or another. Most, if not all, sport and leisure organisations will have managerial structures that attempt to clearly outline lines of authority, unity of command and clear roles and responsibilities. Increasingly there is a need to measure performance at individual, group and organisational levels. In each case, however, there are significant limitations with both classical and scientific notions of management in this regard. Unsurprisingly, other models began to develop which challenged existing orthodoxies and encouraged both owners and managers to take a more holistic and multi-layered view of worker performance and productivity.

The human relations approach was such a response. It was based on the work of Elton Mayo and his 'Hawthorn' studies (1927–1933), where productivity increased regardless of changes in work conditions. It was postulated, therefore, that performance was more related to a perception of the special attention paid to workers by management. The key, according to this thinking, is to focus on social relationships as a vehicle towards organisational efficiency and success. As such, managers should have the highest regard for their employees. The premise was that people need both social interaction and recognition in order to be both socially and psychologically well. This, in turn, would lead to improved efficiency and performance. Therefore, group needs were more important than pay and conditions and it is group behaviour that will strongly influence output and overall performance at work. So the managerial prescription here is that organisations need to be aware of the importance of social needs in order to effectively lead and motivate their employees. These studies also found that workers could restrict and increase workflow based on the influence of group dynamics. This prompted the need for further research into the importance of group behaviour as the key to increasing performance. Of course, there is also a need to keep this dynamic under constant review. For example, Carlo Ancelotti, the former Chelsea Football Club manager, wrote in his autobiography of the pivotal role played by Ray Wilkins during his early time at Chelsea:

> It was tough in the beginning. I didn't speak English that well. One of the reasons I fitted into the locker room was thanks to the fundamental role played by Ray Wilkins, my number two and my friend, because it is one thing to translate words – plenty of people can do that – but translating feelings is the gift of only a select few.
>
> (extract from *Sky Sports Magazine*, December/January 2010:54)

Clearly Wilkins appeared to have a special relationship with Ancelotti, who held him in high regard; all the necessary ingredients for good 'human relations'! However, Wilkins was controversially sacked in November 2010 from his alleged £400,000-a-year role as coach; perhaps considered surplus to requirements now that Ancelotti, who is known to prefer a hands-on approach to training and coaching, had mastered the language!

This highlights how ruthless professional sports business organisations can be and is consistent with a pattern of well established, results-oriented, behaviour at Chelsea Football Club over a number of years. As Ruud Gullit has said, after being dismissed by Chelsea in 1998 after just winning the FA Cup with them for the first time in 26 years, being second in the Premiership and still in the quarter finals of two cup competitions:

> During my life, that [the sacking] had the biggest impact. As a human being, I had never been treated like that. I was shell-shocked for almost three months. I couldn't

believe that people I worked with every day could do that. ... People I played golf with, people I exchanged gifts with, these people were doing things behind my back ... that was the worst thing.

(Walsh, 2007:2.14)

There are some fundamental concepts of behaviour that underpin much of what has been discussed so far. Chester Barnard (1938), for example, elaborates on the human relations school of thought by adding that organisations are made up of small groups and that that the productivity of these groups is dependent upon worker cooperation and acceptance of legitimate authority. In many ways, Bernard reminds us that management is just as much an art form as it is a science. Whilst management 'effectiveness' is important and measures the extent to which outputs and goals are met, Barnard argued that 'efficiency' should be regarded as the extent to which the organisation meets the needs of its stakeholders. This provided a very different way of viewing organisations, as compared with the hard scientific approaches previously postulated. It is also well related to the needs of sports organisations that have to consider the requirements of stakeholders within both their strategic and operational decision-making processes. For example, the Amateur Swimming Association's Strategic Plan (2009–2013) identifies the need 'To develop and deploy a skilled workforce that meets the needs of participants, clubs and employers' as an integral part of its workforce development plan (ASA, 2009:15).

Barnard (1938:235) argues that management decisions require '"feeling", "judgment", "sense", "proportion", "balance", "appropriateness". It is a matter of art and it is aesthetic rather than logical.' Of course, this will always be a matter of opinion and the judgement of the Chelsea FC hierarchy may well be different from that of Ancelotti, the players and the fans. However, the bottom line for most professional sports organisations is to plan for the future by managing in the present. As Ancelotti is reported to have said: 'The club made this decision. ... It was a difficult decision for everyone, but I have respect for this decision. I have trust in all the staff who are working with me, but we have to move on now' (Burt, 2011).

The common thread, in all the models reviewed so far, is that they adopt a unitaristic approach. In other words they tend to be looking at the world from a one-dimensional, reductionist and, therefore, overly simplistic perspective. This, as we know, is unlikely to fully reflect the reality of work life in the twenty-first century. Organisations are multifaceted and a more holistic and expansive approach is needed if we are to understand how sport and leisure organisations operate in practice. This is not an easy feat, as even the smallest of sport and leisure organisations will have their own bespoke culture, features, context and ways of doing things. From the local golf club to regional sport governing bodies, from small leisure businesses to multinational sports retailers, they will all have a very unique way in which things get done.

Organisation theory and systems thinking developed following on from the more traditional management approaches identified above. As outlined in Chapter 1, 'systems thinking' requires organisations to see themselves as part of a whole rather than as an isolated entity. Organisations can be viewed as a closed system, not interacting with the surrounding environment, or as an open system, which responds to external influences. However, it is becoming increasingly difficult for sport or leisure organisations to function as a purely closed system in today's competitive, dynamic, pluralistic and stakeholder driven markets. That said, organisations could have a predisposition to look inwardly rather than externally, depending on the organisation's history, culture and objectives. For example, public sector sport and leisure providers have complex managerial structures that involve paid officers and elected members. This will bring with it a predisposition to move carefully and to consider internal political factors before taking decisions that will interface with the surrounding context. This is not to say that UK public sector providers of sport and leisure work in a closed system, rather that their unique culture may be predisposed to first looking inwardly before then looking to the wider external environment.

4.3 The development of organisational theory

At the outset of this chapter we stated that the key to understanding human resource management is through a recognition that people are different. So far the foundations of management thinking, outlined above, do not fully account for this. The response is the development of organisation theory and associated contingency approaches to solving organisational problems. As we have said, people are different and such differences can be multiplied exponentially within organisations; no two being exactly the same. Each sport and leisure organisation will have its unique history, personalities, politics, competitive context, missions and objectives. In addition, the people that make up the organisation will have different ambitions, skills and personal qualities. This creates real challenges for managers operating within such a complex environment of competing priorities. Contingency theory offers a more holistic approach to this problem.

Concept check

Contingency management

Contingency management is where:

- Managers assess problems and develop best solutions based on this.
- The major assumption is that there is no one best way to manage and no easy quick fix solutions to complex problems and decision-making.
- Solutions to organisational problems will, therefore, depend on the nature of the organisation, its environment, the nature of the problem and the qualities of the people within the organisation.
- A 'what if' approach is adopted, attempting to take into account as many interrelated variables as possible. This could involve many different groups within the organisation including workers, managers and senior executives. The solution should be 'contingent' upon these.

Contingency management also has it limitations. It is very difficult, if not impossible, to account for every possibility in a given set of circumstances. In addition, understanding the external environment is, in itself, a complex activity. How do you define the external environment and how do you identify all of the relevant alternatives in a given set of circumstances? The seminal work of Herbert Simon and James Quinn is useful to discuss here. Simon coined the phrase 'bounded rationality'. What this means, in essence, is that individuals and groups are limited in terms of their ability to identify all of the contributory factors and possible alternatives in a given set of decision-making circumstances. In all but the most simplistic of circumstances, it would be impossible to gather and fully understand all the required information needed to take complex decisions. As a consequence, most decisions are seen to be 'bounded' by incomplete information, time pressures, human limitations and/or disagreements over goals.

As a result, rather than using contingency theory to come to the best solution to complex problems, solutions are frequently agreed that are satisfactory rather than optimal. In other words there is a compromise in the nature of decisions taken: satisficing rather than optimisation. James Quinn's work on logical incrementalism is in a similar vein. Quinn was interested in studying the nature of strategic decisions and, similar to Simon, came to the conclusion that this had more to do with step by step reactive approaches than the existence of perfectly crafted strategic plans that account for every contingency possible. In both cases the thinking tends to be more realistic and less idealistic in terms of what organisations actually do in practice. In addition to these realities, there is also the power and politics within organisations. These can be somewhat irrational and certainly not consistent with more traditional and logical approaches to strategic development. Rational analysis provides the foundation for many approaches to management both in theory and in practice. In fact it is the starting point in most strategic decision-making processes. Rational analysis includes consideration of the following questions:

- Where are we now?
- Where do we want to be?
- How do we get there?
- How long will it take?
- What resources do we need?
- How will we know if we are going in the right direction?

Concept check

Voluntarism vs determinism

The extent to which sport and leisure managers have control over their environment is not clear. Theoretically, this is accounted for in two broad perspectives.

Voluntarism. Sport and leisure managers have control over the environment and can, therefore, be *proactive* in shaping future events.

Determinism. Sport and leisure managers have little control over the environment and can, therefore, only be *reactive* to issues that impact the organisation.

In reality, it is probably a combination of both voluntarism and determinism that drives decision-making in sport and leisure organisations. A good example of this is the 2012 London Olympics. The London bidding team had little control over the outcome of the decision. What they could do was to provide the best bid possible given time, resources and political support. The decision was left to the International Olympic Committee. The London team would have behaved both in a proactive and reactive fashion in relation to the circumstances that they were facing. This can be seen as a realistic and pragmatic approach to the activity. Conversely, the uncertainty of such processes can be illustrated by considering England's bid for the 2018 Football World Cup (see Exhibit 4.2).

Exhibit 4.2

England's Football World Cup bid

Despite having arguably the best technical and commercial bid and a final presentation that was described by FIFA president Sepp Blatter as 'excellent and remarkable', England were comprehensively eliminated in the first round of possible countries to host the 2018 Football World Cup. According to Richard Scudamore, the Chief Executive of the English Premier League:

> What was interesting was what the president said at the end about taking the World Cup to two new territories and, in Qatar's case, mentioning Arab

countries. That was the driver. They have decided to take the World Cups to developing areas.

Source: Gibson (2010b)

Unfortunately, this was never clear to the English bid team who may have decided not to bid if they had understood this earlier in the process. Alternatively, perhaps the decision to develop FIFA's World Cup brand in this way was taken much later in the process following allegations in the British media about corruption at FIFA. Whatever the truth, it is difficult to argue that the pervasive influence of the British media didn't prove to be both decisive and divisive throughout the bidding process and, particularly, in the final few days before the final decision was made at FIFA Headquarters.

Local authority providers of sport and leisure in the United Kingdom have to work closely with central government and react to changing legal requirements. In these circumstances managers do not have a free hand in decision-making, which is set within this political context. For example, local authority sport and leisure managers did not create competitive tendering or best value. These were government initiatives set up to improve efficiency and customer service in local government. Sport and leisure managers, as well as senior local authority officers, then had to decide how to manage this situation given their circumstances and political context. Again this is an example of both voluntaristic and deterministic decision-making.

On the other hand there are events that happen which sit outside any rational planning model and theoretical decision framework. In fact, several decisions may be much more opportunistic in nature, often taken quickly in response to a combination of either internal and/or external antecedents. This is certainly true of the English Cricket Board's 2008 decision to sign a deal with Allen Stanford, a wealthy American philanthropist.

Exhibit 4.3

Allen Stanford and the ECB

In 2008, the English Cricket Board (ECB) were worried about the growing influence of the Indian Premier Cricket League and accepted an offer of a lucrative, winner takes all, Twenty20 cricket series between England and the Stanford Superstars in the West Indies. The series was funded by Allen Stanford, a wealthy and philanthropic American businessman. Of course, it's important to both spot and seize opportunities when they become available. However, the phrase, 'act in haste, repent at leisure' is certainly true of the ECB's decision, as the cricket series proved to be a PR nightmare. To exacerbate such issues still further, the disastrous cricket series was closely followed by the arrest of Mr Stanford on fraud charges. In February 2009, the ECB formally severed ties with Stanford in a humiliating reversal for the leadership team. It is unclear if they will need to pay back some or all of the money received from Stanford, as part of ongoing criminal investigations in the United States into his business practices. This clearly fits into what can be described as an irrational model of organisational decision-making. It is more to do with fear, power, politics and ambition than with more traditional and more rational forms of management thinking.

Exhibit 4.4 illustrates an example of more traditional approaches to management thinking.

NBA referees' strike

In 2009 the National Basketball Association (NBA) referees decided to go on strike over pay and conditions. The negotiations were tense and the thinking in the popular media was that the referees were not performing well and did not deserve an increase in their pay packets.

NBA referees are subject to very close scrutiny and their performance is reviewed following each match. They come in for much criticism. The problem here is that their performance is viewed by millions of fans both at the live matches and on the television. Match commentators also review referee decisions as they occur live on national television. This is unique in terms of performance measurement and puts significant pressure on the referees to perform well. This example also fits well with traditional approaches of scientific management and performance measurement.

The response of the NBA owners was to train alternative referees to take their place. The owners, therefore, took a hard line, which led to the referees agreeing to a lot less money than they originally wanted. This illustrates an example of where fear, power, politics and ambition worked in favour of management, rather than against it, as they outmanoeuvred the NBA referees.

4.4 The nature of groups and group behaviour

It is clear that group development and performance will be the key to organisational success or otherwise. Moreover, it is also clear that improving group performance is not an easy task to achieve in practice. There are many interrelated variables at work here that create challenges for managers and leaders. This includes the managerial leadership predisposition and style, the environment of the organisation, its objectives, people, structures, cultures and we could go on. If we talk about fundamentals we can begin to identify some common threads that may helps us deal with these complexities.

Concept check

Groups and teams

A **group**. A collection of individuals who often have personal and task interdependence.

A **team**. A collection of individuals who share a collective identity, collective purpose and work together to achieve a common goal.

How do groups and teams differ?

- Teams interact to achieve shared objectives.
- All teams are groups, not all groups are teams.
- Team members have to depend on and support each other to accomplish shared objectives – they have interdependency and shared goals.

The effectiveness of team performance will have a direct impact on how well a sport and leisure organisation achieves its mission, goals and objectives. There are many authors who offer ideas, theories and models to help us further understand group dynamics and performance. John Adair's action centred leadership model (1973) combines the three important aspects of the leadership and group situations. These are the team, the task, and the individual. In each case there needs to be a synergy between the elements in terms of skills, clarity of role and emphasis on priorities. For example, if urgent action is needed, then the task would take priority over individual and group needs. On balance though, it is thought that a leadership approach that accounts for all three elements, broadly in equal measure, is more likely to have a positive impact on individual motivation, group cohesion and team/organisational performance.

Another model that highlights the need to take a holistic view, when faced with group and individual dynamics, is the Blake and Mouton managerial grid, which has been well documented in the generic management literature (see Mullins, 2007). The essence of the model is that sport and leisure managers should have high regard for both the task and the people side of delivering objectives; this is termed 'team leadership'. This again makes perfectly good sense and is a prescription that is worth considering; even given the complex nature of most organisations.

During the 1970s Meredith Belbin (2010) provided a useful framework to try to understand the roles that people can play in any group situation. This is important for a sport and leisure manager to understand in order to try, as far as possible, to get a good fit between individual contributions and organisational needs. This also provides an opportunity to build on individual strengths and improve the potential for individuals to make important contributions based on their interests, skills, personal qualities and knowledge.

Concept check

Belbin's team role model

Belbin argued that teams should, ideally, be made from individuals who have complementary roles and personal qualities. These are identified below.

Coordinator. Keeps goals clear, leadership, coordinator style.
Shaper. Overcomes hurdles, leadership, directive style.
Plant. Problem solver, new ideas creative thinking, innovative.
Resource/investigator. Explores opportunities and develops contacts, explores ideas and resources beyond the team.
Team worker. Moderator and worker, promotes team spirit.
Monitor/evaluator. Critically analyses and gives accurate judgements.
Implementer. Moves into the tangible, practical, works within the rules.
Completer/finisher. Reviews work, gets job done. Keeps work on schedule and maintains standards.
Specialist. Focuses on details, strong technical knowledge.

The important thing to keep in mind is that all of the models have value and provide useful frameworks to better understand group dynamics and situations. However, there are no easy quick fix solutions to dealing with group dynamics and performance issues. Like much of the early management theory, the models on their own can only provide a partial explanation for the complexities of group dynamics. The prescriptions are useful but what is needed is an eclectic knowledge of such concepts and an understanding of how these can be applied to real life issues in order to provide a more useful contingency approach to both individual motivations and group dynamics.

Group dynamics is further complicated by the power and political dimension of organisational life. Often it is the leader who sets the agenda for group dynamics and behaviour. If a leader is more of a consensus manager he/she will seek to involve and communicate with subordinates. On the other hand if a leader is more authoritarian, then it is less likely that he/she will seek the advice and input of subordinates in the decision-making process. Of course there will be shades of grey in between and this is well rehearsed in the management literature. For example Tannenbaum and Schmidt (1973) presented their 'continuum of leadership behaviour'. At one end of the scale, management style and decisions are viewed as entirely autocratic. At the other end of the scale, however, there is a much more delegative leadership style, which promotes a strong sense of staff empowerment.

Another important theory to consider during group situations is groupthink. Groupthink is a theory developed by Janis (1972) as a response to group situations that seem to go wrong. He identified several symptoms of groupthink, including those identified by Exhibit 4.5.

Exhibit 4.5

Examples of groupthink

Chief amongst Janis's (1972) conception of groupthink are the concepts of 'invulnerability' and 'rationale' where managers have an inflated sense of confidence; an omnipotence which predisposes them to ignore warnings and take greater risks.

The 1993 Lyme Bay canoeing tragedy, where four teenagers lost their lives, demonstrates this type of behaviour. Two experienced canoeing instructors continually warned the owners of the centre that there were significant health and safety issues that needed to be addressed urgently or someone would be hurt or killed. They provided a strong rationale for their position but the owners and the managers refused to listen to them even though they were the experts in the activities. It would appear that the owners were more concerned with the short-term cost of making changes than longer-term health and safety considerations. Ultimately, the tragedy led to the first successful prosecution in the UK, under corporate manslaughter legislation, and the instigation of a new regulatory framework to govern related practices.

As you can see, from the above description of groupthink, it is a very powerful social psychological construct that can potentially restrict and negatively influence group development and performance. The potential for this to happen will be, to some extent, dependent upon the degree of organisational health.

Concept check

Organisational health

The extent to which individuals and groups are able to share their views, even if they run against the conventional wisdom of the individuals and groups in position power. A healthy organisational culture would, potentially, reduce the negative aspects of groupthink.

4.5 Individual motivation

The key theme of the chapter is that there is no one best way to motivate or manage people. This will all depend of the organisational context, the external environment, the people who make up the organisation and the leadership style. In all of these circumstances, power and micro-politics will also play a role. In other words individuals and groups will look to protect themselves and their interests against the interests of others. So, for example, approaches to management and motivation of employees will be very different in a public sector sport and leisure organisation than it would be in a private sector organisation or a voluntary sport organisation. There are particular management challenges in the voluntary sector as traditional motivational influences such as pay, reward and recognition may not apply as volunteers may be doing this work purely for their own altruistic reasons.

We can look to traditional motivation theories to help us understand and manage in each of the above contexts, although none can provide all the answers. They can, however, provide a framework to effectively guide management in carrying out this very difficult and challenging task.

Individual motivation and performance is complex. There is no one best explanation for behaviour that can account for all circumstances, contexts and people. For some, individual motivation will be about pay, conditions, reward and recognition. For others it may be about the work itself or tied to an individual's life cycle and personal circumstances. For example, John Parrott the one time world snooker champion was reflecting on his career during an interview with the BBC. He was clear that the reason that he is now retired is not the fact that he lost his skill or, for that matter, the love of the game, but that there are now other priorities in his life, such as his family.

The major motivation theories have been well described in the literature to date. It is clear that they remain useful in helping sport and leisure managers to understand and deal with the complex nature of human motivation. There are many such theories but the main authors seem to be the following; Maslow, Alderfer, McGregor, Herzberg, Likert, Argyris, Adams, McClleland and Vroom. To this we can add the work of Hadler, Festinger and the more contemporary work of Ryan and Deci. Such theories can be, broadly, categorised into process and content theories.

Concept check

Process and content theories of individual motivation

Process theories. Focus on the drivers, processes and often the expectations associated with a set of behaviours, i.e. extrinsic motivation. These theories tend to concentrate on the consequences of external measures of performance and equity. As such, 'cognitive' based theories, such as those provided by, *inter alia*, Vroom and Adams, are relevant here.

Content theories. Focus upon an individual's physical and emotional inner drive to achieve things for themselves, i.e. intrinsic motivation. As such, 'needs' based theories, such as those provided by, *inter alia*, Maslow and Herzberg are relevant here.

Content theories appear to have a consistent theme associated with them. They identify a distinction between higher order needs such as self-actualisation, growth, recognition, advancement, independence, need for autonomy, maturity and lower order needs such as physiological needs, pay and conditions, dependence, immaturity, need for control and need for increased supervision. The emerging themes are clear but the solutions to the problem of how best to motivate individuals is not so clear. It would all depend on the nature of the organisation, its relationship with the external environment, the tasks that need to be carried out, the personal histories, skills and ambitions of the individual members of staff and, of course, the relationship between managers and their subordinates. As we said at the start of the chapter, people are different. Whilst some might welcome the opportunities afforded by the increased professionalisation of sport, others will bemoan its effects on the underpinning values, philosophy and integrity. For example, Augustin Pichot, the Argentinean rugby captain, speaking just before the 2007 Rugby World Cup semi-final has argued:

> It is not about the thousands of pounds in a player's pocket or the numbers that fill a stadium. It is about the passion you share when playing, it's about the pleasure you have together...
> We are obsessesed with advertising campaigns, keeping the press out of reach. Remembering that Rugby is first of all a game that should be played with passion and pride has been a victim of this process. We should use the rugby jersey not for how much money we can make but to remember we represent other people, maybe a nation.
> (quoted in Bills, 2007:90)

So once again there are no quick fix solutions as intrinsically motivated sports stars may become seduced by the external motivators associated with fame and fortune. Sport and leisure managers have to consider the individual differences, the context and the task in order to begin to achieve successful outcomes in terms of motivating both individuals and groups. This seems like common sense, but working reality creates situations where common sense may not prevail. As cited above, this may often be influenced by power, internal politics, individual ambition or even a lack of competence and commitment to achieve the desired outcome.

Another major consideration, that will have an impact on individual motivation and performance, is the interface between the individual and the organisation. In sport and leisure organisations, individuals and groups are under pressure to do more with less. Increasingly this is set against a context of the reduction in unit resourcing that, in turn, reduces the ability for the organisation to reward performance based on individual initiative; this is particularly true of the public and voluntary sectors. An irony here is that even the traditional concepts of classical and scientific management recognised the need to reward effort based on individual performance. This in turn creates a tension between attitudes and behaviours. Attitudes are what individuals believe and behaviours are what individuals do. There is no problem if an individual's attitude and belief system is congruent with what they are being asked to do (cognitive consistency). The problem arises when there is incongruence between an individual's attitude or belief system and what he/she is being asked to do (cognitive dissonance).

Cognitive dissonance is based on the seminal work by Leon Festinger (1957). His social psychological theory has relevance today, given the fast-changing nature of sport and leisure organisations coupled with increasing demands to be more competitive and businesslike in all aspects of the industry. Cognitive dissonance occurs when there is tension between what an individual believes, and the nature of the organisation and the task that needs to be carried out. The most notable example of this in the UK is the changing nature of UK voluntary sporting organisations such as national governing bodies for sport. These are complex organisations that work at local, regional, national and international levels. They depend heavily on the work of volunteers in order to survive yet they are at the same time being required to be more businesslike in their approach to the work (see Abrams *et al.*, 1995; Nichols, 2004).

Concept check

Cognitive dissonance

Cognitive dissonance is a psychological concept that denotes a mismatch between what people think and what people are required to do.

The opportunity to experience cognitive dissonance, which in turn may influence job satisfaction and motivation, is particularly acute with sporting structures. For example, a national governing body of sport is not a homogeneous group, it comprises a wide range of interests and standpoints including: 'Elected honorary officers, staff of national body, officers of constituent regional/county bodies, elite performers, recreational performers, coaches, technical officials, voluntary administrators, club owners, men and women, disabled and able-bodied players' (Abrams *et al.*, 1995:45). Rarely does an individual express the viewpoint of the entire national governing body. What we have, instead, are multiple goals and multiple stakeholders with different motivations; all requiring a unique and thoughtful approach to management. Herein also lies a significant managerial challenge. How do you motivate volunteers who may not respond to the traditional theories of motivation outlined in this chapter so far? In addition, how do you deal with the inevitable cognitive dissonance of some volunteers when faced with the requirement to behave in a 'more businesslike' fashion?

This is one of many examples of the tension between individual needs and organisational requirements, often driven by change and external influences. It is not surprising, therefore, that an increasing body of research into the motivations of sports volunteers clearly demonstrates that there is no simple formula for understanding the multiple motivations of sports volunteers (Kim *et al.*, 2010; Busser and Carruthers, 2010; Allen and Shaw, 2009; Lee and Beeler, 2009; Giannoulakis *et al.*, 2007; Downward and Ralston, 2005; Twynam *et al.*, 2002/3).

Likewise, employees in public sector sport and leisure organisations are now required to be more flexible and to work across functional areas. This may include pool supervision, managing hospitality and bars, activities and programme coordination. In addition, as stated previously, this also requires employees to do more with less: sometimes to a higher standard of quality. This adds to the difficulties of first understanding and then managing within such an environment. However, if managers are to effectively manage they need to first understand such issues and then effectively communicate with employees and keep them 'informed of where the business is heading and what the organization is expecting from them' (Levine, 2009:3).

Ryan and Deci have attempted to rationalise many of the previously highlighted tensions with their 'Self Determination Theory' (SDT). This builds upon earlier attempts, through their 'cognitive evaluation theory', to explain the complex relationship that exists between extrinsic and intrinsic motivators; particularly with respect to work performance and behaviour. Whilst they argue that tangible (extrinsic) rewards can undermine intrinsic motivation, this did not explain all instances characterised by such relationships.

In SDT they add to the literature by identifying a relationship between 'autonomous', and 'controlled' motivation. Broadly, both of these variables imply an intention to act and are related to the concepts of intrinsic and extrinsic motivation, respectively. In contrast, 'amotivation' refers to instances where there is a lack of intention/motivation to act (Gagne and Deci, 2005). What is important here is that a continuum exists between situations where there is no intention to act (amotivation) and situations that are entirely characterised by intrinsic motivators. The trick is to understand the relationship that 'controlled' (external) motivators have in mediating such relationships and the position on the continuum. Where possible managers must seek, through a variety of methods, to assimilate work tasks, by pressing the buttons that really engage staff in their work. If management is skilful in this endeavour, this should move staff towards the side of the continuum that is more related to autonomous and intrinsic motivation. This, of course, will vary from person to person and will be dependent upon factors such as leadership style, interpersonal relations and organisational culture. This role is captured by Tony Hall, the Chief Executive of the Royal Opera House who argues: 'my job is to enable as many of their [workers'] dreams to happen as possible' (in Kelleher, 2008:4).

Deci and Ryan argue that in order to achieve optimal psychological development, health and motivation, in any situation, it necessary to fulfil the three basic needs of relatedness (with other work colleagues), individual competence and personal autonomy to act. Furthermore, it is the perception and interpretation of events, combined with the extent to which this mediates individual need, that will dictate subsequent behaviour, overall psychological well-being and work performance. As they argue: 'it is typically people's feelings, beliefs, motives, and goals, and the perceived environment within which these feelings, beliefs, motives, and goals arise, that organize subsequent behavior' (Ryan and Deci, 2008:655).

4.6 Summary and conclusion

The chapter provides an overview of the factors affecting individual and group decision-making and behaviour. It does not pretend to produce a detailed look at each theory, as this has been done many times before by various authors and textbooks. Instead, it seeks to synthesise the lessons to produce a more coherent understanding of the issues as a whole. What is interesting, however, is the extent to which the lessons of the past, whilst being mediated by the present, are still relevant to the current and, probably, future demands faced by sport and leisure managers. It is also true that there is no easy prescription or one size fits all solution to such issues.

Human beings are not robots – sometimes they appear rational, whilst at other times incoherent, particularly if you cannot appreciate the antecedents of their actions. Individuals, by definition, are all different and respond in different ways to different situations. In some sense, this can be aligned to the 'black box' analogy found in the introductory chapter, where the black box represents the way in which internal and external environmental factors (inputs) are both individually and collectively interpreted to produce subsequent actions (outputs).

What is clear is that it is an understanding of the lived experiences both of staff and managers, combined with the influence of the prevailing context, that is likely to lead to better quality decisions, actions and subsequent performance. This makes it all the more important that managers are both reflective and reflexive in their approach to both their own individual development and that of their co-workers (also see Chapters 5, 7 and 10).

The changing nature of sport management and the personal skills required by sport managers

> **Learning outcomes**
>
> By the end of this chapter you will be able to:
>
> - appreciate how the historical context of sport influences sport management and the skills required today;
> - analyse the nature of the contemporary sport manager;
> - review skills policies with regard to sport management;
> - evaluate the personal skills required by sport managers.

5.1 Introduction

Are the personal skills required by sport and leisure managers any different from those valued by other sectors? This provides a key question for HR managers within this sector and the subsequent approach to related areas such as recruitment, retention, development and performance appraisal. The answer, at least in part, relates to the unique context of sport and leisure provision within local, national and international markets. It is also important to remember that the provision and management of sport and leisure, worldwide, is far from uniform, representing a multiplicity of competing markets, demands and priorities both for customers and providers (refer to Chapter 1). For example, the management of a public sector 5-a-side facility will share similarities, but also significant differences, from commercial operators in this area. Moreover, there are likely to be differences at local, regional, national and even international levels. This affects the type of skills required and, also, the prioritisation of such skills within the rubric of the manager's skills toolkit. It is certainly true to say that sport management jobs are becoming more and more attractive to managers from outside of the sector, perhaps driven by the impact of high profile sports events such as the London 2012 Olympics.

The chapter will begin by briefly exploring the historical context of sport management and how this influences the general and sector specific management skills needed today. The chapter will then examine related UK-centric national policy frameworks such as National Occupational Standards. These will be viewed in relation to the literature surrounding skills and competencies and will help examine the numerous claims made by the sector to professional status. Finally an overview of the key sport management personal skills will be provided.

5.2 Defining competencies and skills

Before reviewing the nature of sport management and its associated competences and skills it is important to first define and explain what is meant by the two terms. With regard to competencies there are actually two distinct concepts: competencies and competences, although the two are often used interchangeably.

Competencies were first described by Boyatzis (1982:23) in his book *The Competent Manager: a model for effective performance* where he defined them as 'the behavioural characteristic of an individual which is causally related to effective or superior performance in a job'. Of course, this definition represents a large continuum between role performance that is merely adequate (effective), as opposed to exceptional (superior). Skills can be seen as an integral part of someone's wider competencies, as illustrated by the following definition by Harrison (2005:120) who regards competencies as: 'the set of character features, knowledge and skills, attitudes, motives and traits that comprise the profile of the job holder and enable him or her to perform effectively in his or her role'.

In contrast competences define the tasks and outcomes required of the job (Wood and Payne, 1998) or a system of minimum standards (Hogg, 2009). These form the basis of National Occupational Standards, which represent a UK based approach to skills identification and development. These will be discussed later in this section (also see Chapter 7).

The key difference between the two concepts is that competencies refer to the inputs for effective work performance, whilst competences refers to the outcomes. As a consequence, they are often referred to as 'behavioural competences' and 'outcome based competences' respectively (Pilbeam and Corbridge, 2006). Additionally, competences tend to be job or role specific, whilst competencies can cover a range of different jobs at different levels (Whidett and Hollyforde, 2003).

Competence and competency

Competency (competencies): an ability based on behaviour – how they have to achieve (inputs).

Competence (competences): an ability based on work tasks – what they have to achieve (outputs).

Adapted from Whidett and Hollyforde (2003)

As previously identified, skills can also be seen as competencies, which Harrison (2005) describes as any component of the job that involves doing something. However, the notion of skills has been considerably broadened with regard to management and is now used, almost interchangeably, with competencies. This is exemplified by Whetten and Cameron's (2007:9) definition of management skills: 'Management skills consist of identifiable sets of actions that individuals perform and lead to certain outcomes. Skills can be observed by others, unlike attributes that are purely mental or are embedded in personality.' To confuse things even further the government tend to use the term skills in this broad way; for example, the title of the government 'Department for Business, Innovation and Skills'. Additionally, the government commissioned Leitch Report (2006:6) defines skills as:

> Skills are capabilities and expertise in a particular occupation or activity. There are a large number of different types of skills and they can be split into a number of different categories. Basic skills, such as literacy and numeracy, and generic skills, such as teamworking and communication, are applicable in most jobs. Specific skills tend to be less transferable between occupations.

In Chapter 6, dealing with recruitment and selection, the term competencies is used, as this relates to particular approaches to job analysis and selection. However, as 'skills' appears to be the term of choice, used by related governmental and non-governmental organisations, this chapter will follow such a precedent.

Review question

What is the difference between competences, competencies and skills and how do they manifest themselves in sport management?

5.3 Historical overview of sport management and its changing skill requirements

Employment in sport in the UK can be traced back to two distinct sectors – spectator sports and recreation. With regard to spectator sports, in particular football and cricket, the main motivation was playing success rather than profits; primarily because they were run by unpaid volunteers. Carter (2006) argues that this motivation, and the values of friendship and mutuality, underpinned much of the football league's policy up until 1961. He compares this with the USA and, more specifically, baseball, which had a key objective of delivering a profit for club owners. This led to a clear hierarchical management structure within Baseball clubs: 'the owner who provided the capital and took the risks; the general manager who had responsibility for acquiring and trading players plus salary negotiations; and the manager who was responsible for the team' (Carter, 2006:148). Consequently a sport business industry in the USA can be traced back to the 1870s through baseball. Furthermore, there was also a growing industry in the production and retail of sporting goods. This sport industry was underpinned by a group of entrepreneurs who developed 'techniques and processes to produce products and experiences for the sport and leisure market' (Fielding and Pitts, 2003:42), which highlights a clear contrast with the English traditions of amateurism and volunteerism. As organised sport grew in the USA, it was recognised that there would be a need for professionally prepared administrators and between 1949 and 1959 a Baseball Business programme was established at Florida Southern University (Pitts, 2001). In terms of general sports administration, Ohio University claims to have set up the first programme in 1966 with masters level provision aimed at preparing students for a range of sport related industries (Parks and Quarterman, 2003).

In the UK the roots of sport management can particularly be traced back to recreation in the early 1900s with the establishment of the Institute of Baths and Recreation Management in 1921, and the Institute of Parks and Recreation Management in 1926. In those early days it was very much a technical occupation reflected in the type of qualifications the two bodies provided in swimming pool technology and horticulture respectively (Trimble et al., 2010). During this period, and continuing until the 1960s, sport provision was left to the voluntary and, to a lesser extent, the private sector with regard to spectator sports. However, during this time there was an increasing recognition of the need for more effective management of sport with the Wolfenden Report (1960) identifying that a more professional approach was required (Houlihan and White, 2002).

The public sector's role in UK sport increased during the 1960s and 1970s with the emphasis of provision of recreation as welfare and sport for all. Again there was a call for more highly skilled managers (Sports Council, 1969; Department of the Environment, 1975); furthermore it was acknowledged that there was a lack of appropriate sport and recreation management training and the few sport related courses that did exist were based within physical education programmes.

The Yates Report (1984) was established to examine training in sport and recreation. It identified that a consequence of the rapid expansion of, primarily, public sector sport and recreation provision in the 1970s was a rapid promotion of staff from narrow specialist backgrounds to senior officers. Yates found that many of these staff had limited elementary or secondary education and consequently were perceived as having low status; they themselves acknowledged the difficulty in adapting their technical skills to being more concerned with the management of people's leisure needs. During this time there was also an influx of people from other areas of work in the public sector, particularly teaching, youth and community work and the armed forces, attracted by the changes and expansion that were taking place (Henry, 2001; Yates, 1984; Veal and Saprestein, 1977). An influence of the entry of new people from other professions was the acceleration of the claims for professionalisation of sport management in local authorities (Henry, 2001). Tensions also began to emerge between traditionalist approaches based on technical skills and progressive approaches based on meeting people's needs (Coalter et al., 1986; Braham and Henry, 1985).

Yates also found that there continued to be limited educational provision for sport and recreation management with only 40 colleges in the UK offering relevant sub-degree through to postgraduate courses. The USA was slightly ahead of the UK where graduate programmes in sport grew from provision in 20 colleges and universities in 1980, to 83 in 1985 and 109 in 1988; however, as in the UK, many of the courses had a strong PE orientation (Parkhouse, 2005).

The election of the 'New Right' Conservative government in 1979 created major changes in sport management in the UK, with the introduction of Compulsory Competitive Tendering (CCT) to Local Authority sport in 1988. This led to a very different management culture of cost control and entrepreneurship during the mid 1980s to mid 1990s (Henry, 2001; Roberts, 2004). During this time the commercial sector also became more significant for sport with new employment opportunities being created (Trimble *et al.*, 2010).

Sport management continued to have professional aspirations during this time, despite it running contrary to the Thatcher government's view that professions were a threat to the core New Right tenet of individual freedom (Coalter, 1990). A key element of professionalisation is the educational requirements for entrance (Fleming, 1996; Henry and Spink, 1990); consequently Bacon (1990) argued that the status and identity of sport managers would more likely be enhanced if they were graduates. In contrast, research into the education and training needs of sport managers, commissioned by the Sports Council in Greater London and the South East, concluded that sport managers had relatively low levels of qualifications and that there was no clear educational pathway leading to entrance into the sport profession (Coalter and Potter, 1990). However, within polytechnics and universities there was the start of an explosion in the provision of sport related courses so by 1996 there were 150 degrees in 68 higher education institutions.

Few of these courses were specifically related to sport management and there were concerns raised about their appropriateness to the sport industry (Bacon, 1996). The professional body ILAM attempted to respond to the increase by creating an accreditation scheme with the aim of more tightly controlling the syllabus taught and the skills developed. The scheme was based on the NASPE-NASSM Sport Management Curriculum Standards that had been developed in the USA, but the scheme did not take off. In contrast the USA standards are seen as crucial in ensuring that the knowledge and skills required to work in the USA sport industry are developed in sport management programs (Parkhouse, 2005).

In the UK, a new government in 1997 created further changes for sports management with the introduction of Best Value by New Labour, which led to a more integrated planning approach to the publicly funded sports sector (Henry, 2001). Nevertheless, Henry argues that Best Value created tensions between adopting an enabling role through partnership working, whilst simultaneously promoting competition and market testing. This links back to the discussion in Chapter 1, where it is argued that sports managers are likely to experience 'wicked problems' as a result of competing internal and external agendas.

The historical analysis of sport management, from the late 1800s until the start of the millennium, has shown that since the 1960s sport management has undergone a tremendous amount of change, predominantly driven by government policy. This change has had a significant impact on the fundamental values underpinning the provision of sport in the public sector and consequently the skill set that sport managers require to work effectively. Also, it would appear that, compared to the USA, the UK had a fairly incoherent approach to the development of sport management skills, although both experienced massive growth in course provision from the mid 1980s onwards.

Review question

How has sport management changed since the 1950s and how do you think this has impacted on the values underpinning sport management and the skills required?

5.4 Contemporary sport management skills

The historical analysis of sport management focused on the public sector as this was the main sector initially employing sport managers and, also, there had been very little research regarding sport employment in the commercial and voluntary sector during this time.

Since the beginning of this millennium the commercial sector has grown rapidly, mainly through the health and fitness sector where private health club membership grew by 28 per cent between 2002 and 2006 (Mintel, 2007), creating an increase in the number of sport and leisure managers in this sector. There has also been growth in management opportunities in spectator sports in the management and marketing of professional sports clubs.

The voluntary sector has also changed, particularly national governing bodies who have received substantial lottery funding through World Class Performance Funding. This has placed pressure on them to modernise and become more accountable by improving the quality of their management through the implementation of business practices such as strategic planning, human resource management processes, target setting and monitoring and evaluation (Houlihan and White, 2002; Cuskelly *et al.*, 2006). A major outcome has been an influx of paid staff into the sector creating the need for more developed management skills.

Finally, there has been a growth in opportunities in mega event management exemplified by the London Olympics. In this sector, sport managers travel around the world, from one event to another, using their skills in bidding and event delivery. An example is the number of Australians working on London 2012 who were involved with the Sydney Olympics (Braid, 2008). Similarly, Mike Lee, the former director of communications at UEFA, was central to the successful Olympic bids of both London 2012 and Rio in 2016.

The changes and growth in the sport sector have meant that management jobs are seen as being more attractive, even sexy, with sport being perceived as more professional as evidenced by the following quotes from the *Sunday Times*: 'many in the sport sector report a trickle-down effect that is taking the amateur out of sports management' and 'it's seen as a business not a hobby' (Braid, 2008:7). Thus the status of sport management in the UK would appear to be changing, with managers such as Paul Deighton, former chief operating officer with Goldman Sachs Europe, being appointed as chief executive of London 2012. It also seems to support Smith and Stewart's (2010) contention that sport management's claim of a unique status has been substantially eroded and that it is becoming very much like running any other business. This new perception is shown by the newspaper article found within Exhibit 5.1.

Exhibit 5.1

Sporting managers spot gap in the field; a sector that businessmen once ignored is suddenly proving attractive as revenues increase

MARK Waller is vice-president of sales and marketing for the US's biggest sporting institution, the NFL, the American football governing body. Waller is British and was recruited from Diageo, the UK drinks company, in 2005 and his move has proved a clear success. In leading the global expansion plans of the NFL, Waller masterminded the two American football games played at Wembley, London, in 2007 and 2008, which attracted crowds of over 80,000.

He was at Diageo's marketing department in the US, and for him the challenges posed by the two industries are the same. 'It's still about keeping consumers happy, which is the fans', he explains. 'It's great because fans are so passionate, they build their lives around it.'

Management jobs in the sport sector are proving more attractive to business people who, in the past, have turned their noses up at sport. Increasing revenues has meant increasing professionalism and salaries, once a stumbling block, are rising to levels which can compete with the City.

However, the idiosyncrasies in the sector and its high profile also mean that recruiters look for more than basic management and corporate skills. There has to be a cultural fit too. Businesses and bosses range from the corporate plc's to entrepreneurial mavericks while stakeholders include not just shareholders but a complex mix of fans, lenders, and media.

'Saying you work in sport is good to talk about in the pub, but it's not always the best career move', says Will Lloyd, a director at Sports Recruitment. 'It takes a special sort of person to progress in the sector.'

Personality and flexibility are key attributes for sports executives, but commercial acumen is as pivotal as in any sector. For the leading businesses, their most valuable asset is their rights – whether broadcasting or sponsorship – and this can be worth up to 80pc of revenues.

'In the end, when you break it down, it's a commercial deal like any other commercial deal', explains Paul Nolan, founder of sport-focused headhunters Nolan Partners. With this sentiment, and with the sports industry still considered to have enormous growth potential, it is no surprise that a number of top executives are leaving the corporate world for the sporting one.

Source: summarised from Ruddick (2009)

Review question

To what extent do you agree that business people, from outside sport, can be successful sport managers?

The article summarised in Exhibit 5.1 suggests that people from generic business backgrounds can effectively undertake these executive level sport jobs. However King, managing director of Sport Recruitment International, cited by Braid (2008: 8), argues that those with experience of public–private partnerships are more likely to be successful in the sport sector as 'those who come in from a purely commercial background can find the wait for approval from a number of parties rather frustrating'. This links back to the discussion in Chapter 1, which identified that sport managers often work in a context of multiple and competing objectives. However, it is also the case that managers, recruited from the public sector who are, supposedly, experienced at handling a number of stakeholders, can become increasingly frustrated by the embedded historical and cultural idiosyncrasies found within areas such as sports administration. An example of this can be seen by the resignation of Ian Watmore, who was a former civil servant before becoming Chief Executive of the Football Association (see Exhibit 5.2).

FA fears row over Ian Watmore may leave chief executive role empty

The Football Association said it would not appoint a full time chief executive, to fill the hole created by the resignation of Ian Watmore, for several months, amid fears that it will struggle to attract high-calibre candidates for the job that may be seen as a poisoned chalice.

Following an emergency board meeting at Wembley to discuss the departure of Watmore after less than ten months, the FA made its chief operating officer, Alex Horne, acting chief executive and sought to quell talk of a dysfunctional board structure that had compelled his predecessor to quit.

It is understood some senior FA figures fear that Watmore's departure, which has left the organisation looking for a fifth chief executive in eight years, will make it difficult to attract the best candidates for the job. Watmore's resignation came three months before the World Cup and in the middle of a debate about football's future. The bruising treatment of Lord Triesman and Watmore could, it is feared, dissuade applicants from inside and outside football.

In what appeared to be an attempt to portray Watmore's actions as being out of step with the mood of the rest of the board, an FA statement said there was no need for a substantial overhaul of the way the game is governed.

'The board strongly believe that the FA and all of English football's stakeholders are strong and capable enough of changing and developing the game under their own authority', the statement said. 'The board will always try to act in ways that are right for the game. The FA is stable, working normally, and as an organisation we are geared up for success.'

It is understood, however, that Watmore came to believe that only a complete modernisation of the FA's structure, giving it independence from what he saw as 'vested interests' on the board, would leave it with enough power to govern English football. The board currently has five representatives from the professional game – including three from the Premier League – and five from the amateur, plus Triesman and the chief executive.

Frustrated with the extent to which his reforms were blocked by the professional game, and after several clashes with the Premier League chairman, Sir Dave Richards, Watmore resigned on Friday.

Source: summarised from Gibson (2010a)

Furthermore, Francis Baron the chief executive of Rugby Union and a former director at W.H. Smith and First Choice reflects,

Don't get involved in sport if you don't want to occasionally take some flak. That's the nature of sport, it doesn't matter which sport you are in. You are a hero one day and a villain the next. You don't have that in business. You meet your shareholders once or twice a year. You don't have this democratic accountability all the time.

(Ruddock, 2010)

However, these sorts of executive and high profile jobs are seen as very different from grass roots sports trust and local authority sport management jobs where there has been difficulty in attracting appropriately skilled people. This is illustrated by the following article by Cartlidge (2009), an experienced leisure professional, which shows the rapid change that sport and leisure managers have been subject to and that these managers are under very different pressures – a clear contrast to the sexy, exciting work environment suggested by high profile sport jobs.

Exhibit 5.3

The hardest job in leisure?

Receptionists are the face of a business and have to deal with complaints on a daily basis. Gym instructors are challenged with converting couch potatoes into athletes and producing programmes for people with every imaginable injury or illness. And lifeguards face possible prosecution and manslaughter charges if they fail in their duties. All three often work seven-day shift patterns and are paid little more than the national minimum wage.

These are all respectable and often undervalued professions, with many challenges and stresses, but they aren't the hardest jobs in leisure.

The hardest job in leisure is one that has existed as long as there have been swimming pools and leisure facilities, but is also the one job that has changed the most in recent years and which is fast becoming an unattractive career choice for many young professionals.

The hardest job in leisure is the multifaceted role of centre manager.

In recent years the traditional centre manager roles of leader, organiser, motivator and coordinator have been extended to include accountant, IT expert, illusionist and magician! Budgets have been cut and income targets inflated beyond what is reasonably achievable. As energy costs soar and sport and leisure receives more political focus, the pressure on managers to do the impossible is threatening a mass exodus of skilled professionals from our industry.

As well as the introduction of British Standards PAS39 (2003) and PAS65 (2004), managers have had to learn, implement and manage a whole library of new legislation and best practice. Recent additions to the Health and Safety at Work Act 1974 include: the Working Time Directives 1998; The Disability Discrimination Act 1995; Hazardous Waste Regulations 2005; The Control of Asbestos at Work Regulations 2002; and the Work at Height Regulations 2005. Not to mention the relentless stream of updates and amendments.

The recent tendency to devolve personnel functions, placing responsibility back on managers, has also taken away some of the professional support and guidance. There is a genuine fear among young managers that they are operating within a minefield of potential prosecution.

Typically, a centre manager can expect to earn somewhere in the region of £20,000 to £30,000 a year, depending on the employer and the size of the facility. The private sector may offer performance-related bonuses, but it also offers redundancy to those who fail to meet targets. This means that they lure ambitious managers and keep the good ones.

I am not aware of a single council that offers performance-related pay, nor am I aware of a single local authority manager ever sacked because of poor performance. I have worked for and closely with around 20 local authority leisure centre managers. All had strengths and weaknesses, but how many would I describe as good at their job? Maybe four.

Around half the managers I have worked with had no ambition to progress and are simply treading water, content with their salary and comfortable status. At a time when we need proactive, forward thinking, dynamic individuals leading operational change, many of our facilities are infested with dead wood that hasn't adapted to new challenges – and in many cases, doesn't want to.

Good managers are a valuable commodity and, if you're lucky enough to have one, you should be doing everything to keep them.

Unfortunately, far too often employers seem to believe that personal development lies with the manager and their role is simply to set targets and direct their work. They have the qualifications to do their job, so there is little support for them to attend seminars and courses to broaden and refresh their skills.

There are very few aspects of a manager's work that could be classed as enjoyable. In order for them to stay motivated and able to persevere with the often difficult and frustrating elements of the role, managers need to be given the freedom and the opportunities to express themselves and explore new and exciting development options. They need support and assistance to battle through the red tape that saps the strength of even the most determined manager and they need to feel their employers trust and believe in them.

I see a lot of similarities between centre managers and football managers. If we are to avoid similar levels of retention we need to change the way that we treat our managers and let them lead developments. We need to let them have an input into our destination then leave them to choose the route. The role of senior management should be more akin to a car rental company than satellite navigation, dictating their boundaries, not their every move.

Source: Cartlidge (2009:24)

5.5 Skills development and National Occupational Standards in sport

Over the last decade there has been an increased focus on the skills of the UK workforce (also see Chapter 7). This has led to an analysis of the operational and management skills required by different occupational sectors. In this context, National Occupational Standards (NOSs)

> define the competences which apply to job roles or occupations in the form of statements of performance, knowledge and the evidence required to confirm competence. They cover the key activities undertaken within the occupation in question under all the circumstances the job holder is likely to encounter.
>
> (Skills for Business, 2010)

The NOSs for Managing Sport and Active Leisure are from levels 1 to 4, with level 4 relating to more complex and management related roles. These levels are not the same as those used for National Qualification Frameworks and are illustrated by Exhibit 5.4.

Interestingly, the NOSs used for Sport and Active Leisure share several standards with those available for general business management, as below:

- managing self and personal skills (Unit A323)
- providing direction (Unit A13)
- facilitating change (Unit A512)
- working with people (Unit A327)
- using resources (Units A29 and C240)
- achieving results (Unit A511).

Exhibit 5.4

Level 4 National Occupational Standards – managing sport and active leisure

A13   Influence, develop and review strategy for sport and active leisure (SkillsActive)

A29   Manage finance for your area of responsibility (Management Standards Centre)

A323   Manage your resources and professional development (Management Standards Centre)

A327   Manage an effective workforce for sport and active leisure (SkillsActive)

A511   Develop, implement and review operational plans for sport and active leisure (SkillsActive)

A512   Initiate and manage change to improve sport and active leisure structures and services (SkillsActive)

C240   Manage health, safety, security and welfare in sport and active leisure (SkillsActive)

Source: SkillsActive (2006b)

Despite the Sport and Active Leisure standards being similar to the standards for management and leadership, as articulated by the Management Standards Centre (MSC), they do highlight the need to apply those skills in the context of sport. This, to some extent, supports the arguments put forward for the uniqueness of sport management and Smith and Stewart (2010) interpretation of Hoye *et al*.'s (2008:2) analysis that: 'the management of sport invokes the same basic considerations as any other form of business management, but the specific application is subject to a range of contextual quirks that demand customised adjustments'.

The question at the start of this chapter asked how does sport and leisure management differ from management and how does this affect the personal skill requirements of sport managers. The analysis of sport management both historically and with regard to contemporary sport management suggests that there is not one homogeneous occupation of sport management. As a consequence, it is impossible to establish one set of skills that can be applied uniformly across the whole sport industry. This is highlighted by McLean *et al*. (2005) in their analysis of the required competences of public park and recreation CEOs. In their research they found a multitude of differences in the structure of agencies, making the identification of common competencies extremely problematic.

Sport is complex and is provided in many different ways, to many different people, for many different reasons. Nevertheless, it could be argued that the fundamentals of management act as a unifying agent for sport and leisure managers. The MSC standards, for example, can be applied across sport management. However, it is crucial that the skills identified are applied to the specific context of sport in which the manager is working; in effect this is the approach of this book. If the SkillsActive NOSs are broken down then three particularly apply to HRM:

1 manage an effective workforce;
2 initiate and manage change;
3 manage your resources and professional development.

Different chapters within this book cover all these important elements. The rest of this chapter will focus of the skills of managing yourself in the context of sport management.

5.6 Management of self and personal skills for sport management

Couzins and Beagrie (2005) argue that self-awareness is an important skill with regard to managing our own behaviour alongside colleagues in order to achieve organisational goals. Within the SkillsActive NOS unit 'Manage your resources and professional development' a range of areas are covered that can be related to self-awareness and reflection. Couzins and Beagre maintain that this is crucial to effective leadership and enables more effective reflection on performance and identification of areas for development. This is supported by Whetton and Cameron (2007:59) who argue that the knowledge we have of ourselves is crucial in the development of our management skills. They also identify that there is considerable empirical research that supports the notion that 'individuals who are more self-aware are more healthy, perform better in managerial and leadership roles and are more productive in work'. Consequently, it can be argued that self-awareness is fundamental to the subsequent development of all the personal skills required by a manager.

Self-awareness is a term that is frequently used without clarity of what it means and is often based on assessing your own strengths and weaknesses, usually at a superficial level. However, Whetton and Cameron (2007) have developed a useful framework from which to develop a more in depth understanding of self-awareness with regard to management. They propose that there are five critical areas of self-awareness that impact on management effectiveness:

1 emotional intelligence;
2 personal values;
3 learning style;
4 orientation towards change;
5 core self-evaluation.

Each will be outlined, but the main focus of discussion will be on emotional intelligence and personal values as the other areas are discussed in more detail in other parts of the book (see Chapters 4 and 10 in particular).

5.6.1 Self-evaluation

This construct relates to personality, which was discussed in Chapter 4. Whetton and Cameron (2007:82) describe core self-evaluation as the 'fundamental evaluation each person has developed about himself or herself' and they explain that most people are not aware of their own core self-evaluations and how they influence their perceptions and behaviour. It comprises four components:

1 Self esteem – the extent to which a person see's themselves as capable, successful and worthy
2 Self efficacy – sense of one's ability to perform
3 Emotional Stability – low level of neuroticism and less likely to have a negative outlook on life
4 Locus of control – a person's beliefs about the extent to which they can control their own experiences.

(Whetton and Cameron, 2007:82)

It is suggested that those with a positive core self-evaluation have sensitivity towards others and the environment, and are more able to lead, manage and form supportive relationships with others (Whetton and Cameron, 2007).

5.6.2 Emotional intelligence

Classical management theories have traditionally emphasised the need for rationality and that organisational leaders should 'manage emotions out of the organization' (Cartwright and Pappas, 2008:151). Over recent years there has been a growing interest in emotions in the workplace, due to the increasingly dynamic nature of organisations and the stresses people are placed under, and there is some evidence that emotional intelligence (EI) may be associated with readiness to change (Cartwright and Pappas, 2008). It has also been argued that emotions are an important influence on service encounters and client customer interactions, a key aspect of the sport and leisure industry (Pugh, 2001). For instance research suggests that in situations of extended service transactions the development of an employee's abilities to recognise customer's emotions and adapting service delivery accordingly could improve the service offered (Cartwright and Pappas, 2008). From this interest in emotions the concept of EI has been developed.

EI was first identified by Salovey and Mayer in 1990 and popularised by Goleman in 1995 (Armstrong, 2009). However, there is considerable difference in the definitions, models and measurements of EI, which has to some extent created scepticism of its existence. Cartwright and Pappas (2008) identify two fairly distinct approaches to EI: ability based models, which include those developed by Salovey and Mayer, and mixed method models, including those developed by Goleman and Bar-On. The two approaches will be briefly outlined before going on to discuss the implications of EI for sport management.

Mayer *et al.* (2008:503) define emotional intelligence as the 'ability to engage in sophisticated information processing about one's own and others' emotions and the ability to use this information as a guide to thinking and behaviour'. They see EI as a form of intelligence involving (a) the capacity to reason with and about emotions and/or (b) the contribution of the emotions system to enhancing intelligence. Their Four Branch Model of Emotional Intelligence (Mayer and Salovey, 1997) has the following components:

- managing emotions so as to attain specific goals;
- understanding emotions, emotional language and the signals conveyed by emotions;
- using emotions to facilitate thinking;
- perceiving emotions accurately in oneself and others.

The model illustrates Mayer and Salovey's view that emotional abilities fall along a continuum with 'perceiving emotions accurately' being a lower level fundamental skill and the 'management of emotions' a higher level one. Mayer *et al.* (2008:511) argue that managers with high EI are more able to 'cultivate productive working relationships with others', and is associated with peers and supervisors having a positive view of the individual's work behaviour.

Mixed models are termed thus because they mix personality traits with socio-emotional abilities, and they draw on the personality and competency literature as opposed to the intelligence literature (Cartwright and Pappas, 2008). The two main proponents are Goleman and Bar-On and their definitions of EI are: 'abilities such as being able to motivate oneself and persist in the face of frustrations; to control impulse and delay gratification; to regulate one's moods and keep distress from swamping the ability to think; to empathise and to hope' (Goleman, 1995:34), and 'An array of non-cognitive capabilities, competences and skills that influence one's ability to succeed with coping with environmental demands and pressures' (Bar-On, 1997:14).

Goleman's model of EI provides a framework that consists of four key domains of self-awareness, self-management, social awareness and relationship management. Bar-On's model views EI as a model of psychological well-being and adaptation which consists of the following five domains (Bar-On, 1997; Arnold *et al.*, 2005):

1 intrapersonal emotion skills (including self-actualisation and independence);
2 interpersonal emotion skills (including empathy and social responsibility);

3   adaptability (including reality testing and problem solving);
4   stress management (including stress tolerance and impulse control);
5   general mood (including characteristics such as optimism and happiness).

This has led to criticism of EI as being 'preposterously all encompassing' (Locke 2005:428) and Mayer *et al.* (2008:512) have complained that, 'the acceptance of the construct is threatened less by critics, perhaps, than by those who are so enthusiastic about it as to apply the term indiscriminately to a variety of traditional personality variables'.

Mayer and Salovey's model has received significant theoretical support, however it is 'the mixed model that has been arguably more influential in the measurement of EI in the workplace' possibly because this model has been marketed more aggressively and received more media coverage (Cartwright and Pappos, 2008:155). This may also be because Goleman refers to behaviours in the workplace and is based on analysis of competences in several organisations (Arnold *et al.*, 2005).

Despite the differences in the models there does seem to be consensus that it involves two broad components; namely, awareness and management of one's own emotions (Cherniss *et al.*, 2006). In Cannell's (2009) review of EI for the CIPD he concluded that:

> Arguably, the concept of emotional intelligence is useful because it draws attention to the following in particular:
>   There are aspects of management, leadership and teamwork in which competencies owing their origin to emotional states are at least as important as technical abilities.
>   Managing personal emotions and adapting them to circumstances, and understanding others' emotions, is an important aspect of leadership and teamwork.

With regard to sport, research has been undertaken on emotional intelligence and sport performance but not how it relates to sport management. However, studies which have identified the managerial qualities required within sport have highlighted the need for leadership, persuading and conflict resolution and communication and influence (Crilley and Sharp, 2006) which arguably require high levels of EI. Moreover, the discussion earlier in the chapter regarding the requirement for sport managers to manage the competing needs of a number of different stakeholders and also the high profile and political nature of sport jobs, further supports their need to develop EI.

5.6.3 Learning styles

Whetten and Cameron (2007) include understanding of learning style as a fundamental aspect of self-awareness as managers need to be constantly learning to be effective; if they are not they will quickly become out of date. In the UK and many other countries, lifelong learning forms a key part of government policy in that people need to continue learning throughout their lives. There are a number of models of learning styles that cover a 'spectrum of modalities, preferences and strategies' (Fleming, 2008). Whetten and Cameron's (2007) model refers to the fundamental dimensions of learning in terms of the way a person gathers information and how they then evaluate and act on that information.

5.6.4 Values

Chelladurai (2006:85) defines values as beliefs 'about what ought to be, what ought not to be, what is right, or what is wrong. Values are relative enduring traits that influence our thoughts, feelings and actions'. Values are really derived from fundamental beliefs formed through socialisation processes. As a consequence, beliefs may be more enduring than values, the latter being more prone to change over time. However, the two terms are frequently conflated, as with the quote above. Likewise, Cameron and Whetton (2007) argue that values are generally taken for granted and people are often unaware of how they underpin the basis of the decisions they make, their personal tastes and the life directions taken. It could be argued that values play a large part in the management of sport and the decisions managers make will be affected by what they value about sport; for example, sport for profit or sport as a right of citizenship, competition, fair play and cheating. The analysis of the historical context of sport identified how the philosophy of the provision for sport, in both the public sector and spectator sports, has changed through time. This has implications for how the value systems of a sport manager relate to the outcomes of those changes and the aims and objective of the provision of sport. This links to the notion of organisational values, which was discussed further in Chapter 3, which deals with organisational structure and culture. Unsurprisingly, individuals who have values that fit with those of their organisation have been found to be more productive and satisfied (Whetten and Cameron, 2007).

Concept check

Values

Values are beliefs about what should be and what is desirable.

Values are affected by a number of factors such as nationality, ethnic group and religion. Girganov *et al.* (2006) undertook a study of the cultural orientation of sport managers from seven different countries and found different perceptions regarding the role of human relationships, time and the environment. They concluded that the cultural orientations of sport managers influenced their interpretation and practice of management and that a single best way of managing does not exist. For example, the consideration of sport management skills identified in this book are located in the UK cultural context and influenced by research and writers from the USA and Australia. Linking back to the discussion on emotion, Girganov *et al.* (2006:54) suggest that in Western cultures management tends to be viewed as instrumental and task-oriented whilst in other cultures (eastern and southern Europe, Asia and Latin America), 'successful sport management is about human relationships, which includes the whole spectrum of emotions and displaying them on the job is not deemed unprofessional'. Consequently, with the increasing globalisation of sport, it is important that sport managers recognise the importance of managing across cultural boundaries or 'transcultural competence'. This alludes to an appreciation that cultural differences offer a different, equally effective, style of management (Girganov *et al.* 2006).

5.6.5 Attitudes towards change

As illustrated in the historical analysis of sport management, sport is a dynamic industry in which managers need to respond positively to change. The management of change is dealt with in more detail in Chapter 9. However, Whetten and Cameron (2007) argue that having awareness of your own orientation to change is fundamental to coping with change. They identify two dimensions of change orientation: tolerance of ambiguity and locus of control. Locus of control has been discussed under core self-evaluation. Tolerance of ambiguity refers to: 'the extent to which individuals are threatened by or have difficulty coping with situations that are ambiguous, where change occurs rapidly or unpredictably, where information is inadequate or unclear, or where complexity exists' (Whetten and Cameron, 2007:85). In summary, Whetten and Cameron's model is useful in unpicking what is meant by self-awareness in relation to management and enables a much deeper analysis compared to a more typical and yet superficial review of strengths and weaknesses. A key issue is how can self-awareness be developed? This will be examined in the next section.

5.7 Developing self-awareness

Megginson and Whittaker (2007:29) have identified six different sources that enable us to develop our sense of self:

1 Work itself – key questions are identified to enable analysis of self with regard to work:
   • What are the issues at work that cause you sleepless nights?
   • What are the challenges that are difficult to think about because you are embarrassed about the weaknesses that they demonstrate in you?
   • What are the opportunities that lie outside your grasp because you dare not stretch out to grasp them?
2 Reflection by self – this is seen as a crucial skill in developing self-awareness and will be discussed further in the next section.
3 Feedback from others – this puts a check on our capacity for self-delusion. Within organisations the appraisal system is the main opportunity for feedback.
4 Individual psychometric and self-diagnostic measures – there are a wide range of self-assessment metrics that can be used to build a realistic picture of yourself. These include Myers-Briggs Type Inventory (MBTI), Belbin's team roles, EI assessments.
5 Organisational metrics – assess ourselves against organisational expectations in the form of organisational goals and competencies.
6 Professional metrics – you could assess yourself against industry standards such as the National Occupational Standards for Managing Leisure.

5.8 Reflection

A fundamental technique for developing self-awareness is reflection. Edwards (1999) argues that reflection is a core management skill that has an essential role in professional practice; and yet he observed reflection had not been examined with regard to sport management. Since then the notion of reflection has been applied to sport performance and a critical mass of research has developed within sport psychology. However, there still remains a paucity of evidence applied directly to the sport management context. Despite this, there is a overall 'belief' that 'values' its importance, as evidenced by its permeation throughout nearly all management related NOSs in the UK.

Like self-awareness, it is a term that is often used in modern management but it is not always clear what it means, as there is a range of meanings. Edwards (1999:67) identified three definitions of reflection:

1 the ability to analyse one's practice – the common sense view;
2 a process incorporating a problem setting approach and learning by doing;
3 critical enquiry, which extends beyond technical expertise and focuses on objectives, situational context and ethical issues.

Gray's (2007:496) explanation relates to Edwards' third definition of reflection when he explains that reflection is

> the bridge between experience and learning, involving both cognition and feelings (Boud *et al.*, 1985), aiding managers in achieving emancipation from 'perspective-limiting assumptions' (Kayes 2002:138). It is important because it allows us to critique our taken for granted assumptions, so that we can become receptive to alternative ways of reasoning and behaving.

Thus reflection enables us both to develop and to use the self-awareness identified in the previous section. Moreover, it allows us to consider how our sense of self influences and constrains the decisions and actions we take. Hunt (2005:222) explains this well when she says,

> the main reason for consciously and systematically engaging with the process of reflection is to learn how to identify, articulate and take ownership of, and begin to control that which constitutes the 'baggage' – habits, ideas, assumptions, preferences, needs and so on – that would otherwise control our thoughts and actions; and to consider to what extent, and with what effect, the influences from our past interact with the requirements of the environment in which we now live and work.

An example of this can be found in research undertaken by Minten (2007) on the transition of graduates into sport organisations. The UK sport industry has not been a traditional graduate employer and thus many of those in senior management positions are not graduates. This is reflected in the case studies cited in the research, where none of the managers employing graduates were graduates themselves. Some of those managers had a negative perception of graduates, often based on a view of them having no common sense. However, when this was explored more deeply, this was not based on experience but on basic assumptions or beliefs. On the occasion where they did employ graduates, who were on the whole effective, they were seen as 'not typical' graduates. Despite the employer having no particular negative experience of graduates there was still this assumption, which influenced the recruitment and selection decisions they made. This assumption appears to pervade the sport industry within the UK creating individual and collective baggage about graduates that may influence decisions and behaviour and yet when working with employers through placements, student projects and alumni the experience employers have is, often, very different from this negative perception.

5.8.1 The reflective practitioner

A key theory relating to reflection is the notion of the reflective practitioner proposed by Donald Schön in his seminal 1983 book. Informing this theory was his work with Chris Argyris, which identified two distinct learning patterns; namely single and double loop learning (see also Chapters 9 and 10). Argyris (1977:116) gives the following useful illustration of double and single loop learning.

> Single loop learning can be compared with a thermostat that learns when it is too hot or too cold and then turns the heat on or off. The thermostat is able to perform this task because it can receive information (the temperature of the room) and therefore take corrective action. If the thermostat could question itself about whether it should be set at 68 degrees, it would be capable not only of detecting error but of questioning the underlying policies and goals as well as its own program.

Single loop learning involves correcting actions in order to achieve goals. It does not, however, involve reflection; in other words there is no or limited learning and transfer of learning taking place. Thus any changes are made within the context of the person's existing ways of viewing such experiences; their assumptions, goals and fundamental work/thought processes are simply not questioned. In contrast, double loop learning does involve deeper levels of questioning/reflection. As a consequence, assumptions and beliefs are both recognised and questioned (Edwards, 1999). The process of recognising the potential impact of underlying personal assumptions, values and beliefs, upon any given situation, has been termed reflexivity. The iterative process of critically reflecting upon existing and/or previous experience, whilst simultaneously recognising the influence of personal assumptions, promotes higher levels of personal learning and understanding. As a consequence, this improves the likelihood that more appropriate decisions are taken, being cognisant of a wider variety of variables that are likely to positively impact upon subsequent performance.

Edwards (1999:71) suggests that many managers do not undertake double loop learning so that they can 'avoid embarrassment, threat, feelings of vulnerability or a sense of incompetence'. In other words some find reflection intimidating and actively choose to avoid such processes. Hunt (2005) notes that there is not always a need for double loop learning and that single loop learning is appropriate when situations are predicable. However, whilst operational issues should be predictable, quality assured and, wherever possible, run like clockwork, the same cannot be said for strategic considerations. Regardless of the sport and leisure sector under consideration, it is rare for organisations to operate within a predictable external environment. Like it or not, double loop learning is essential in every sector (also see Chapter 10).

Another element of Schön's work was the notion of reflection in action, which involves the practitioner thinking about and modifying what he/she is doing whilst engaged in an activity. This occurs in real time so can impact on the problem solving process. This is often what we term thinking on our feet and is usually a feature of experienced practitioners. This involves 'tacit' knowledge, in that the practitioner may not actually be aware of what she/he is doing. Edwards (1999:73) explains that Schön's model views reflective practice as a 'creative blending of theory with experience that has been reflected on', as opposed to just the application of theory to practice. An example can be seen in Sir Clive Woodward's approach with the 2003 World Cup winning England rugby team when he says,

> A prime example of this was when the World Cup final went to extra time. I don't think that I had ever played in a game that went to extra time and I certainly had never coached one. Of course we had the possibility of extra time – we'd considered all options! We were able to respond to that extension of play more effectively, and that is probably where Johno is coming from. The concept of a 'game-plan' to me is very regimented. This philosophy is not just about 'pressurised' situations though; it is about encouraging players to think rather than just do!
>
> (Lee *et al.*, 2009:307)

With regard to sport managers, Edwards (1999) suggests that reflection-in-practice is beneficial to a sport manager. Given that a key characteristic of their work is multiple stakeholders, reflective practice would enable the manager to take the range of interests into account. He contrasts reflection-in-action with the 'burned out' practitioner whose practice is 'repetitive and routine'. This perhaps explains the issues highlighted in Bennett's article referred to earlier in Exhibit 5.3.

Another aspect of Schön's reflective practitioner is reflection on action, which is the practitioners' analysis of their practice after the event, in order to review what did and did not work and to identify where things could have been done differently with regard to future planning. This is again illustrated by Sir Clive Woodward:

> I think allocating time to sit down and analyse a video of a game in order to understand why things happen. 'Why didn't you do that? Did you think about this?' You need to ask the right questions and challenge the players to think about the decisions they make.
>
> (Lee *et al.*, 2009:299)

There are a number of techniques that can facilitate reflection:

● reflective journals are a write up of personal anecdotes, stories or descriptions, which enable the analysis of work related problems;
● critical incident technique – involves an interpretation of the significance of an event with regard to the analysis of significant underlying trends, motive or structures;
● a good practice audit.

Review question

To what extent can knowledge of self and reflective practice help the sport manager become more effective?

5.9 Summary and conclusion

This chapter has consisted of two fairly distinct, but interlinked halves. The first part examined the changing nature of sport management and how this has influenced the approaches taken and the skills needed. The second part focused on the fundamental importance of self-awareness and its impact upon the identification and subsequent development of necessary personal skills in this area.

Chapter 6

Recruitment and selection in sport and leisure

Learning outcomes

By the end of this chapter you will be able to:

- provide an overview of the recruitment and selection process with regard to sport and leisure organisations;
- critically analyse how sport and leisure organisations define their recruitment requirements;
- evaluate the recruitment methods used by sport and leisure organisations;
- discuss the validity, advantages and disadvantages of key selection methods with regard to sport and leisure jobs;
- appreciate how the recruitment and selection process may impact on the future behaviour of sport and leisure staff.

6.1 Introduction

The recruitment and selection of appropriate staff is crucial to the success of sport and leisure organisations and has been identified as a key priority for the industry within the UK (Studd, 2008). Over a number of years, sport and leisure organisations have struggled to recruit appropriately skilled staff (SkillsActive, 2006a). This is also a problem for other industry sectors: in 2009 68 per cent of organisations experienced difficulties in attracting people with appropriate skills, despite the dramatic decrease in the number of vacancies due to the economic downturn (CIPD, 2010a). A further issue for sport and leisure is that, in contrast to other areas of the economy in the UK, it is predicted that there will be continued growth in the sector meaning that the skills shortages are unlikely to ease (SkillsActive, 2009a).

Recruitment and selection is fundamental to the formation or modification of the characteristics and competences of an organisation's workforce (Price, 2007), and if there is not a basic match between people and work then organisations will not maximise their human assets (Roberts, 2005). On another level it is not only who is selected but how it is done, as the process may impact on an employee's future behaviour and psychological contract well beyond the recruitment and selection stage. Thus the process has consequences for the retention of staff, which is also an issue for sport and leisure with many organisations experiencing high staff turnover (SkillsActive, 2006a).

Despite the problems of recruitment in the industry there has been limited research into the activities and processes used. The approach taken in this chapter is to provide a critical overview of the generic recruitment and selection process in relation to sport and leisure. Throughout the chapter case studies will be provided of recruitment and selection processes within sport organisations, not necessarily as prescriptions of best practice, but to highlight the importance of fitness for purpose and how factors specific to the situation influence the processes used (Nieto, 2006).

6.2 Overview and definitions

Recruitment and selection are terms that are often used interchangeably, but it is important to distinguish between the two as they are very different activities (McCormick and Scholaris, 2009). Barber (1998:5) defines recruitment as the 'practices and activities carried out by the organisation with the primary purpose of identifying and attracting potential employees'. Wood and Payne (1998) take a wider view and also include induction into the organisation. They describe selection as focusing on the decision of who to recruit and the instruments and methods used to assess candidates.

Concept check

Recruitment and selection

Recruitment is the process of generating a pool of capable people to apply for employment to an organisation.

Selection is the process by which managers and others use specific instruments to choose from a pool of applicants a person or persons most likely to succeed in the job(s), given management goals and legal requirements.

Source: Bratton and Gold (2007:245)

McCormick and Scholaris (2009) argue that recruitment has been a neglected area in the human resource management (HRM) literature, where it is often combined with selection to the detriment of recruitment. However, they note that in recent years greater attention has been given to the attraction of applicants, possibly as a response to the problems that organisations have identified in recruiting appropriately skilled staff. This has led to new areas of investigation such as employer branding which will be discussed later in this chapter with regard to sport and leisure.

Despite the difference in recruitment and selection it is important to recognise that they form part of an interconnecting process: this is illustrated by the process used by the Leisure Services Department of Preston City Council in Figure 6.1.

Armstrong (2009) identifies that there are two ways that organisations define their recruitment requirements. First, there is a planned approach with detailed human resource workforce plans. Second, and much more common, is an ad hoc approach where demand for new staff arises due to the replacement of those who have left, or expansion into new activities/areas, leading to the creation of new posts.

Before a decision is made to start the recruitment and selection process it is important to review whether there is a need to fill a post. As the Preston City Council example illustrates, in the case of replacement staff, it is important to explore if there are alternatives to recruiting a new person: for example in leisure facilities, shift systems could be changed or the tasks could be included in other staff's responsibilities. Newell (2006) suggests that by undertaking such reviews there may be opportunities for the development of other employees.

6.3 Job analysis

Once it has been established that a post exists then a job analysis is undertaken to identify the main tasks. This obviously needs to be undertaken for a new post; however, it is also important for an existing post as there are likely to be changes in job requirements, particularly if the former post holder had held the job for a long time. Job analysis is not only important for recruitment and selection, but can also form the basis for performance management, training and development and reward management (see Chapters 7 and 8).

> ### Concept check
>
> ### Job analysis
>
> A **job analysis** is a detailed and systematic review of any job related information, including the knowledge, skills and competencies required to undertake a job.

Pilbeam and Corbridge (2006:147) have outlined the type of information that needs to be collected to complete a job analysis:

- data which identifies the job and locates it in the organisational structure;
- job objectives and performance measures;
- accountability, responsibilities and organisational relationships;
- job duties and content;
- terms of employment and work conditions;
- skills, knowledge and competencies required;
- other distinctive job characteristics.

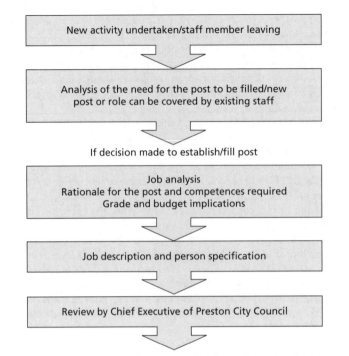

If decision made to establish/fill post

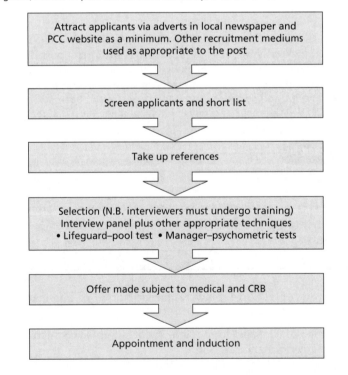

If agreed, review of post can be filled internally, if not, then advertised externally

Figure 6.1 Preston City Council Leisure Services Recruitment and Selection Process.

Over the last 30 years a number of job analysis techniques have been developed such as the Position Analysis Questionnaire (PAQ), Fleishman Job Analysis Survey, Repertory Grid Technique (RGT) and Critical Incident Technique (CIT) (Cook, 2004). There has been criticism of job analysis, particularly those that are based on lists of tasks or detailed descriptions of what the job holder does (Voskuijl, 2005). A key weakness of job analysis, identified by Voskuijl (2005), is that it supposes or creates job boundaries This could hinder innovation and flexibility in industries with dynamic environments such as sport and leisure, where rapid change constantly affects organisations and the nature of their work. This view is put forward by Cook (2004) who suggests that organisations require adaptable staff who can problem solve, work in teams and define their own direction, rather than focus on task specific skills. Another criticism is that traditional job analysis techniques have not linked to business goals and strategies (Voskuijl, 2005).

An alternative to job analysis is competency modelling which focuses more on the worker and the core competencies, personality and values they possess and how they relate to a range of jobs and the long-term organisational fit (Voskuijl, 2005) (see Chapter 4 for a discussion of competencies).

A key point that Voskuijl (2005) makes is that the relevance of job analysis will depend on the work setting. Where the description of tasks and duties needs to be tight, particularly with regard to health and safety, then a job analysis is critical; for example, in the case of a lifeguard or outdoor activities instructor. Where work situations are more ambiguous and there is a need for flexibility and resourcefulness, then job analysis may be less effective; such as in the case of senior managers within sport and leisure.

An output of job analysis is the job description and person specification. Taken together, these should then underpin the selection techniques used by the interviewer/panel in assessing the candidates' suitability for the job.

6.4 Job descriptions, person specifications and role profiles

Pilbeam and Corbridge (2006:147) identify that the objectives of person specifications and job descriptions with regard to recruitment and selection are:

● to provide an objective focus for the matching of applicants to the job requirements;
● to communicate a clear idea of the job to the applicant – what is termed a realistic job preview (RJP);
● to provide a basis for appraising performance and identifying training needs during the transition from candidate to effective employee.

> ### Concept check
>
> ### Job descriptions and person specifications
>
> A **job description** provides a description of the purpose of a job and the activities, duties and tasks that are undertaken.
>
> A **person specification** provides a profile of the characteristics required in order to do the job effectively.

An illustration of a typical job description used within sport is shown in Exhibit 6.1.

Example of a job description

Post: Community Sports Coach

Purpose of the post: to lead sport schemes throughout the Borough and encourage individuals to participate in sport by providing leadership and coaching expertise.

Duties:
- Plan, prepare and deliver sessions as directed by the Borough Sports Development Unit;
- Undertake the recording and monitoring of sessions in accordance with the Sports Development Units procedures;
- Create a friendly and professional environment where participants are able to enjoy their sport and improve their skills;
- Work in designated communities and with target groups throughout the borough; to be responsible for the health and safety of course participants and undertake risk assessments as appropriate;
- Ensure that all accidents and incidents are recorded according to Sports Development Unit procedures;
- To be responsible for the setting up, maintenance and putting away of course equipment as appropriate;
- Undertake any other duties appropriate to the post.

As with job analysis, there has been debate about the value of job descriptions within organisations exposed to rapid change (Pilbeam and Corbridge, 2006; Armstrong, 2009). Armstrong (2009:188) argues that they are too prescriptive and inflexible, 'giving the opportunity to say "it's not in my job description"'. In order to counteract this attitude, organisations often develop job descriptions that list all the things a person might be expected to do with no identification of the frequency or importance of activities (Cook, 2004). It has also been suggested that job descriptions are more focused on undertaking the tasks and duties.

An alternative to job descriptions are role profiles which define the 'outcomes, accountabilities and competencies for an individual role' (Armstrong, 2009:188). Armstrong contends that the focus on outcomes provides clearer guidance for the expectations of those undertaking the role and means that people are not constrained to undertaking a prescribed set of tasks. This enables greater flexibility than job descriptions as they can be more easily updated to reflect the changing environment and needs of the role. The outcomes are either expressed as key result areas or accountabilities.

Concept check

Key result areas and accountabilities

Key result areas are defined as 'elements of the role for which clear outputs and standards can be defined, each of which makes a significant contribution to achieving its overall purpose' (Armstrong, 2009:452).

Accountabilities are 'areas of the roles for which role holders are responsible for in the form of being held to account for what they do and what they achieve' (Armstrong, 2009:445).

The main advantage of talking about roles, as opposed to tasks and duties, is that their emphasis is on people, which reflects the view that organisations are made up of people who achieve outcomes by working together, rather than 'impersonal jobs contained in boxes on an organisational chart' (Armstrong, 2009:445). This coincides with Robert's (2005) view that in the twenty-first century there is a need for selection processes to look beyond the twentieth century approach of matching people with specific jobs and to assess people more strategically against such things as future work environment and interaction with a wide range of potential colleagues. To some extent Pilbeam and Corbridge (2006) appear to agree with this view but they question the extent to which a person should fit the job or the job should fit the person and suggest that it should be a combination of the two. This ensures that the focus is on the achievement of business objectives and does not pre- scribe and, hence, restrict the methods/processes used to achieve this.

Within sport and leisure in the UK, the predominant approach is still job descriptions, although role profiles are beginning to be used by some organisations. This is illustrated by the extract of a role profile used by Sport Hampshire in Exhibit 6.2.

Exhibit 6.2

Summary role profile

Department: Recreation and Heritage
Section: Sports
Role Title: Sports Development Manager
Reports To: Senior Sports Officer/Partnership Director

Role purpose

- To manage Sport Hampshire and IOW and its programmes in Hampshire and the IOW.
- To implement and manage the Sport Hampshire and IOW strategy.

Accountabilities
Strategic planning

- To research, develop and implement strategic sports plans in consultation with Local Authorities, Governing Bodies of Sport, Sport England and the voluntary sector.
- To negotiate, agree, manage and monitor partnership agreements with NGB's.

Staff management
To recruit, manage and develop staff, both full, part-time, sessional and voluntary. This work includes:

- Overseeing the processes required to employ over 200 coaches and volunteers to deliver activity sessions
- Day to day management of staff, including implementation and monitoring of the staff performance management programme
- Managing the recruitment of staff and overseeing the recruitment practices surrounding all new staff, e.g., Job specs, advertising, interviews etc.
- To deputise for the Partnership Director, when required.

Source: extract from a Summary Role Profile for Sports
Development Manager, Hampshire County Council (2008)

In an overview by the authors of online applicant packs for job vacancies on the Leisure Opportunities job vacancies website, during February 2010, it was found that there are a significant minority of sport and leisure organisations using some elements of the role profile approach, as evidenced by the inclusion of terms such as accountabilities within job descriptions.

In terms of identifying the skills, background and experiences of the ideal candidate, many sport and leisure organisations use person specifications. However, Pilbeam and Corbridge (2006) suggest that person specifications can over specify characteristics thus creating a profile of a 'super-human' candidate and excluding people who have appropriate competencies. Roberts (2005:63) uses the acronym PERSON to identify the key elements of a person specification as outlined below.

- **P**ersonal qualities and attributes which are inherent in the person's character, not easily changed, and pertinent to good work performance.
- **E**xperience, whether of a particular industry or type of work, or dealing with certain types of customers.
- **R**ecords of achievement or evidence that the potential has been applied and realised, such as projects completed or income targets achieved.
- **S**kills or qualifications needed to perform the role.
- **O**rganisation-match, may include fit with the style and culture if significant or more usually, and particularly appropriate to sport and leisure, aspects such as shift work or travelling requirements.
- **N**eeds and expectations of the candidate, for example is the candidate looking for long-term work, routine, or new challenges.

With regard to role profiles, as compared to person specifications, their focus on the essential requirements of what is needed to operate effectively within a role means that the issue of over-specification is to some extent avoided. Consequently 'desirable' attributes are not included which helps prevent the depiction of a 'super-human person'. For example, the Sport Development Post at Hampshire Sport includes a straightforward list of relevant entry requirements (see Exhibit 6.3).

Exhibit 6.3

Entry: necessary role-related knowledge, skills and experience at selection

- A degree or equivalent qualification, preferably in a related subject area e.g., leisure, recreation, business management
- A minimum of 5 years working in sports development
- Sound sports development knowledge with a proven track record of achievements
- Understanding of the structure of sport and in particular the work of governing bodies of sport
- A proven track record in sports/project planning and development
- Understanding of the role of local authorities and political awareness
- Understanding of budgets and their management
- Staff management
- Current valid driving licence and access to a motor vehicle
- Strong interpersonal skills and written skills with the ability to motivate,

---

negotiate, persuade and influence others in order to establish and maintain good working relationships

● Able to assess priorities and work to strict deadlines
● Able to work under own initiative as well as part of a team
● Strategic thinker
● IT skills
● Committed with a willingness to work extra and some unsociable hours
● Working knowledge of Health and Safety at work
● Understanding and experience of the issues surrounding equity within sport.

Source: extract from a Summary Role Profile for Sports Development Manager, Hampshire County Council (2008)

When identifying attributes it is important that any form of discrimination is avoided – this is a particular issue when identifying personal characteristics and person–organisation fit. For example, it is important to consider whether requirements to travel or to work unsociable or irregular hours are necessary as they could constitute indirect discrimination against those with caring responsibilities. This is not in itself illegal provided it can be justified, and in the case of many sport and leisure jobs there is an absolute need to work unsocial hours (Department for Business, Innovation and Skills (BIS), 2010b). A similar situation could arise if the term 'physically fit' is used, which again may be a requirement in many sport and leisure jobs, but again it is important that it is justified as it may be an offence under the Disability Discrimination Act 1996 (Cook, 2004). BIS (2010b) suggests that to reduce the possibility of discrimination it is best to explicitly describe the tasks involved; rather than identifying the need to be physically fit, the person specification might state the ability to set up and put away large pieces of gym equipment.

Concept check

Direct and indirect discrimination

Direct discrimination means treating one person less favourably than another on the grounds of sex, race, disability, sexual orientation, religion/belief or age (BIS, 2010a).

Indirect discrimination refers to applying a provision, criterion or practice, which disadvantages people of a particular group (defined by sex, race, disability, sexual orientation, religious belief or age). Indirect discrimination is illegal if it cannot be justified as a proportionate means of achieving a legitimate aim (BIS, 2010b).

Over recent years organisations have begun to use competencies to develop their person specifications to enable the isolation of the key characteristics to be used for selection (Cook, 2004). Wood and Payne (1998:23) suggest that there are four major advantages of a competency approach to recruitment and selection:

1 increased accuracy of predictions about suitability;
2 facilitates a closer match between the person's abilities and demands of the job;
3 helps prevent the interviewer from making 'snap' judgements;
4 can be used to underpin and structure selection techniques.

Cook (2004) suggests that using a competency framework enables different parts of the selection process to target particular requirements of the role, as illustrated in the following example for an event manager. He argues that using a competency framework:

- enables the identification of the most appropriate selection technique by which to assess each competency;
- reduces conflict between the techniques;
- enables a better overview of the candidates.

The strengths and weaknesses of the major selection techniques will be discussed later in this chapter. Cook also suggests that an advantage of the competency approach is that it creates a thread through the recruitment and selection process to training and development.

Concept check

Competency

Competency is an ability based on behaviour (plural competencies).

Review question

Go online and look at job vacancies, for example http://www.leisureopportunities.co.uk. Find one that uses a traditional job description approach and one based on role profiles. Compare, contrast and critique the differences.

6.5 Recruitment

McCormack and Scholaris (2009) believe that recruitment is a neglected part of HRM literature with greater emphasis being placed on selection. However, over recent years there has been increasing interest in the area (Breaugh, 2008; Saks, 2005). This may be (in)directly related to the skills shortages identified by Chapter 2 and at the start of this chapter. This has led to greater emphasis being placed on the 'applicant's perspective' which acknowledges that recruitment and selection, is a two-way relationship between the organisation and the applicant.

McCormack and Scholaris (2009) argue that the decision made by the applicant is critical to the success of the recruitment process and that this is influenced by their perception of the

Table 6.1 Example of event management competency framework

	Individual exercise	Group exercise	Interview
Planning	X		
Leadership		X	X
Problem solving and decision-making	X		
Communication		X	
Motivation			X

opportunities that are offered. However, Billsberry (2007:23) highlights that there is a power relationship between the recruiter and candidate in that 'the salvation or opportunity that a new job offers means that recruits are rarely able to exercise their prerogative fully'.

The discussion so far has tended to view recruitment in terms of external candidates. Before looking at this process in detail, however, it is important to first examine the recruitment of internal candidates. As the recruitment and selection process at Preston City Council (Figure 6.1) shows, some organisations prefer to identify whether there are suitable internal candidates before advertising a post externally. Others advertise externally and consider internal candidates alongside external ones (Torrington *et al.*, 2007).

There are a number of advantages of internal recruitment: it is considered cheaper, the candidate can often start more quickly and they are also more knowledgeable about the organisation and its culture and rules (Torrington *et al.*, 2007). In addition, internal recruitment can reduce uncertainty as the candidate is already known to the organisation (Newell, 2006). Torrington *et al.* (2007) also believe that it enables management to show employees are valued and the career opportunities within the organisation; thus creating an incentive for staff that may increase their motivation and organisational commitment (see, also, Chapter 4).

There are however a number of disadvantages of recruiting internally: the field is more limited and there may also be issues regarding equal opportunities and creating a diverse workforce. Torrington *et al.* (2007) make the point that if an internal candidate is not selected then this may impact on morale, therefore it is important that feedback is constructive, honest and accurate.

In terms of external recruitment, Roberts (2005) argues that organisations need to develop a recruitment strategy and compares the approach with the development of a classic product marketing strategy. He suggests that, traditionally, selectors have been seen as buyers and the candidates viewed as sellers of labour; however, he believes that recruiters should see themselves as sellers and thus develop an employment brand strategy.

The initial step in this strategy is to research the market in order to identify the labour pool from which the organisation will recruit the eventual staff member. The general characteristics of the sport and leisure labour market are discussed in Chapter 2, but it is important for an organisation to identify the characteristics specific to the labour market for the particular job they are recruiting for. Consequently, they need to look at the potential sources of labour including the effect of geography and demographics, the other competitors for that labour and also any legislation that may influence recruitment from that labour market (Roberts, 2005).

Roberts (2005) also suggests that product research should be undertaken, the product being the nature of the job or role and how attractive it is. It should also review the positives and negatives of working for the organisation. The product forms part of, what is in essence, the marketing mix and also includes the design of the job/role and the career opportunities available. Other parts of the marketing mix include pricing (the salary, rewards and benefits) and promotion (Roberts, 2005).

A key part of promotion is employer branding where organisations attempt to position themselves 'as employers of choice' in their particular labour market, in order to attract the best candidates (Torrington *et al.*, 2007:159). This means that the organisation is likely to receive more unsolicited applications, which will reduce recruitment costs. Creating a positive brand image is obviously something that could help sport and leisure organisations attract stronger applicants. This, in turn, may help address previously identified skills shortages in this area. There is evidence of this in larger sport and leisure organisations whose websites include pages dedicated to highlighting the available career opportunities. An example is Virgin Active Health Clubs who have a comprehensive section dedicated to promoting themselves to potential employees – http://www.virginactive.co.uk/Content/Careers/Careers.aspx.

A key aspect of employer branding is identifying the unique selling proposition (USP) for the organisation. However, this must be 'rooted in the actual lived experiences' of staff, otherwise it could be counterproductive (Torrington *et al.* 2007:159). A key USP for Virgin Active appears to be the culture of the organisation and the opportunities available, as

Exhibit 6.4

Example of employer branding: Virgin Active Health Clubs

Careers
What you can get from us

1 Flexibility

Not interested in the 9 to 5 routine? Then you'll be pleased to know a lot of our jobs offer shift patterns that allow you to be flexible. Finish early and enjoy the most of your afternoon, or have a lie in when you're on the late shift.

2 Variety

There are loads of different roles in our clubs – and you can start in one department and move on to where you want to go. So if you start in front of house and want to move into sales or fitness, just show us you have the potential and we'll get you sorted.

3 Feedback

We like to ask, 'How are you doing?' and we also like to let you know. We offer regular one-to-one sessions as well as quarterly and annual evaluations. We also like to talk about your hopes and ideas for the future, so we can help you plan your moves.

4 A career

We take people development pretty seriously. Why? Because it's one of the reasons great people join us and stay with us.

It makes sense for us to have a team of engaged, talented, high performing people at the top of their game. That's why our training team is dedicated to helping you go further, and play a bigger part in a growing and successful business.

We are very keen on recruiting and promoting from within, that's why we advertise all our positions internally on our employee website. We also provide our people with a career path that shows them all the different opportunities available, and we offer them the training and development required to get there.

Benefits
We want to provide our people with 'value for money', so if you work for us we will offer you:

Free gym membership for yourself (so no excuse not to hit the gym!)

Free off peak membership for a nominated other or a discounted peak membership

Pension contribution
Tribe card that gives you discount with all Virgin businesses and more

Childcare vouchers (so we can help you look after your little bundle(s) of joy!)

Source: Virgin Active (2010) http://www.virginactive.co.uk/Content/Careers/WhatYouGet.aspx

indicated in Exhibit 6.4. It also illustrates Robert's (2005) point about the application of the marketing mix with regard to the rewards that are available to Virgin staff.

A positive brand image can also create issues for sport organisations, as strong brands, particularly in professional sport, can mean large numbers of people being attracted to jobs within those organisations. For example UEFA receive 100–120 applications for each position they advertise (BBC, 2010). Todd and Kent (2009) suggest that the high numbers of applications to sport organisations, particularly those that have a high profile and media exposure, reflect the notion that membership of those organisations can impact positively on an individual's social identity. Consequently, the key objective in the recruitment and selection strategy in these organisations is to manage the large number of applications they receive in order to ensure the most appropriate people are selected; as opposed to those who want to work for them just to be associated with the brand. This reflects Pilbeam and Corbridge's (2006:151) view that there is a 'tension between ensuring sufficient applicants and a sharp targeting of the relevant labour market'. In contrast smaller and more specialised sport and leisure organisations may find it more difficult compared to larger organisations (Torrington *et al.*, 2007).

Employer branding can be seen as part of the notion of realistic job previews (RJPs) which provides 'applicants with accurate information about what a position with an organisation involves' (Breaugh, 2008:103). This is based on the premise that because employers want their organisations to appear good places to work they can inflate applicant's expectations. If these expectations exceed the reality of working for the organisation then it may affect employee retention as they may feel that the organisation has been dishonest and it may create a breach in their psychological contract. Breaugh (2008) suggests that candidates should be given candid information about jobs in order that they have realistic expectations and are able to decide if there is a good person–job/organisation fit. If the RJP does not appeal to the potential candidate then they would not apply in the first place or withdraw from the recruitment and selection process thus saving time and resources for both the organisation and the candidate. RJPs occur throughout the recruitment and selection process and include the employer website, job adverts and the selection techniques.

Review question

Choose a health and fitness organisation and compare its employer branding to that shown by Virgin Active. Based on that analysis which would you choose to work for and why?

There are a number of methods of promoting vacancies to potential candidates, the most effective of which will depend on the nature of the post. The methods used by organisations in the UK are indicated in the 2009 CIPD Resourcing and Talent Planning Survey in Table 6.2. This demonstrates, when compared to previous surveys, the increasing importance of professional networking sites, such as Linked In, which are featured more highly.

Armstrong (2009) suggests the most appropriate method should be decided by an evaluation of the likelihood of it producing strong candidates, and its speed and cost. As has been identified in the case of Virgin Active many sport and leisure organisations use their own websites to advertise vacancies. Likewise, many local authorities, such as Preston City Council, are required to target the local workforce by advertising job vacancies through local newspapers.

Recruitment/executive search agencies and headhunters are often used for more senior posts and over recent years a number of sport and leisure specific agencies have been established in the UK. An example is Knight, Kavanagh and Page (KKP) who managed the whole recruitment and selection process for the Rugby Football Union (RFU) England academies.

> **Table 6.2** Most effective methods for attracting applications

Own corporate website
Recruitment agencies
Local newspaper advertisement
Employee referral scheme
Commercial job boards
Specialist journals/trade press
Encourage speculative applications/word of mouth
Job Centre Plus
Search consultants
Links with schools/colleges/universities
National newspaper advert
Professional networking such as (Linked In)
Apprenticeships
Secondments
Local employment partnership
Alumni (previous employees)
Social networking sites such as Facebook

Source: CIPD (2010a).

Exhibit 6.5

Using executive recruiters for RFU England academy staff

KKP developed the job evaluation and person specifications and managed the international recruitment process for RFU England academy management staff. This incorporated national and international adverting, executive search and the conduct of informal and formal interviews with candidates from all over the world, as well as KKP's own extensive UK networks. We managed candidate evaluation, short-listing, interview panel formation at each club, in situ formal interviews and the initial stages of negotiation in relation to the terms and conditions for each appointment.

Source: Knight, Kavanagh and Page (2009)

More generic recruitment agencies have also been involved in the recruitment of sport and leisure staff: the headhunter's Odgers, Ray and Berndtson were tasked by the FA to search for the chief executive and five directors for the FA's bid to host the 2018 World Cup; Munro Consulting were the headhunters for Glasgow's 2014 Commonwealth Games and were tasked to find four directors, three managers and two PAs (*Recruiter*, 2008). The London 2012 Olympics are using the recruitment company Adecco to recruit the 3,000 paid staff required (London 2012, 2009a).

There are also specialist recruitment organisations for coaches and outdoor activity instructors such is the demand: these include Sports Coach Recruitment and Adventure Jobs. Additionally, there are a number of specialist trade journals that advertise sport and leisure jobs, the main one being *Leisure Opportunities*. Sport and leisure organisations are also increasingly using links with colleges and universities for recruitment, particularly for the high numbers of seasonal staff. These include Manchester United Soccer Schools and children's activity camp providers in the USA. In the UK, Kings Activity Camps are working with higher education institutions such as Leeds Metropolitan and Loughborough universities in order to recruit and train their future staff.

As mentioned earlier, effective recruitment activities need to provide a RJP to ensure suitable candidates are retained within the process and unsuitable candidates self-select so that they do not apply. It is also important to consider the impact of recruitment activities on creating a diverse workforce. Breaugh's (2008) overview of employee recruitment identified that recruitment material, that included pictures of people from different ethnic groups, increased the number of applications from the featured groups; particularly if those shown are in supervisory posts. However, Breaugh also identified that if related diversity information, received as an integral part of the recruitment and selection process, did not match the reality of working for the organisation, this may lead to employees perceiving a violation of their psychological contract and subsequently leave. This is illustrated in the following quote from the Diversity and Inclusion strategy of the London Organising Committee of the Olympic and Paralympic Games (LOCOG, 2008:21):

> Recruitment activities are a critical component in achieving the diversity objectives. We intend to be an organisation that is knowledgeable and committed to best practice for inclusive recruiting and development techniques. For example, we will guarantee an interview to any disabled or deaf candidate that meets the essential criteria set out in the person specification for a vacancy.
>
> Demonstrating diversity is essential in order to demonstrate the seriousness and success of the diversity strategy. But simply attracting diverse talent is never sufficient of itself.
>
> If diverse individuals are attracted to LOCOG, but once here, find their diverse perspectives, background and approaches are not valued and/or a lack of support for their growth, it could be worse than not attracting them at all.

Review question

Undertake an analysis of current sport and leisure recruitment literature and evaluate the extent to which they encourage applications from a diverse range of people.

6.6 Shortlisting

Shortlisting involves screening applications in a consistent way to reduce them down to a more manageable amount. Shortlisting should be based on specific criteria that relate to the person specification or competencies. If there are clear criteria then the process can be undertaken in as little as two to three minutes per application. The main methods of screening are identified below:

● Application forms/CVs: these are matched against the person specification.

- Telephone screening: rather than complete an application form applicants are asked to phone during a defined period. The operator is provided with a script and scoring system and based on this the applicant is asked to attend a face to face interview, further phone interview or to send a CV. However, this approach is expensive and tends to be only be undertaken by larger organisations.
- Online screening: can be used where there is a large volume of applicants and key words can be used to filter applications. However, there is the real potential of over-looking appropriate candidates if their application does not exactly match the criteria used.
- Biographical data (Biodata): uses an inventory of objective questions such as qualifications held or hobbies undertaken and subjective questions such as preferred job features. There can be 150 plus questions and it is based on the assumption that past actions and behaviours are the best predictors of future behaviours such as work performance or absenteeism (Arnold *et al.*, 2004). Biodata is not commonly used; however, Breaugh (2009) suggests that this is surprising given the evidence of its value in predicting performance.

From the screening, a manageable shortlist of candidates is then drawn up for the selection stage of the process. Pilbeam and Corbridge (2006) make an important point that only those that are genuinely going to be considered should be shortlisted, as by inviting candidates for the next stage will raise their expectations and will also mean that they are expending time and effort to prepare for and undertake the selection process.

6.7 Selection

The selection process is based on discriminating between the applicants with regard to their ability and suitability for the job. The issue of strong brands attracting high numbers of applicants very much emphasises Newell's (2006:66) view that selection is a 'process of selecting the correct jigsaw piece (the "right" individual) from the incorrect pieces (the "wrong" individuals) to fit into a particular hole in the jigsaw'.

The process should be structured, consistent and based on the job criteria that emanate from the person specification or competencies. There is a range of selection methods that can be used and the following list from the CIPD (2010a) survey shows those favoured within the UK, with competency based interviews being the most used:

- competency-based interviews
- interviews following contents of a CV/application form
- structured interviews (panel)
- tests for specific skills
- telephone interviews
- personality/attitude/psychometric questionnaires
- literacy and/or numeracy tests
- assessment centres
- pre-application elimination/progression questions
- group exercises (for example role-playing)
- general ability tests
- pre-interview referencing
- video CVs.

The remainder of this section will examine the main selection methods. However, before doing this it is important to examine the notions of validity and reliability as this provides a basis from which to examine the effectiveness of selection methods.

> ### Concept check
>
> ## Validity and reliability
>
> **Validity** is the extent to which the selection method measures what it is intending to measure.
>
> **Reliability** is the consistency of the selection method between different candidates and the same candidate at different times.

Validity in selection methods is attempting to measure or predict the performance of the candidate within the actual job – this is termed the predictive validity. Other types of validity are face validity and construct validity: face validity refers to the connection between the method and the job (for example, a swim test for a lifeguard position), construct validity is the extent to which a method is based on sound theory or evidence (for example, in the case of psychometric tests for a senior leisure manager).

Reliability is where a selection method produces the same result regardless of who the interviewer is or when the method was undertaken.

6.7.1 Interviews

As the results of the CIPD (2010a) survey identified, interviews are the most popular form of selection method and there are many different types. Over a number of years, there has been much criticism of interviews for being subjective, unreliable and open to bias (Arnold *et al.*, 2004; Newell, 2006). However, increased training of interviewers and more structured approaches, such as competency based interviewing, have improved their validity (Arnold *et al.*, 2004).

Where interviews are unstructured and based on probing the application form/CV, with the candidate talking freely, then this creates inconsistency. Consequently, it is difficult to compare candidates and relate their answers to the job. These issues can be reduced by having a more structured approach, where the questions are based on the job analysis and have consistency across the interviewees.

There are different approaches to structured interviews that are split into situational and behavioural; though in practice interviews often combine both approaches. Situational interviews require candidates to describe how they would handle a hypothetical future situation; for example, dealing with a customer complaint. The approach is based on the premise that intention to behave predicts future behaviour (Arnold *et al.*, 2004). However this does not mean that the candidate will actually behave in the way he/she says when actually placed in that situation.

Behavioural interviews entail candidates recalling specific past experiences; for example, how they handled a customer complaint. The difficulty with this is that this could disadvantage candidates who may not have had relatable experiences but are more than capable of doing the job. Also, it does not take into account the context/environment in which the individual has been working; for example, risk taking may have been discouraged and the question is asking for a situation where a risk was taken. Competency based interviews use the behavioural interview technique but the questions are structured around the competences.

Roberts (2005) suggests that structured interviews are more highly perceived by candidates than unstructured as they feel that the interview has been more relevant to the job. Moreover, structured interviews enable selectors to provide more meaningful feedback. However, a problem with overly structured interviews is that they may be too rigid, meaning that there is less opportunity to probe and they may be less effective at putting the interviewee at ease.

A key strength of interviews is that they enable interaction between the candidate and members of the organisation. This allows the candidate to make a more informed judgement, as the interview enhances the RJP.

Despite the improvements to validity by the use of structured interviews, they are still based on human decisions and it is important that interviewers recognise their fallibility. The main problems that can affect interviews are:

- snap judgements: it is said that interviewers make up their minds in the first two or three minutes then the rest of the interview is used to confirm their first impressions;
- halo or horns effect: where either one or two positive/negative points overshadow everything else in the interview;
- mirroring: the candidates are rated in relation to how similar or dissimilar they are to the interviewer in terms of background, personality and attitude;
- stereotyping: where it is assumed that certain characteristics are typical of members of specific groups, i.e. sex, race, disability, marital status or ex-offenders;
- likeableness of the candidate may also influence judgements.

Pilbeam and Corbridge (2006) also warn against risk aversion by interviewers, where negative indicators are given greater weight than the positive aspects of the interviewee.

6.7.2 Telephone interviews

Telephone interviews are useful where speed and geographical distance is an issue. Torrington *et al.* (2007) argue that telephone interviews are most effective when they are part of a structured selection procedure: they are particularly important in jobs where telephone manner is critical to the job, for example, a receptionist. Many children's activity camps, both in the UK and the USA, use this technique as an integral part of their early selection procedures.

6.7.3 Testing

As indicated in the CIPD (2010a) survey (Table 6.2), there are different types of testing that are used for selection. The basis of testing is that the tests provide reliable predictions of behaviour or performance and therefore enhance the process of making objective and reasoned selection decisions. The three main types of tests are:

1 **Cognitive ability tests.** These measure the candidate's development potential and fall into two categories: mental ability or general intelligence, and those that measure specific abilities or aptitudes (Torrington *et al.*, 2007). Arnold *et al.* (2004) believe that these tests are the best predictor of job performance, as all jobs require some cognitive ability to learn and perform effectively; although they acknowledge that predictive validity tends to be higher with more complex tasks.

2 **Personality tests.** Personality is an attribute that is often seen as important when working in sport and leisure, yet there is debate over the effectiveness of using personality tests in selection processes. Arnold *et al.*'s (2004) overview of the literature on personality testing suggests they are effective as a basis for selection when used appropriately; however, he does note that there may be cross-cultural issues. Within sport and leisure, cognitive ability and personality tests are more likely to be used in more senior posts as indicated in the case study of PCC.

3 **Attainment/aptitude tests.** These measure skills that candidates already have and usually consist of work sample/in-tray tests, for example the lifeguard test at PCC.

In all three approaches to testing they should be administered and interpreted by people who have had appropriate training. Also there have been concerns raised about the fairness of tests and whether there could be indirect discrimination if there is a social, sexual or racial bias either in the set up of the test, the questions asked or the scoring system. Thought also needs to be given to whether the test may disadvantage a person with any disability (Torrington *et al.*, 2007).

Assessment centres are becoming increasingly popular as a method of selection. They should not be perceived as a place, but a process which usually consists of multiple assessments using a range of methods; including interviews, aptitude, personality and attainment tests, as well as group discussions and role play exercises. These activities are rated and then these are typically combined into a single overall assessment rating which is used in making the selection decision (Thornton and Gibbons, 2009). The activities used need to be based on the competencies required for the job and because of the combination of methods that are used they have a fairly good predictive validity (Arnold *et al.*, 2004; Thornton and Gibbons, 2009).

Assessment centres are resource intensive as the process itself is quite lengthy, usually one or two days, and consequently it is quite costly. However, there is high face validity, meaning that applicants' reactions are quite positive as they can see the linkages between the exercises and the requirements of the job (Arnold *et al.*, 2004; Torrington *et al.*, 2007; Thornton and Gibbons, 2009).

References are frequently used to inform the selection process in sport and leisure organisations. There are two types: the factual check, which is usually undertaken after the interview, and the character reference which involves asking, usually a previous employer's opinion, about the candidate. The main problem with character references is it is generally the candidate who identifies who will act as referee; they will obviously choose someone who will give positive feedback. Interestingly there has been little research into the validity of references given their high usage (Arnold, 2004).

6.7.4 Other methods

There are a number of other methods that can be used in selection including graphology (handwriting analysis), astrology, polygraphy (lie detector test) and body language. Graphology is used fairly regularly in France and to some extent in Holland and Germany (Thatcher, 1997, cited by Torrington *et al.*, 2008).

An interesting and innovative alternative method used by the Queensland Academy of Sport (QAS) can be seen in Exhibit 6.6.

Exhibit 6.6

Selection for head coach baseball role at Queensland Academy of Sport

The advert

You must include a 30 minute DVD or video demonstrating your ability to perform the following:

1 Demonstrate how you coach a baseball specific technical skill. The skill must be demonstrated in an individual (one to one) coaching session.
2 Demonstrate the technical skills and your ability to coach an athlete in this skill.

3 Demonstrate your ability to communicate and deliver a Baseball training drill for a group (three to six athletes) and/or individual (one to one).

4 Identify and issue and demonstrate your ability to provide motivational and psychological coaching skills to an athlete/s. These skills should be demonstrated in either a group (three to six athletes) or individual (one to one) coaching session.

5 Demonstrate an important aspect of a strength and conditioning program that you utilise to help develop functional qualities specific to baseball that enhances athlete performance.

6 Demonstrate your strongest coaching attribute, identifying your strengths and why it is crucial to the sport you coach.

N.B. the language spoken in the DVD or video must be English.

Why this approach
QAS supports 600 athletes across 21 sports through individual scholarships providing them with access to world-class sporting facilities, coaching and support services.

Coaches are employed on a four year agreement coinciding with the Olympic Games cycle. Prior to 2004, the screening and selection methods used for coaches were: submission of a CV, responses to a set of selection criteria, interviews and reference checks. However, this was costly and insufficient in assessing coaching skills. For the 2004 cycle, which aimed to employ 24 coaches, QAS wanted to improve the predictive validity of the selection methods and also reduce applicants' and selectors' travelling costs.

The pool of suitable talent for this post was located abroad so after consultation with HR specialists, QAS chose the above approach as it allowed them to assess competency based areas without requiring candidates to come in for assessment.

The method was very successful in terms of appointing the most appropriate people and reducing costs. They also found that it enabled them to identify people with potential – for example a Croatian candidate who has now become an assistant national coach. QAS stated that 'if we had continued with the previous processes he may not have made it past first base because of his English and writing skills, and his lack of elite experience'.

Source: summarised from Queensland Government Public Service Commission (2008) Recruitment and Selection Case Studies

6.7.5 The selection decision

The final selection needs to be based on the evidence gathered from the selection methods and candidates need to be assessed against the person specification/competencies identified at the beginning of the process. In many sport and leisure related jobs there is a need for the person selected to undergo a medical and a CRB check. This provides a formal check and clearance, as appropriate, for people who will be working with children or vulnerable adults. Legal requirements, surrounding such issues, are continually under review and it is necessary to make sure that organisations are clear about the current regulations. For example, in England, Wales and Northern Ireland it would have been a legal requirement for all newly appointed staff and volunteers, who are working with children, to register with the Independent Safeguarding Authority from November 2010 (National Society for the Prevention of Cruelty to Children, 2009). However, this was a policy of the previously incumbent Labour administration, which the current UK coalition government have now decided not to implement.

Review question

Identify the strengths and weaknesses of the selection method used by the Queensland Academy of Sport.

6.8 Summary and conclusion

This chapter has provided an overview of the recruitment and selection processes with regard to sport and leisure. It has shown how the processes are interconnected and that it is crucial that there is a clear identification of the organisation's requirements. This generally involves the use of job analysis techniques, although in sport and leisure, role analysis and the competencies required to undertake a job are beginning to be used.

The chapter identified that there is increasing focus on recruitment methods in order to generate more appropriate candidates, but also that there is a realisation, by recruiters, that it is a two way process. In order to attract staff, there is a need to understand the process from the applicant's perspective. This has led to a more marketing-oriented approach that emphasises the need for a positive brand image. However, for sport and leisure organisations with a strong and positive brand profile, this may lead to excessive interest and, therefore, applications.

An overview was provided of a range of selection methods that are used in sport and leisure organisations including interviews, telephone interviews, testing and assessment centres. Additionally, this overview identified that sport and leisure organisations were also developing innovative methods of selecting staff.

Learning, training and development

7.1 Introduction

It is widely recognised that learning, training and development activities are crucial in sustaining ongoing organisational performance. At the level of the organisation and the economy, learning, training and development increases skill levels which leads to increased productivity and competitiveness (Grugulis, 2009). For the individual, developing a higher level of competence increases job satisfaction, enhances promotional prospects and consequently leads to higher rewards (Arnold *et al.*, 2004; Armstrong, 2009; Grugulis, 2009). The benefits of learning, training and development are summed up by the British government's Skills Strategy, 'Skills for Growth' (2009):

> We know that investing in skills pays a double dividend for society. Skilled individuals have more options and climb higher. They earn more, get greater satisfaction from their jobs, and the wealth they help to create stimulates the creation of more jobs. Skilled people are the building blocks of successful businesses, especially businesses built on sophisticated services or complex processes.
>
> (Department of Business, Innovation and Skills (BIS), 2009)

Despite the benefits of a highly skilled workforce a fundamental concern, outlined in Chapter 2, is that UK skill levels are lower that its main competitors and are not evenly distributed amongst the population (Grugulis, 2009; BIS, 2009). At present the concern is that sport is a low paid, low skilled industry with many organisations competing on cost (Lloyd, 2005a). This has implications for learning, training and development in that those organisations may see it as an unjustifiable cost rather than an investment. In contrast the UK government has been urging organisations to compete on quality in which they see highly skilled staff as essential (Grugulis, 2009). Consequently, for a number of years there has been pressure on the sport industry to develop a more highly skilled workforce (Department for Culture, Media and Sport (DCMS), 2003; Sport England, 2004; SkillsActive, 2009c). However, as will be discussed later, what may be holding back this fundamental aspect of HR is that there is not a simple relationship between higher level skills and quality.

This chapter will explore learning, training and development on a number of levels. First it will provide an overview of current national policy and will examine how this impacts on sport and related leisure organisations. It will then outline and explain the key theories in order to provide a framework from which to discuss learning, training and development HR practices within such organisations.

7.2 Learning, training and development at a national level

As outlined in the introduction to this chapter, a fundamental policy of the previous UK Labour government (1997–2010), and governments elsewhere in the world, is the improvement in skill levels of the workforce in order to increase national competitiveness, productivity and also social inclusion (Payne, 2008). Over a number of years it has been recognised that Britain has lagged behind other countries in the quality of skills within its workforce (Keep and Mayhew, 1999; Leitch, 2006; BIS, 2009). The concern has been that unless skill levels are improved then Britain will become trapped in a low wage, low skills economy competing on price rather than quality. Arguably, sport exemplifies this problem with large parts of the sport workforce characterised by relatively low pay and low levels of qualifications (Lloyd, 2005b).

Before analysing the issues of skills, learning, training and development in the sport industry, it is important to provide an outline of the national training framework in the UK and how it relates to sport. In contrast to many countries the UK national training framework is voluntary in nature. Consequently, the government's role is based on encouraging training rather than more direct interventionist approaches, such as a licence to practice, statutory rights for paid study leave or, as in the past, levies for training (Torrington *et al.*, 2008). The approach taken is demand-led with the aim of directly responding to employers' and individuals' needs. This contrasts with a supply-led system based on 'the Government asking employers to articulate their needs and then planning supply to meet this', which, it is argued, hinders flexibility to changing demands (Leitch, 2006:74). The demand based system is based on the principle that suppliers are only funded when they attract customers, thus the system is market driven underpinned by the notion that businesses will shape training through the choices that they make.

Despite this demand-led approach, Payne (2008:94) argues that the idea of it being employer led is 'something of a misnomer' as the English education and training system is subject to a high amount of centralised state control. A core part of this system is the Skills for Business Network that is led by the Sector Skills Development Agency (SSDA), which coordinates 25 sector skills councils (SSCs). SkillsActive is the SSC for the active leisure, learning and well-being sector. This consists of an interesting combination of sport and recreation, health and fitness, outdoors, playwork and the caravan industries. The vision and goals of SkillsActive can be seen in Exhibit 7.1. As can be seen, their role is critical in ensuring employer engagement in the skills agenda. In order to achieve this, key employers sit on their board and consultation is also undertaken with sport and active leisure employers nationally. However, it has been argued that in reality these state created organisations are actually delivering government determined policy goals and targets, often with little or no employer input (Payne, 2008; Torrington *et al.*, 2008). Payne (2008) argues that employers do not want to take a lead role in the skills agenda and to some extent this is highlighted by the CIPD (2009a) learning and development survey that found that 53 per cent of respondents' learning and development activity had not been influenced by the Leitch agenda.

Exhibit 7.1

SkillsActive vision

A highly skilled and competent workforce in an industry equipped to fulfil its potential at the centre of the social and economic development of the UK.

SkillsActive goals

- To involve more employers and their workforce in best practice based training and development programmes, thereby reducing skills gaps and shortages, improving productivity and lifting business and public sector performance.
- To take a strategic lead in developing a new, demand-led flexible supply of learning and skills development that meets the needs of workers (paid and unpaid) and organisations, as well as providers from the active leisure and learning sector.
- To work with partners across the UK to agree common messages, as well as cohesive, innovative ways of boosting the skill of the active leisure and learning workforce.

Source: Gittus (2007)

A major part of the SSCs' work has been to develop Sector Skills Agreements in order to help employers identify their current and future skills priorities. However, with the emphasis now on a demand-led approach there is a question mark over how this work is to be used, given that there has been criticism of approaches that are 'over reliant of centralised planning mechanisms' (Payne, 2008:98). Nevertheless, the work undertaken for the sector skills agreements has been valuable in enabling SkillsActive to identify five skill priorities for the sector:

1   To improve recruitment and retention of the workforce.
2   To upskill and professionalise the existing workforce.
3   To match training supply to employer demand.
4   To redirect and secure new funding for training to meet employment needs.
5   To increase sector investment in our people.

(SkillsActive, 2009c:19)

As identified earlier, despite the emphasis on upskilling, a key problem is that many firms are competing successfully on price, using low skill business strategies (Payne, 2008). If this is the case there is a danger of an oversupply of those with higher level skills as indicated by the UK Commission for Employment and Skills: 'the growth in our numbers of high skilled people significantly exceeds the growth in our numbers of high skilled jobs. The growth in high skilled jobs is also occurring at a slower rate than in other countries' (UK Commission for Employment and Skills (UKCES), 2009:10). This concurs with the evidence reviewed in Chapter 2 which looked at the market for labour in this area of the economy. Lloyd (2005a:16) undertook some interesting research into the health and fitness sector in an attempt to unpick the relationship between business strategy and skill levels, the question she asked was: 'Are those that compete at the high-quality end making use of a workforce with higher levels of skill, thereby confirming the relationship between product market strategy and skill?' In her review of the literature she found a lack of research, particularly on the service sector, demonstrating a link between high-quality and higher level skills. Her own research examined 11 different types of organisations (local authorities, private sector, corporate and hotel providers of gyms), which covered over 600 clubs, employing more than 20,000 people. She found that there is a complicated relationship between high quality and a high skilled workforce, in that there were companies operating at the top end of the market that were 'not utilising skills at a higher level than some of those clubs at the bottom' (Lloyd, 2005a:27). The main reason for this was high quality tended to be related to the tangibles of the services, such as the attractiveness of fixtures and fittings and the range of facilities and services provided. Where employees' skills were seen as important this was generally in relation to their customer service with a senior HR manager claiming that alongside technical skills, 'we also want to be famous for service: We are looking for people who show empathy with the members.... It's about eyes and teeth with a bit of depth' (HR manager quote from Lloyd, 2005a:24).

Despite SkillsActive's attempts to address the issue of low skills within the sector, through the Register of Exercise Professionals (see Chapter 2), Lloyd (2005b) believes that this is unlikely to lead to improvements unless statutory regulations create a legal requirement for instructors to undergo training. Given the employer led, demand-led approach to education and training in the UK, this is unlikely to happen. However, it does have implications as the consequences of poorly trained staff could be far reaching; for example, in terms of injuries and the central use of fitness and fitness clubs in government health strategies.

Lloyd's research also raises questions relating to the UK government's approach to mass higher education. Chapter 2 identified that the UK sport labour market is suffering from the joint challenge of an oversupply and under utilisation of its graduates. Lloyd's (2005a:30) research illustrates that rather than those graduates providing a catalyst to upskill the sport workforce, in some parts of the health and fitness industry they could actually be fuelling the problem, 'It could be argued that the stream of young people coming out of educational institutions, who may have completed industry vocational qualifications, provides little incentive for companies to change their current employment practices.' This is supported by Minten's (2010) case study research that found that graduates are being underutilised within the sport industry. She concluded that this has implications for SkillsActive's priorities of upskilling and professionalising the industry and also improving recruitment and retention.

Another issue Lloyd raises is the low level of management training undertaken within health and fitness organisations, as illustrated in another quote from her research: 'If someone wanted a GM position, there is coaching and extra responsibilities but generally it is sink or swim. We leave them there and wait for them to yell if they are not coping' (HR manager quote from Lloyd, 2005a:27).

The Working in Fitness (2009) survey indicates that this is still a problem with 31 per cent of those surveyed, who were duty managers, identifying a need for more training (SkillsActive, 2009a). This reflects the CIPD's view that the government skills agenda has focused on the lowest level of qualifications and omitted management and leadership skills. Paradoxically, there is a link between poor productivity and poor management and leadership training (CIPD, 2010c). To address this issue the SSDA have tasked SkillsActive to lead an initiative to develop leadership and management skills across all sectors.

7.3 Investors in People

A government skills initiative that has had a major impact on sport is Investors in People (IiP) which was introduced in 1990, although there have been major revisions since then. Robinson (2003) identified that IiP is used within a large number of public sector leisure providers and more recently Leeds Rugby became one of the first professional sports clubs to receive IiP in 2008. Richards and Hogg (2009) describe IiP as

> a national quality standard which sets a level of good practice for improving an organisation's performance through its people. It provides a framework for improving organisational performance and competitiveness through a planned approach to setting and communicating business objectives and developing people to meet these objectives.

As IiP links learning, training and development to organisational objectives, it means that these activities should relate to the organisation's needs. In the early days of IiP a large amount of paperwork was required to produce a portfolio of evidence that was then assessed in order to achieve accreditation. This has now been simplified to reduce bureaucracy. The focus of the new standard has also moved more to employee involvement and engagement (Foot and Hook, 2008). The CIPD believes that IiP has encouraged organisations to undertake a much more strategic and detailed view of their learning and development processes. Bourne and Franco-Santos undertook a review of the impact of IiP and found that such organisations:

- Have more capable managers – assessed in terms of their knowledge, experience and skills
- Exhibit a stronger organisational learning culture
- Deliver more effective managerial development practices
- Develop a managerial context that encourages high performance working practices
- Have managers that benefit from more autonomy and freedom to decide what to do and how to do their jobs
- Generate higher management performance
- Achieve higher non-financial and financial performance.

(2010:13)

The review found that companies with IiP had performed better financially. An example of its impact in a sport organisation can be seen in Exhibit 7.2.

Exhibit 7.2

Investors in People case study: Skern Lodge

Skern Lodge sails to success through staff investment

An outdoor activities centre with a difference, Skern Lodge offers schools, businesses and the public a comprehensive range of sports coupled with the highest professional tuition.

The educational adventure complex, which has operated since 1976 in Appledore, North Devon, where the River Torridge meets the Atlantic, is ideally located for outdoor pursuits such as surfing, abseiling, archery, high ropes courses and kayaking.

Investors in People (IiP) discovered committed, dedicated and knowledgeable staff, who were led by a supportive management team keen on developing its workforce.

By adopting these IiP principles, Skern Lodge has created a happy working environment in which staff feel empowered to make decisions and clearly contribute to the group's business strategy and aims.

The centre's renowned reputation as a leading sector employer is supported by its staff retention rates. On average instructors working in this type of post are expected to stay six to 12 months or one or two seasons, at Skern the average length of employment is three to four years.

As well as developing its own in-house training programme to ensure staff reach a competent level, it also advocates a summary skills matrix which goes a long way towards providing a clear personal development programme for individuals.

There are opportunities for instructors to be course directors, which provides real stretch and skills building, while staff are encouraged and supported through external training and learning. One staff member was even supported through an MBA.

Operational manager Barry Kaufman-Hill attributed the success of the centre to the staff. He said:

> The IiP has proved a useful and important tool in the continued success story of Skern Lodge. The accreditation has helped guide us in the right direction on a whole range of issues such as management strategies, staff development and business growth. We will continue to work within the framework of IiP to ensure we get important feedback on our management style and delivery.

Skern Lodge excelled in its approach to business, leadership style and communications strategies. Staff commented: 'There's no management and workers. They treat everyone the same.' 'I've never looked back since I came here. It's a fantastic place to work.' 'Some of my friends moan when they have got to go to work. I don't think of it as work. I think of it as socialising. It's professional but fun.'

Source: Quality South West

7.4 Using sport for training and development

Sport is not only an end user of national skills strategies it also forms a basis for delivery. It has been found that sport can be used to attract young people who are educational underachievers to educational environments enabling them to improve basic skills including maths, literacy, spelling and ICT (Coalter, 2005). For example, many football clubs have developed community or education trusts to facilitate schools' national curriculum delivery through the environment and medium of football. A fundamental objective of London 2012 is its skills legacy as illustrated in Exhibit 7.3.

Exhibit 7.3

Using the 2012 Olympic and Paralympic Games to develop skills

2012 presents exciting skills challenges and opportunities. We need to ensure that we have enough skilled individuals to take full advantage of these opportunities as we prepare for and deliver successful Games. We will use these opportunities to secure a lasting skills legacy; supporting businesses in key sectors and helping individuals to develop skills that will help them progress long after the Games have ended. To do this we are working with key partners to provide:

a Apprenticeships in construction, sport, and hospitality, leisure and tourism
b Employment opportunities in retail, security and construction
c Opportunities for the unemployed to use a structured programme of volunteering – the Personal Best Programme – as a way back into employment.

Source: BIS (2009:39)

7.5 Definition of terms

This chapter has been entitled learning, training and development. However, many human resource texts refer only to training and development; often interchangeably. This chapter will examine these key terms in relation to human resource development (HRD), it will also explain why the terms learning and development will be used in this text. Learning and development is one of two components of HRD, the other being organisational development which is covered in Chapter 9.

The term training can be subsumed within wider notions of learning and development. It refers to more prescriptive levels of skills acquisition and often relates more directly to the performance of a specific function or the acquisition of a specific skill. As such, the term training is more likely to be associated with lower order skills and is seen as one of many tools providing a foundation for deeper learning and development. In this context, Armstrong (2009:665) sees training as 'the application of formal processes to impart knowledge and help people to acquire the skills necessary for them to perform their job satisfactorily'. Hence, training activities can be associated with the acquisition of prescriptive competencies, whilst wider notions of learning and development relate to the more outcomes driven and integrative notion of competence (see Chapter 5 for a fuller discussion of such concepts).

In contrast, HRD is strategic and the terms learning and development are often used as they provide a much broader approach to the acquisition of knowledge, skills, behaviours and attitudes. However, Sadler-Smith (2006) highlights that there are national cultural difference in terminology, and training and development are used interchangeably with learning and development.

There is much debate about the precise definition of learning. From his review of the debate, Sadler-Smith (2006:4) provides a synthesis of related literature and proposes the following definition that will be used to inform this chapter:

> Learning is a longer-term change in the knowledge possessed by an individual, their type and level of skill, or their assumptions, attitudes or values, which may lead to them having increased potential to grow, develop and perform in more satisfying and effective ways.

Development is defined by Sadler-Smith (2006:10) as

> an increase over the longer term of the capacity that an individual has to live a more effective and fulfilling professional and personal life as a result of learning and the acquisition of knowledge, skills and attitudes. It is a directional shift towards a higher condition or state of being and in this sense is concerned with an outcome.

With regard to the focus of this chapter it will examine the processes that are used by individuals, organisations and economies to ensure they have the appropriate knowledge, skills, behaviours and attitudes.

7.6 The learning process

As identified in Chapter 5, an important skill of self-awareness is the ability to understand how you learn. As a manager it is also important to understand how others learn in order to identify and design the most appropriate methods for the learning and development of staff. There is not one singly accepted theory of learning and Sadler-Smith (2006:99) argues that each provides only a partial insight into human learning in the workplace and in order to understand learning and development it is necessary to take an 'eclectic and integrated approach across a variety of perspectives'. Consequently this section will outline the following three main theories, particularly focusing on experiential learning theory:

1 reinforcement theory;
2 cognitive theory;
3 experiential learning theory.

7.6.1 Reinforcement theory

This theory is rooted in the behaviourist approach to learning, which is based on the notion of stimulus and response. This maintains that behaviour change occurs as a 'result of an individual's response to events or stimuli, and the ensuing consequences' (Armstrong, 2009:703). Therefore we use feedback from our past behaviour to modify our future behaviour. If the behaviour is rewarded then it is likely to be repeated in the future, if it is punished or ignored then that behaviour will be avoided. It is accepted that feedback is very important in the learning process but a criticism of reinforcement theory is its belief that learning mainly takes place through trial and error and it ignores the cognitive components of learning new concepts (Arnold *et al.*, 2004).

7.6.2 Cognitive theory

Cognitive theorists believe that reinforcement works in much more complex ways than behaviourists suggest. They see the learner as an information processing machine and, rather than just a stimulus – response behaviour – we process information by perceiving, interpreting, ascribing meaning and then using it in decisions about future behaviour. Huczynkski and Buchanan (2007:116) explain that 'behaviour is purposive' in that to achieve those purposes we formulate plans which are a set of mental instructions for guiding the required behaviour. They also identify that feedback has a motivating effect on behaviour rather than simply reinforcing.

7.6.3 Experiential learning

Experiential learning is also known as learning from experience and has been particularly influential in learning and development in workplace settings. It is based on the notion that people learn from their experience by reflecting on it so that it can be understood and applied (Armstrong, 2009). The main proponents are Kolb *et al.* (1974) and Honey and Mumford (1996) who both suggest that people have preferred styles of learning (see also Chapter 5). Both Honey and Mumford and Kolb *et al.* identify the concept of the learning cycle (see Figure 7.1).

There are four different learning styles that link with the learning cycle, although none of these are exclusive and it is possible for a person to exhibit more than one. Each learning style is linked to different learning techniques:

1 **Activists** – act first and then think about their actions later, they seek challenge and immediate experience and are open-minded and enthusiastic about new ideas. Favoured learning techniques: role plays, group discussions, case studies.
2 **Reflectors** – tend to stand back and observe experiences from different angles, they like to gather data and analyse before reaching conclusions, they tend to listen and take in other people's perspectives before making their point. Favoured learning techniques: lectures, films, reading.
3 **Theorists** – think things through in logical steps and synthesise disparate facts into coherent theories. They tend to be rational and objective and are often perfectionists. Favoured learning techniques: lectures, reading.

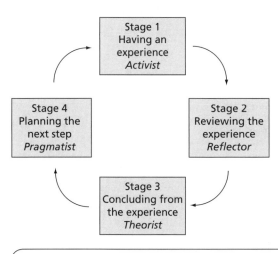

Figure 7.1 Honey and Mumford's (1996) learning cycle.

4 **Pragmatists** – are keen to seek out and try new ideas, they enjoy problem solving and become bored with long discussions. Favoured learning techniques: case studies, role play in-tray exercises.

7.7 Learning and development in organisations

As outlined in the introduction, learning and development is critical for organisations in order to meet their strategic objectives and improve productivity. It creates a safer working environment, improved employee well-being and reduced absenteeism and staff turnover (Arnold *et al.*, 2004). It also helps to attract and retain high-quality staff and is seen as an important part of total reward policies (Armstrong, 2009; Taylor, 2009). It also forms a crucial part of the psychological contract (Conway and Briner, 2005). SkillsActive found that within the health and fitness sector there appeared to be a link between training and recommendation of an employer to others: 'approximately two-fifths of respondents who had undertaken no training would not recommend their employer whilst 81 per cent of respondents who had spent 11 or more days training would refer them' (SkillsActive, 2009a:3).

Despite the value of learning and development many sport organisations still appear not to recognise it as a priority, leading to SkillsActive identifying that progress still needed to be made in encouraging employers to develop their workforce. For example the Working in Fitness survey found that one-fifth of those surveyed reported a lack of training (SkillsActive, 2009b). This links to the research by Lloyd discussed earlier which suggested that health and fitness employers do not necessarily see a relationship between higher level skills and quality.

Learning and development processes and activities should relate to the organisation's strategic objectives. In order to achieve this and to ensure the effectiveness of learning and development there is a need to undertake a systematic approach; as illustrated by Figure 7.2.

This approach dates back from the 1960s and has continued to have an influence, underpinning the development of National Occupational Standards in the late 1990s (Harrison, 2009). More recent models recognise that training is a narrow term and use the broader notion of learning and development (Foot and Hook, 2008). Each part of

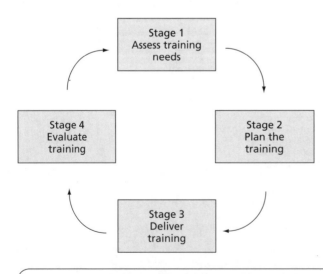

Figure 7.2 Traditional training cycle model.

the model will be discussed in more detail. However, it is important to note that although the model shows the learning and development tasks taking place in sequence, in real life the context in which learning and development takes place is messy and complicated and is often influenced by political factors (Harrison, 2009). For example, if there is not a buy-in by key stakeholders such as line managers, staff may not be freed up to attend training activities. It is likely that such decisions are influenced both by practical considerations, such as staff cover, and by overall perceptions of the added value provided by the learning, training and development activities on offer. In this context, shorter-term training activities may be favoured over longer-term learning and development opportunities that may struggle to justify the cost when measured against more intangible benefits.

> ## Review question
>
> Outline the main differences between learning, training and development. What are the main advantages and disadvantages afforded to each?

7.8 Assessing learning and development needs

This is also known as training or learning needs assessment and involves the systematic analysis of gaps in the existing skills, knowledge and attitudes of organisation employees in relation to the business strategy (Taylor, 2009). The analysis should include both short- and longer-term needs. Taylor (2009) stresses the importance of assessing long-term needs as it can take a long period of time to recruit people with appropriate skills or to develop them in the existing workforce. In sport this is particularly important with the ever changing trends in types of exercise; for example, the move towards personal trainers and the trend for activities such as boxercise or pole dancing means either that staff are trained to keep up to date or that qualified staff are bought in. There may also be strategically based organisation development initiatives such as diversity training.

Within many sport organisations a detailed learning needs analysis would be too complex to undertake centrally. Consequently, it should take place at department/team level with support from HR whenever possible. Learning needs may also be analysed at an occupational level where there are a large number of homogeneous jobs (Palmer, 2005); for example, a chain of health and fitness clubs may review the needs of fitness instructors across the organisation with regard to changing approaches to exercise and/or health and safety.

For individuals it is important that their personal learning links to the needs of the business. The assessment of individual needs usually comes from the performance management/appraisal process and a useful foundation is a job/role analysis as outlined in Chapter 6. An example of a training needs assessment for a pool supervisor is shown in Table 7.1. A job/role based learning needs analysis is best used for those in lower level jobs, as the problems identified with job analysis techniques in Chapter 6 also relate to learning and development; i.e. managerial roles are often dynamic and the job analysis may not be flexible enough to identify the training needs of such complex roles.

Palmer (2005) highlights that there can be a danger of focusing learning, training and development purely from the perspective of the organisation. He argues that organisations need to take into account employees' own development needs, which may not relate directly to current organisational/department objectives, but may still impact staff motivation levels. This is also important in relation to succession planning within the organisation.

Table 7.1 Extract of learning needs analysis for a pool supervisor

Activity	Competence	Skills				
Swimming pool programmes	Develop swimming programmes	Develop activities to meet recreation needs	Plan programmes and activities	Implement programmes and activities	Coordinate programmes and activities	Evaluate programmes and activities
Assessment score						
	Administer swimming programmes	Develop schedules for pool use	Supervise the pool, facilities and staff	Remain current with programmes and services	Maintain office files	Prepare month end reports
Assessment score						
Maintenance of swimming pool and surrounds	Maintain the facility	Ensure cleanliness of pool and surrounds	Ensure cleanliness of changing rooms	Ensure facility is safe for use	Inspect facility at the agreed times	
Assessment score						
	Water quality	Test for chlorine	Test for PH levels	Monitor temperature		
Assessment score						

Source: adapted from Training Needs Assessment Evaluation Form, Government of NW Territories, Municipal and Community Affairs, Canada.

> ### Review question
>
> What are the strengths and weaknesses of using job/role analysis as the basis of a learning needs analysis?

7.9 Planning, delivery and evaluation

From the needs analysis it should be clear what is required with regard to the learning and development of the individual team or organisation. It is important that this is used to set the aims and objectives for the learning or development event or activities to ensure the needs identified are met and also to provide a basis for evaluation. This should ensure that the aims and objectives are met in the most effective way in terms of addressing the need identified and also cost. This may involve decisions regarding whether it should be delivered in-house or by an outside organisation. Also, if the initiative involves an event then within many sport organisations logistical planning will be needed to ensure staff are available, perhaps using off-peak periods, or covering their jobs.

There are an enormous range of learning and development techniques that are available, as indicated by the list of techniques below indentified by the CIPD's (2010b) survey of learning and training methods, with in-house development programmes being the most used techniques:

- in-house development programmes
- coaching by line managers
- on-the-job training
- job rotation, secondment and shadowing
- coaching by external practitioners
- action learning sets
- external conferences, workshops and events
- internal knowledge sharing events
- mentoring and buddy schemes
- instructor led delivery on the job
- formal education courses
- e-learning.

It is beyond the scope of this chapter to explain each in detail, however Taylor (2009) provides a useful list of specific techniques:

7.9.1 Work-related learning techniques

- **Action learning and learning projects** managers are placed into cross-functional groups or sets that enable them to broaden their experiences, exposing them to different functions, which enables them to learn about other aspects of the organisation. Learning occurs from the managers

  questioning their own and others' proposed actions, identifying courses of further action and a time scale. It can make a major contribution to freeing up inflexible or traditional thinking, but needs top level management support if radical outcomes could be threatening.

  (Taylor, 2009)

- **Coaching and mentoring involve** improving skills and performance, usually for the current job, but also to support career transitions. These techniques are discussed in detail in Chapter 10.
- **On-the-job training**. As the CIPD survey shows, on-the-job training is a popular method of learning as it is seen to be immediately relevant. In the past this may have been undertaken in an unstructured way where, for example, a new member of staff would be told just to watch a more experienced member of staff. More recently, the introduction of NVQs has meant that those experienced employees have learnt how to train others (Foot and Hook, 2008).
- **Knowledge management**. This occurs at the end of projects where teams review how they have worked and the 'lessons learned'. This technique is discussed further in Chapter 10.

7.9.2 Off-the-job learning

- **Bite-sized learning involves** small chunks of formal training of an hour or two and in varying formats sometimes linked with other techniques such as e-learning.
- **Classroom training** these are instructor led and formal courses: they can be internal, which give the opportunity to focus on organisation specific problems; or external, which involves people from other organisations and may help individuals see things in a different context.
- **Distance learning** involves learning materials delivered either by mail or increasingly electronically (e-learning).
- **Education** through formal vocational and management courses.
- **Outdoor training/development** includes team building, problem solving or leadership exercises, usually in the open air. These should not emphasise physical challenge and should be seen to relate back to the work environment using reviews.

Obviously it is crucial that the techniques used meet the aims and objectives of the learning and development initiative and they must be appropriate for the needs of individual learners, e.g. their learning styles, educational background etc. The case study of FA learning (Exhibit 7.4) provides an example of the range of learning and development techniques used by a sport organisation. It also illustrates how national governing bodies have to develop learning, training and development strategies both for their own paid staff and also for the volunteers who are involved in the sport.

Exhibit 7.4

FA Learning case study

FA Learning, the Football Association's training arm, was established in 2003. It covers everything from coaching to management qualifications; level 1 courses right up to post graduate studies. Danielle Every, Head of FA Learning, manages a team of 12 staff, including specialists in marketing, course development, e-learning and conference organising, as well as managers who run a national network of around 2,000 freelance trainers delivering courses to local clubs and community centres.

FA Learning complements the in-house training done by the association's own HR department, which mainly covers generic office based skills, such as using PowerPoint. Every year FA Learning trains around 25,000 individuals as amateur status coaches to levels 1 and 2. A further 1,500 professional club coaches are studying for levels 4 and 5 coaching qualifications to equip them for jobs in the game's upper echelons. Across England there are also 30,000 people training as referees. All levels are compatible with UEFA recognised qualifications and are intended to increase international job mobility.

Every states: 'Our courses draw on the experience of top professionals from other sports and disciplines, for example sport psychology and dietetics. If we're to improve the quality of players, we need to improve the quality of coaching.' She sees FA Learning's role as bringing training up to date and giving time pressured individuals more flexible study options. Hence online courses as well as videos and DVDs have been developed to supplement existing taught courses.

With all the millions from commercial sponsorship flowing into the game, rigorous business management is a priority. As Every says, 'It is important for managers as well as finance and commercial directors to understand player valuation, board structure, contracts and corporate governance.'

With regard to learning and development within the FA itself it is felt that FA Learning will complement the work undertaken to strengthen management and leadership skills. A number of senior managers have undertaken a leadership programme at Cranfield University and middle managers have taken part in an executive development programme tailored for the FA by Henley Management College.

In 2006 a learning and development manager was recruited to link staff appraisal with training opportunities offered in-house, and monitor people's professional development. An aim was to push learning to the top of the FA's people agenda with the strategy being about building a high performing environment and organisation which builds the business skills and leadership of the FA's top people.

Source: summarised from an article by Hoare (2006)

Delivery of learning and assessment activities needs to be undertaken by appropriately trained people whether they be learning and development managers or line managers. Learning and development activities need to have some flexibility built in to take account of learning styles (Foot and Hook, 2008).

Dee and Hatton (2006:40) describe evaluation as the 'holy grail' of learning and development due to the difficulties in measuring its effectiveness. A satisfactory return on investment calculation has not been developed and effectiveness tends to evaluated by a post-course questionnaire, often called a happy questionnaire due to the halo effect of staff having a break from their work routine (Torrington *et al.*, 2008). Additionally, Torrington *et al.* (2008) point out that such questionnaires tend to evaluate the quality of the delivery of the course, rather than what has been learnt and how this relates back to the learning and development aims and objectives.

The most commonly cited framework for learning and development evaluation is Kilpatrick's (1959) four levels of evaluation (Arnold *et al.*, 2005):

1 **Reaction level:** data collection from the participants on their reactions to the training – the post-activity/event questionnaire
2 **Learning:** the new knowledge acquired by the participant – may be assessed using a pre and post-programme test or assessment process.
3 **Behaviour:** a test of the new skills in relation to whether the participant can perform to the appropriate standard, for example the effect on the number of customer complaints.
4 **Results:** the extent to which the learning/development activity produces results in the workplace, for example in a health and fitness club this could be the number of memberships sold or member retention.

A key criticism of Kirkpatrick's model arises from the implication that the four levels are hierarchical. Organisational performance measures are perceived to be more important than reactions. Moreover, each level is associated with the previous or next level (Tamkin *et al.*, 2002). For example, learning of training material is dependent on enjoying the training. The model has also been criticised for being too simplistic by failing to take account of intervening variables that may affect changes in work performance following training.

Arnold *et al.* (2004) conclude their review of the evaluation of learning and development by arguing that it is not possible to evaluate using a single method and a multi-method approach should be used.

7.10 Continuing professional development

The starting point of continuing professional development (CPD) is self-awareness and reflection (see Chapter 5). CPD focuses on the individual and is defined by the Institute of Sport and Recreation Management (2009:3) as

> the systematic maintenance, improvement and broadening of knowledge and skills, relevant to the sport and recreation industry and the development of personal qualities necessary for the execution of professional, managerial, developmental, administrative, coaching and operational duties throughout a member's career.

A key part of CPD is that individuals take responsibility for their own learning. This involves setting development objectives and related plans over the short, medium and longer term. Consequently, according to the CIPD's (2010d) essential principles of CPD, it should ensure that:

- Development should be continuous in the sense that the professional should always be actively seeking improved performance.
- Development should be owned and managed by the individual learner
- CPD is a personal matter, and the effective learner knows what he or she needs to learn.
- Development should begin from the individual's current learning state.
- Learning objectives should be clear and, wherever possible, should serve organisational or client needs as well as individual goals.
- Regular investment of time and learning should be seen as an essential part of professional life, not as an optional extra.

There is a range of benefits of CPD for the individual, including remaining competent and contributing to overall levels of employability and career mobility. Additionally, Sadler-Smith *et al.* (2000) highlight that CPD may impact on an individual's self-worth and thus motivation and job satisfaction levels.

CPD also has benefits for employers as it ensures an organisation's staff skills and knowledge are up to date and also aids with succession planning. However, Irvine and Beard (2005) warn that by focusing responsibility for learning and development on the individual, an organisation may use this as a means of abdicating responsibility for the learner in order to reduced expenditure.

CPD is critical in sport employment, as highlighted in SkillsActive's (2009b) *Working in Fitness* survey, which found that 58 per cent of the fitness workforce paid for their own training. This rises to 75 per cent in the private sector, prompting Irvine and Beard (2005:360) to apply the term 'abdication of responsibility' to industries who rely on their workers to pay for their own learning, training and development in this way. Within coaching, the UK Coaching Framework highlighted the importance of CPD for coaches and many national governing bodies (NGBs) have developed CPD activities that run alongside their coaching qualifications.

> **Review question**
>
> Identify and discuss the key learning and development issues within the sport industry.

7.11 Summary and conclusion

This chapter has provided discussion of the learning, training and development in sport at the level of the economy, the organisation and the individual. It has explored UK government strategies for learning and development in terms of upskilling the sport workforce. Additionally, it has identified that trying to move forward from a low paid low skilled workforce is a complex issue. A key problem appears to be that sport organisations do not necessarily see a clear relationship between upskilling and improving the quality of the product.

The chapter examined the definitions of learning, training and development and discussed how there had been a move from using the narrow term training to the broader notion of learning. It then examined the range of approaches to learning and development that are used within sport organisations. Overall, the evidence suggests that sport and leisure organisations adopt a lukewarm approach to this area, many failing to recognise the potential benefits of embedding a learning culture into the overall performance of the organisation (also see Chapter 10).

Evaluation and performance appraisal in sport and leisure organisations

---

Learning outcomes

By the end of this chapter you will be able to:

- demonstrate an understanding of what is meant by 'performance appraisal' within a sport and leisure context;
- appreciate the differing sport and leisure contexts in which performance appraisal can be applied;
- provide a critical appraisal of the different options available to organisations;
- appreciate the pivotal role of the customer in this process;
- develop an insight into the wider systems context of evaluating and rewarding performance.

8.1 Introduction

In this chapter we draw, once again, on the theories of individual, group and organisational behaviour (see Chapter 4). These are important in order to understand the antecedents of performance and as a necessary adjunct to the critical application of the differing approaches available to a variety of stakeholders in the sport and leisure sector. Clearly, the term 'performance' can exist at the level of the industry, the organisation, the facility, the department, the team and the individual. It can be measured in a number of ways including financial, economic, customer and in more human/qualitative terms. Moreover, it can also be applied to the local, regional, national and international contexts.

Of equal significance, is the nature of the relationship between the organisation and the individual. By this we are broadly referring to the nature of the employment relationship, which could vary from full time (salaried), to full time (piece-rate), to part time, to casual, to temporary, to seasonal, to volunteer, to amateur status, to contract worker. In addition, the level, context and relative importance of individual staff members, within both the internal organisation and the wider external environment, may also have an impact on the dynamics of such relationships. This, in turn, mitigates the power differentials at play and the potential impact of this on the allocation of appropriate pay and rewards for any given level of performance. For example, how many times do senior managers award themselves the smallest wage rises and bonuses? In professional sport, who has the power when negotiating contracts and bonus payments? What happens in voluntary sport and leisure when the more traditional rewards of money and perks are not really on offer? In truth, there are many potential responses to such questions. For our purposes, however, and in line with many previous assertions during this book, the only real answer is that it depends!... But on what?

To help unpack such questions we must first be clear what we mean by performance and who it is applied to. For example, are we talking about the performance of senior managers, middle managers, first-line managers, supervisors, team leaders or front line players, staff and/or volunteers? What impact do such status differentials have upon issues of performance evaluation and reward? What impact do geographical differences, such as the 48-hour maximum working week in Europe or minimum wage levels in the UK, Europe, Africa, India, Asia, North and South America have upon absolute and comparative measures of both individual and organisational effectiveness? Hopefully, you will be forming the impression that the concept of performance can be a tricky and sometimes extremely illusive concept to define. Of course, clarity and agreement around a working definition of performance represents only the first step in the process of evaluation and subsequent reward allocation!

For the purpose of this chapter, it would be unrealistic to deal with every possible permutation, as the number of contributory variables could be voluminous. Instead it is necessary to provide a framework in which a variety of possibilities can be conceptualised and applied to the systems context in which organisations operate. Given the focus of the book, we will favour performance appraisal at the level of the individual and team; although this will be related to more expansive notions of overall performance where applicable. Organisations in general and HR departments in particular should look to establish systems and procedures that seek to appraise, develop, reward, retain and motivate employees in ways that are aligned to the enhancement of overall organisational performance. However, as with most other HR issues, this process is complex and is not easy to do well. Employee and team evaluations rely on a combination of general managers, line managers, functional managers, HR managers and related staff. However, there are many factors that can conspire against its effective conceptualisation and subsequent implementation.

8.2 The context of performance appraisal

Within the sport and leisure sector any review of this concept must be mindful that there are a variety of contexts in which this can be applied, each revealing a plethora of objectives; some complementary, whilst others may be in conflict. Some of these have been covered both during the introduction to this chapter and during related chapters such as Chapter 1. However, for the sake of clarity, the differing contexts are further embellished below.

8.2.1 Commercial sector

Much of the generic literature and understanding of performance is specifically orientated towards this sector. Pick up most General Management or HRM textbooks and they will present models of performance evaluation, appraisal and reward based on the generic assumption that the primary purpose of both an organisation and its staff is to make money. However, there is an increasing tendency for the dominant management hegemonies espoused by Western business schools to be challenged (Coahen, 2008; Parker, 2008). Profit maximisation is no longer the only game in town! However, prevailing orthodoxies relating to this area are still, largely, predicated upon this primary assumption.

8.2.2 Public sector

The public sector exists to provide products and services for the collective good of a given population. As a consequence, the public sector works in areas where, at least historically, it has been considered uneconomic for the commercial sector to operate. This does not mean, however, that any consideration of the public sector will be devoid of revenue, cost and profit considerations: far from it! Rather it means that the public sector objectives should be fundamentally different from those of a commercially orientated organisation. What, where and how public money is spent has to be justified against wider and more inclusive notions of the public good. In this sense the local councillors and citizens are the ultimate judges of provision and performance in this area.

In recent years, there has been a more overt overlap in the provision of sport and recreation facilities between the public, commercial and voluntary sectors. What was once only provided by the public sector is increasingly being provided by the private sector. For example, swimming pools are now found within many private health and fitness clubs and are no longer the exclusive preserve of the local publicly funded sport and leisure centre. The public sector needs to be prepared to respond to such external changes; not least anticipated reductions in public funding and associated services as the world responds to the massive costs of the global financial meltdown during 2008/2009.

8.2.3 Voluntary sector

This sector includes the greatest number and the widest variety of people who are actively engaged in the sports and leisure sector. Broadly, their objectives are related towards the fulfilment both of individual and group interests in the not-for-profit pursuit of sport and leisure challenge/enjoyment. The sector, through its numerous governing bodies, is also inextricably linked to the professional sports context.

8.2.4 Professional sports

In many ways this represents an amalgam of several of the above categories. Some professional sports are highly commercial in their orientation, whilst others are not but would like to be! Many professional sports, in their present format, are unable to survive on the basis of market appeal and profitability alone. Some are inextricably bound into the cultural fabric of a country or community, whilst many rely upon public subsidy, fundraising and sponsorship. In the UK, sports such as table tennis and swimming require public subsidy to survive. The more subsidies they have the more potential there is for performance improvement. UK swimming, for example, has benefited from a relatively large increase in their funding over recent years in the run up to the 2008 Beijing and 2012 London Olympics. Performance, measured in terms of the number of competitive finals reached and medals won, has improved significantly over this period. Similar arguments could be used for areas such as the investment of the Lawn Tennis Association (LTA) in British tennis over recent years. However, the performance improvements have been somewhat disappointing over the short and medium term. What this means is that having the right capital resources is rarely the only ingredient to sporting success. These must be blended with human resources to create a winning formula. If only there were standard ingredients and complementary recipes! As Gratton and Taylor (1985:136) contend:

> Even when all the right technical ingredients for successful production are present, it is possible that output is not maximised or is of unsatisfactory quality. This can occur because of a lack of motivation, or 'human error' and it is termed X-inefficiency. According to Liebenstein (1966) it is in competitive environments that managerial incentives are most likely to keep this problem to a minimum, and produce X-efficiency.

Like it or not, many governing bodies of sport exist in an external context that is increasingly viewed as part of a wider and more competitive entertainment industry. There is now very real competition between sports and a whole range of alternative leisure choices. This level of competition exists in all areas of the sports economy, including the public and voluntary sectors. Governing bodies increasingly represent hybrid institutions that feel they have to act commercially whilst also acting as the sport's administrators and custodians. Moreover, they tend to be largely staffed by enthusiastic amateurs, although there has been a relatively recent move towards their more professional administration. As a consequence, governing bodies may be forced to consider radical alternatives or watch their sport continue to lose popularity both with audiences and participants. Unsurprisingly, many are reacting by introducing new business models and different types of competition. In cricket, the Twenty20 model has led to a dramatic upsurge in the number of fans attending county games. Netball have introduced format changes within their 'world series' where game times are halved and scoring regimens altered in an effort to make the sport more popular and commercially attractive to audiences and the media.

Within individual sports, competition may come from alternative governing bodies, as is the case within boxing and darts. Within the professional side of sport there is an evolving battle for the hearts and minds of existing stakeholders from both internal and third party influences. In 2009, the FIA (governing body of motor racing) battled with the constructors of Formula One for control of the sport. Likewise, in the summer of 2010 John Davidson battled Barry Hearn for control of professional snooker. Similarly, the International Amateur Athletics Federation (IAAF), responding to pressures and ideas from athletics promoters, sanctioned the biggest shake-up in the sport for 25 years. The 'Diamond League' series represents 14 events across four continents, with the world's top athletes free to negotiate their own central contract based on their perceived economic value. Sport truly has moved on with the likes of Kevin Pietersen (cricket) and Usain Bolt (athletics) now reported to be earning over £1 million (Kimmage, 2009) and £3 million (Leonard, 2010) respectively, mostly through associated endorsements and sponsorships. At the turn of the millennium such figures would have been unthinkable in all but a handful of sports throughout the world.

Enthusiastic amateurs and willing volunteers now share the same governing bodies as professional sports stars earning millions of pounds. The ability and power of governing bodies to act in the best interests of all stakeholders is now likely to have a very real impact upon the perceived success of such entities. This represents a difficult balancing act that must be solved if sport continues to be governed in this way. Of importance for this chapter, however, is how governing bodies choose to reconcile their objectives in a way that is seen to be complementary and not contradictory to the different stakeholders involved.

8.2.5 International context

International variations may also have a significant impact upon the variety and nature of organisations in which performance evaluation should be considered. For example, public–private partnerships are common in France, where the movie industry is regarded as part of the cultural fabric and is thus awarded requisite public subsidies. Similarly, many French Professional Rugby Union teams exist in a partnership with local authorities. It is problematic, therefore, when comparing the performance of French professional rugby clubs with those in the UK as it is not comparing 'like with like'. Similarly, in the United States, the collegiate sports system is fundamental to the US sports industry and significantly differs from virtually any other sports sector in the world in this regard. Broadly, sport within US educational institutions operates in the charitable sector, but is often managed in a highly commercial manner with a variety of lucrative alumni, sponsorship and media deals. Make no mistake about it, US collegiate sport is big business, whilst their major stars exist as amateurs, not professional athletes. This affects the business models used and the extent to which its major assets, i.e. the players, are forced to take a longer-term view of their performance and earning potential during the formative and crucial stages of their sports careers.

There is also a need to consider the impact that globalisation is having upon sports and how its performance is assessed. As with most organisations, there are many alternatives when looking for ways to expand the business. We have already alluded to some of these with respect to the product differentiation that now takes place within a growing number of sports. Increasing the number of formats available has the potential to make the sport or leisure activity more attractive to a greater number of potential customers. Another way is to grow outside national boundaries that offer only limited growth potential. We can see this trend with football clubs such as Manchester United and Real Madrid touring the globe during the close season. We can also see this with American football and basketball which are doing the same with tours of Europe and Asia. Similarly, the European Tour, in golf, now has a truly worldwide reach with ranking events in Africa, Asia, the Middle East, Australasia and Europe.

8.2.6 Pay

Although strong links have been established between performance and monetary reward (Rynes *et al.*, 2005; Mulvaney *et al.*, 2008; Lussier and Kimball, 2009; Rial *et al.*, 2008), this does not reflect the reality of several sport and leisure organisations and those individuals who help them function. For example, in the voluntary sector, coaches, athletes, treasurers and secretaries all give up their time either free of charge or for minimal out of pocket expenses. As Old (2004:70) argues:

> managers sometimes wonder why they cannot 'motivate' their employees by offering them more money for more, or 'better', work – after all this is the way things work in markets. But inside organisations it is much more complex. Do we know in advance what 'better' work will be? Who will say whether it is 'better'? Can the manager monitor precisely what has to be done, and will they be judged by the employee to assess it impartially? To what extent is the performance of the employee under their control, and to what extent is it affected by the performance of others – including crucially, the manager?

Judgements concerning the relative performance of a variety of sport and leisure organisations, including their managers and associated staff, should be based upon a number of interrelated criteria, not purely money. One organisation is not necessarily better than the other based only upon profitability and pay packets. What is clear, however, is that in order to professionally manage and reward performance, from an HR perspective, requisite systems and processes have to be measured against the overall objectives of the organisation in some meaningful way.

8.3 What is performance?

Performance can be defined as the measure of relative success against predetermined objectives over a given period of time. Organisational objectives and performance, taken both individually and together, may also attempt to take into account the internal and external context in which they are formulated, measured and assessed. Once the organisational mission and objectives are established, performance indicators (PIs) can be developed which provide signposts along the road to the ultimate realisation of such objectives. However, this is contingent upon the ability of PIs to accurately represent organisational objectives at the level of the individual and the team.

The application and use of PIs will be dependent upon the scope of the services under scrutiny. Small leisure facilities and the staff who work within them, may require a relatively small number of PIs when compared with larger facilities. In all cases, however, the starting point should be the overall organisational objectives and their subsequent operationalisation. This requires the allocation of individual and/or collective responsibility at various levels of the organisational hierarchy. It also requires the rationalisation and targeting of objectives to appropriate units of performance. These could be at several levels including individual and team and could be measured discretely and also in a more aggregated format; for example, where individual and team performance are combined to allocate bonuses and rewards. Responsibilities, based upon job descriptions and organisational objectives, can then be used as a basis to develop individual and team based performance targets. However, the bigger the organisation the more problematic this process becomes as individual performance, particularly at lower levels, may become detached from the overarching objectives that are designed to drive the organisation forward.

It is useful to place any discussion of performance review in the context of the anticipated outcomes and their antecedents. As highlighted by Chapter 1, 'black box' processes are critical to the conversion of inputs (resources, including staff) into performance outputs (profit, customer numbers, customer satisfaction levels etc.). This is applicable to the evaluation of concepts such as 'efficiency', 'effectiveness', and 'value for money'.

Concept check

The 'e' factors

Efficiency. The relationship between inputs and outputs, e.g. the achieval of specified outputs for minimum cost. 'Value for money' indicators could be measured in this way. These are particularly important in the public sector where accountability for public money may be crucial in securing additional awards.

Effectiveness. Concentrate on output measures, e.g. an additional 1,000 school children signing up for a specified sports scheme.

Economy. The acquisition and use of inputs at minimum cost, e.g. the decision to purchase sports equipment for a school from the lowest cost supplier. This may or may not have implications for quality and measures of efficiency and/or effectiveness over the longer term, i.e. if inferior equipment has to be replaced earlier, hence the phrase 'false economy'!

Equity. The equality with which inputs and outputs are allocated. These are important within the public and voluntary sectors. They are also important within the commercial sector where equity considerations between different parts of the organisation may have both a direct and indirect impact upon relative levels of performance.

Efficacy. The ability to produce a desired output/outcome. Often this may be measured against alternatives. This is very much related to the concept of effectiveness but it has a more qualitative dimension and is perhaps more applicable where value judgements are also integral to measures of performance.

However, it would be wrong to focus solely upon inputs and outputs, in isolation, without using such information to reflect upon the wider and systemic processes that are connecting one to the other. It is inevitable that attempts to establish PIs, based around the above criteria, become somewhat distorted and skewed in favour of the money side of the equation. Value assessment is fraught with problems of subjectivity and, therefore, remains a more contentious issue. It is easier to control and manage outputs that can be readily ascribed with numerical and thus monetary value. As a result, performance evaluation, in the commercial arena, is a more simplistic process, as public and voluntary sector concerns with social objectives are, generally, considered to be relatively unimportant. Moreover, in the public and voluntary sectors, there is a very real danger that inputs are used as the main monitoring currency, as outputs may be difficult to define and subsequently evaluate in any substantive and meaningful way. For example, it is a commendable social objective to promote greater public health through the provision of related facilities: but how is this measured? We can measure the cost, but how do we measure the wider impact? If this were an entirely commercial venture, run by a pharmaceutical company, development costs would be clearly monitored relative to revenue and profit.

When one considers the non-mandatory status of public sector sport and leisure provision in the UK, in tandem with the continuing levels of financial stringency, there is little wonder that the objectives of sport and leisure departments may be subject to value realignment. In this context, it is likely that ways of minimising costs (inputs) and maximising efficiency (ratio of inputs to outputs) will be sought. However, this is often to the detriment of effectiveness and overall considerations of quality and absolute performance (outputs). The Audit Commission is the government body responsible for auditing public sector spending and provision in the UK. In this context they have several recommendations for the provision of local sport and recreation provision. They argue that councils should:

Improve the strategic planning of sports and recreation provision and increase overall efficiency by:

- assessing current and future sports and recreation needs locally and their relationship to regional and national needs;
- collaborating with the private, voluntary, health and education sectors and working across administrative boundaries in the planning, procurement and delivery of services;

- appraising the options for delivering sports and recreation services systematically in an open and transparent way and testing the market to ensure that the best value option is identified; and
- improving the collection, analysis and use of performance information in order to demonstrate value for money, for example by including financial performance and social outcomes in all contracts.

(Audit Commission, 2006:4)

Accountability is often a key justification for performance appraisal in all sectors. However, managers of public and voluntary sector organisations need help in such endeavours as inertia created by bureaucratic red tape and the need to justify every pound of public money spent may stifle motivation, innovation and progress. This view is shared by Michael Higgins, the Audit Commission Chairman, who is reported to have labelled the administration of the £1.6 billion grants system for sports and leisure projects in the UK as 'a dog's breakfast' (Beckford, 2009). Project managers are often reluctant to complicate issues with elaborate and costly methods of performance appraisal when social objectives are difficult to pin down and every penny counts. In this way, an opportunity to better understand the 'black box' processes involved may be lost unless the funding agencies instigate a separate evaluation of what and how objectives are met. Ideally, such issues should be agreed upon in advance as an integral part of the learning processes and legacy of the project. If not, managers may become suspicious of the real value of placing the performance of the project under the microscope. This leads to defensive behaviours that may undermine attempts to learn the lessons and apply them to future projects.

Clearly performance appraisal, particularly in the public sector, must walk a tightrope between a range of different and often competing stakeholders and objectives. Measures of efficiency, effectiveness, economy, equity and efficacy are therefore of crucial importance in this endeavour. With this in mind, there should be a balanced portfolio of PIs designed to accurately portray the performance of sport and leisure organisations and the managers and staff who work within them. Perhaps, in an ideal world, notions of efficiency should remain subordinated by the concept of effectiveness. Unfortunately, we are still a long way away from utopia; it costs too much!

8.4 The characteristics of performance indicators and SMART objectives

For each individual or team it is necessary to monitor, review and prioritise the actions that contribute to overall organisational performance. In order to do this it is useful to focus upon the key goals of the organisation and turn these into more specific SMART objectives at a more local level. SMART objectives should clearly articulate what is required and how performance should be measured. They should be:

- Specific, but also Standardised (well defined and appropriately detailed; where possible capable of comparison through the standardisation of specific measures).
- Measurable, but also Monitored (should be capable of measurement, preferably within the normal process of the management information systems available within the organisation; this allows for regular monitoring to take place).
- Achievable, but also Agreed, Appropriate, Accurate, Aligned. (There is little point establishing objectives that are not achievable. As such, it is highly preferable that all parties agree such measures as this improves the level of commitment and motivation.

It is also important that the measures used are both appropriate and accurate; otherwise they will be of spurious value. Individual development needs should be aligned with those of the team and the overall organisation. Similarly, team objectives should be aligned with the skills and needs both of the individual and the organisation.)

- Realistic, but also Resources, Relevant, Relative, Requirements, Review. (Objectives should be realistic in terms of the resources available to the individual or team. This includes human, capital and time resources. They should be relevant to the motivations of team members and, ideally, should be prioritised in terms of their relative importance. Above all the requirements of the task ahead should be clearly articulated and be subject to continual review.)
- Time bound, but also Targeted. (Most things are possible given enough time. However, it is highly preferable that objectives are given time limits. Typically, this will be during a review period of up to one year, although shorter increments of time are preferable, where possible. This ensures that effort is targeted in appropriate ways and at appropriate times. It also provides greater clarity with what and when targets should be achieved.)

In establishing accountability for performance there are several factors that should be considered. Accountability is mitigated by a number of factors such as organisational constraints and the effects of the external environment. It would, therefore, be wrong to ascribe individual responsibility for variables that occur outside the realm of individual and/or team control. Performance indicators and, ultimately, overall operating objectives must be under continual review in order to ensure that the targets set are both achievable and realistic. This requires a workable balance between competing and often contradictory organisational priorities.

Exhibit 8.1

Performance review in action

Consider a leisure organisation that wants to increase its profitability by 50 per cent over a three-year period. As part of this wider strategic objective an individual multi-sports facility, controlled by the organisation, has been set more specific SMART targets of increasing throughput by 25 per cent whilst maintaining existing expenditure levels. This is reflected in the management and staff performance targets for the facility and is one of the factors dictating managerial bonuses at the end of the year. A similar facility has opened up within a two mile radius and the pricing policy is broadly equivalent to existing levels.

Specific – 25 per cent increase in admissions; 0 per cent increase in costs.
Measurable – against recorded admission numbers and cost allocations.
Accurate – the overall accounting procedures of the facility will be independently audited at the end of the year.
Realistic – the target has been agreed by an ambitious but very inexperienced newly appointed manager of the facility.
Time bound – the targets will be measured during a normal financial year for the organisation.

Review questions

What are the options available to the manager?

What are the implications of each option both for the manager and for their staff?

What could be the implication for admissions over the short and medium term?

Some of the options are reviewed below:

It may be necessary to reduce prices in order to encourage greater throughput. However, by how much? Previous information relating to price changes may help here and it may be better to target those facility activities that are more sensitive to such changes. This may also require a change in the programming policy of the facility where more popular activities are given greater priority. However, this may alienate a proportion of the existing users, many of whom could be regular attendees. They may choose to switch to similar local provision.

Likewise, one would have to consider the extent to which costs are either largely fixed or flexible over the review period. This dictates how much flexibility the manager has to control such costs. With increased throughput, associated costs will also increase, e.g. more instructors, more water/shower use etc. This will have to be balanced by any increase in revenues dependent upon the combination of throughput and prices. Clearly, it would be unrealistic to target a substantial reduction in costs; particularly if they are largely beyond the control of the individual and/or team. Attempting to control costs in this way may also lead to reductions in service quality levels, a reduction in staff morale and a subsequent reduction in attendances as reduced standards and staff disaffection is translated into a reduction in the overall levels of customer care and, thus, repeat attendance. Customer attendance frequencies are important for throughput, cost, pricing, revenue, retention and profitability considerations. Staff disaffection may be also be affected by management style and the extent to which they are included in any rewards available for achieving such targets.

There will always be consequences and trade-offs when looking to set up systems to monitor and reward appropriate levels of performance. Targets and PIs should not only be achievable in the short term, but should also be balanced with a consideration of the medium- to long-term effects, where possible. In establishing SMART objectives one should be aware that several targets would be inextricably linked together. For this reason, one must be careful not to develop a total reliance upon PIs. This may induce managerial myopia and a reluctance to consider the wider picture through a narrowly focused and short-term conception of performance; particularly in situations where the media is always looking for a new angle. The LTA, for example, point to the fact that they have been successful in encouraging new participants into tennis and argue that their plans for elite tennis should be measured over a much longer time frame. The ingredients to success are rarely straightforward and it is necessary to consider an appropriate balance between performance appraisal and performance development. A better understanding of such 'black box' processes is needed.

8.5 Lifting the lid on the 'black box' of performance appraisal, evaluation and development

In a systematic review of the literature surrounding organisational effectiveness, Lee *et al.* (2007:S180) argue that very little evidence exists in relation to such processes, specifically applied to sports organisations. Of the existing evidence, they identify several factors that they claim impact the organisational effectiveness of sports organisations, including

> organizational culture, resources and support, communication and atmosphere, long-term planning, internal procedures, activity level, efficiency of throughput process, realization of aims, interest in athletes, and caliber of board and external liaisons. These findings suggest that both interpersonal and environmental dynamics facilitate the effective running of an organization. Consequently, practitioners must be aware that internal processes rather than inputs and outputs are essential to success, with discrepancies imposing undue demands upon athletes.

This implies that there are many facets to organisational effectiveness and these are inextricably linked with wider systemic work processes. However, some of these factors may be difficult to define and directly correlate with measures of individual, team and organisational success. One such issue relates to the quality of relationships, particularly between managers and their staff (Baptiste, 2008; Lussier and Kimball, 2009).

Concept check

Organisational citizenship

The concept of **organisational citizenship** represents the altruistic and often tacit actions that enhance organisational effectiveness. Such actions are rarely overtly monitored or rewarded and yet have been shown to make a significant impact upon overall organisational performance. Whiting *et al.* (2008:125) argue that Organisational Citizenship Behaviours (OCBs):

> have been shown to enhance organizational effectiveness (cf. Dunlop and Lee, 2004; Koys, 2001; Podsakoff, Ahearne, and MacKenzie, 1997; Podsakoff and MacKenzie, 1994; Walz and Niehoff, 2000). For example, OCBs have been shown to increase both the quantity and quality of work group performance, efficiency, customer satisfaction, profitability, and revenue per full-time employee; and decrease customer complaints and employee turnover.

In some ways OCBs represent the oil that lubricates the dynamics of the organisations and, according to Whiting *et al.* (2008) can be divided into three areas, as below:

1 helping behaviour such as supporting colleagues and reducing destructive conflict;

> 2 voice behaviour such as constructively challenging prevailing ortho-
> doxies held within the team and/or organisation;
>
> 3 organisational loyalty including behaviours that are supportive of the
> organisational position, strategies, reputation and rules.
>
> Such concepts also extend to a wider discussion of management practices
> in general and HRM practices in particular. For example, Baptiste
> (2008:284) highlights that the: 'HRM practices adopted have a significant
> impact on employee wellbeing at work and tend to be more positive than
> negative ... management relationship behaviour in the form of support
> and development of trust, promoted employee wellbeing at work
> amongst workers'. Although OCBs are difficult to measure they appear to
> be positively related to individual performance ratings (Whiting *et al.*,
> 2008:132).

Hoye (2006) applies leader member exchange theory to the workings of voluntary sports organisations in Queensland, Australia. Each Australian state has slight variations in the way that such voluntary sport organisations must be legally operated. However, all will have constitutions that establish that the ultimate responsibility resides with the executive board. The maturity of the relationships between chairs, paid executives and voluntary board members was seen to be pivotal to the effective functioning of the executive and the concomitant achievement of organisational objectives. Performance appraisals (PAs) have a role to play in such processes. For some, such as Jawahar (2006:213), PAs make a clear contribution to more expansive notions of organisational success:

> One of the primary purposes of formal performance appraisals is to provide clear, performance-based feedback to employees (Carroll and Schneier, 1982; Ilgen et al., 1979; Larson, 1984). Almost 45 years ago, Maier (1958) highlighted the crucial role of appraisal feedback in the performance appraisal process ... from the organization's point of view, feedback keeps both its members' behavior directed toward desired goals and stimulates and maintains high levels of effort (Lawler, 1994; Vroom, 1964). From the individual's point of view, feedback satisfies a need for information about the extent to which personal goals are met (Nadler, 1977), as well as a need for social comparison information about one's relative performance (Festinger, 1954).

However, whilst Lussier and Kimball (2009:201) concede the importance of PAs in both understanding and managing people, they highlight the potential complexities by discussing the tensions that can exist between HR processes designed for development and those designed for more evaluative purposes. They contend that:

> Developmental PAs are used to improve performance. Evaluative PAs are used to decide pay raises, transfers and promotions, and demotions and terminations. Evaluative PAs focus on the past, whereas developmental PAs focus on the future. However, developmental plans are always based on evaluative performance. The primary purpose of both types is to help employees continuously improve their performance. Most firms place the biggest emphasis on evaluation, which is a mistake because it doesn't develop employees.

If the organisation and its managers have a genuine desire to develop their teams and employees, then an annual appraisal interview, in isolation, is unlikely to be the best way of achieving this. Individual employees, at any level, are unlikely to volunteer their own and/or organisational weaknesses if the consequences are perceived to be important with respect to pay rises and/or promotional prospects and/or the day-to-day realities of everyday work life, i.e. work relations. Feedback should be a positive two way process between employees, teams and the organisation. It should be both frequent and timely. Feedback should not be restricted to an annual PA and, instead, should form part of the natural daily flow of conversations designed to progress both individual and organisational development. Moreover, regular feedback should be supplemented with other related and concurrent methods of employee development. These should be designed to complement PAs and engage staff in more reflective and discursive behaviours relating to their own development and that of the wider organisation (for a discussion of related issues see Chapter 10).

Kline and Sulsky (2009:161) posit that PAs are 'one of the most researched topics in industrial and organisational psychology'. They argue that most organisations have formal evaluation systems in place. However, as we have already established in Chapter 1, a large proportion of sport and leisure organisations exist in either the voluntary sector or are SMEs. Under such circumstances, both are unlikely to have dedicated HR expertise and, thus, both are less likely to have formal PA systems in place. This is particularly true of the voluntary and private sectors. If the argument is that PA is important within a systems context of managing people, then there are, potentially, a variety of negative consequences for organisations that are unable to fulfil this function. For sport and leisure organisations this may mean that a substantive number are unable to engage in what is considered to be best practice with regards to performance appraisal and development. Unsurprisingly, a notion of best practice is somewhat spurious and represents a contested area of both literature and related practice.

8.6 Methods of performance appraisal

Kline and Sulsky (2009) identify two broad approaches to performance appraisal; rater formats and rater training. Rater format refers to the ways in which managers are asked to make judgements about either the behaviour or traits/competencies of their staff. These could be judged either in absolute terms, against related criteria, or in comparative terms where some form of ranking is preferred. Such judgements can be made either externally (through league tables or world rankings) or internally (through managerial perceptions and related PIs). Broadly, Kline and Sulsky argue that there is no clear evidence that favours either the behavioural or trait approach. However, behavioural methods are more favoured where there is potential for litigation as there is considered to be a more direct and defensible link between observed behaviour and overall performance. Furthermore, when rater formats are used for developmental, rather than purely evaluative purposes, they argue that comparative assessments may not provide enough detailed feedback and depth to effectively facilitate this.

There are advantages and disadvantages to both systems and no single method will fit every situation (Hamilton *et al.*, 2007). In professional sport, for example, there is a frequent need for value judgements to be made about internal selection decisions: who plays and who doesn't. More subtle variations of this are also in evidence and these can exist both through explicit systems of PA and implicitly through more informal methods. In Formula One motor racing each team has two drivers. However, when it comes to race tactics, or how the cars are developed, one driver may be more favoured than the other. This can be extremely significant for both current and future performance. This has consequences in terms of individual motivation, team harmony and ultimately the overall performance both in the individual drivers and in the team based constructors championship at the end of the race season. In this sense, particularly in areas such as professional team sports, internal comparator ratings are often unavoidable.

Although such internal issues are not always directly relatable within individual sports, this will continue to generate competitive internal tension within team based sports. This needs to be skilfully managed. Where possible, competition should be used to harness both individual and team performance. However, if not handled sensitively this could very easily prove to be both divisive and destructive on several levels.

Rater training, on the other hand, concentrates on the ways in which appraisers are trained to improve the quality of the PA process through the psychometric rating systems used. Overall, according to Kline and Sulsky (2009), the literature in this area identifies three main methods, as below:

1 **Rater error training (RET)**. This helps appraisers understand common mistakes in the psychometric rating process. A 'halo' error is made where ratings are influenced and often inflated by general impressions. This leads to a positive bias in favour of certain members of staff relative to others. In this sense such errors could be related to the previously reviewed OCBs. 'Leniency' errors yield inflated psychometric impressions across all candidates. This may, at least in part, be more to do with the appraisers' need to be liked, than any desire to provide more objective and meaningful feedback. 'Range restriction' errors refer to a tendency to grade within narrow margins; for example, the majority are poor or average or good. Given that psychometric PA systems are generally based on numbers, one would expect a typical sample of staff to show a normal distribution of scores. That is to say they will be evenly distributed from top to bottom with the majority somewhere in the middle. Highlighting the potential for a variety of errors does appear to positively influence the objectivity of such evaluations. Kline and Sulsky (2009) argue that this could also result in appraisers looking to artificially avoid such situations by forcing a more even distribution of scores when the vast majority are really good or really bad or simply all mediocre.

2 **Behavioural observation training (BOT)**. This taps into the psychological processes involved in observing and rating behaviour. This demonstrates how individuals may process information differently which can lead to errors. Although there is only limited evidence in this area, it does indicate that there are potential benefits to training appraisers in this way.

3 **Frame-of-reference training (FOR)**. This training ensures that the appraisers give more accurate ratings based on individual impressions of each of the dimensions of performance. In order to accomplish this, a degree of standardisation is necessary around issues that link such behaviours with performance. This necessitates agreement around an appropriate system for identifying behaviours, determining both their relevance and effectiveness, before combining such factors to create an overall scorecard of individual performance (Sulsky and Day, 1992, 1994; in Kline and Sulsky 2009:162).

FOR training is really about developing a taxonomy or rubric that can be used for overall performance assessment. This can be accomplished through more traditional top-down processes, based on generic competency models, or through a more inclusive bottom-up approach based on critical incidents (Kline and Sulsky, 2009:163). This can be much more time consuming, but because it tends to involve more staff, it encourages a greater acceptance of the processes involved. An example of this process can be found by the approach taken by Elmhurst Park and Recreation Service in the United States (see Exhibit 8.2).

Exhibit 8.2

Elmhurst Park and Recreation Service

Elmhurst Park District, Illinois, United States, were looking to integrate a PA process into their strategic HRM framework. In doing this managers wanted to promote a high-performance culture by improving the staff perception of the PA system and using this as a tool to develop a more customer focused approach to their service. The park service is governed by elected officials and has 58 full-time staff, 235 part-time and 325 seasonal employees. The existing system was based on annual performance reviews and a skills matrix that was not considered 'fit for purpose' and did not accurately represent the diversity of jobs within the District. The new system was constructed, bottom-up and consisted of the following process:

1   Job analysis: current job descriptions were reviewed both by appraisers and by staff. Six to ten job areas were identified from which a more specific range of 10–15 tasks were agreed under each heading based on what the employee actually did to perform the function.

2   Rating of task statements: each task statement was rated independently both by the appraiser and by the member of staff based upon its perceived importance and the time/frequency taken for each task relative to all other tasks. Each were rated on a scale of 1 = 'low', 7 = 'high'. These were then combined to create a score ranging from 1 to 49, i.e. low importance, low time/frequency to high importance, high time/frequency. A meeting between employees and appraiser was held to combine, normalise and agree final weightings. The appraiser had the casting vote where any disagreement occurred.

3   Creation of appraisal instrument: this can be used to anchor employee performance relative to some performance model and/or relative to other employees. According to Arvey and Murphy (1998, in Mulvaney et al., 2008) a performance scale of between three and seven descriptors is best. Elmhurst selected a three point system consisting of (1) below standard, (2) meets standard and (3) exceeds standard. There was also a 'not applicable' box included to cover all other eventualities.

4   Identifying raters: in line with the majority of existing research in this area, it was decided that existing supervisors were best placed to provide an accurate appraisal of individual performance against the criteria.

5   Rater training: it is not unusual for many supervisors or managers to be offered either no or very limited training in order to fulfil this very important but potential problematic task of PA. However, the Elmhurst training had three components:

   a   rater error: e.g. halo effect etc.
   b   performance dimension: a collective discussion on the application of the performance dimensions between the appraisers and the appraisees.
   c   performance standard: a collective discussion about how standard categorisations would be interpreted. This allowed for a further degree of standardisation to take place before any appraisals had actually taken place.

6   Performance appraisal interviews: a pilot was conducted where employees first completed the appraisal forms and used these as a basis for discussion with the appraiser. A rating is then agreed for each task area. Each score was then multiplied by the weighting factor to generate an overall performance figure represented as a percentage of the total possible score.

7 A model for the distribution of merit increases: this consisted of three considerations, as below:

  a pay differentials: these need to distinguish between differing levels of performance. Arvey and Murphy (1998, cited in Mulvaney *et al.*, 2008:137) argue that this should be at least 3 per cent between the levels for this to be recognised as qualitatively different by employees.

  b forced distribution: statistical techniques were then applied to consider the performance position of each individual relative to the average through the computation of Z scores (standard deviations). This resulted in approximately 11 per cent being categorised as below standard (−1.0 Z score), 61 per cent meeting standards (−1.0–0.5 Z score) and 28 per cent exceeds standard (>0.5 Z score). Although staff recognised that subjective judgements would always be part of the system, they were happy to endorse this way of distributing merit pay increases. On balance it was considered to yield more objective judgements.

  c pay adjustment matrices: the final amendments were related to necessary adjustments to account for those already at the top of the pay scale.

Levy and Williams (2004; in Kline and Sulsky, 2009:165) suggested many social-contextual variables that may play a role in determining the utility of a given system in a given context including, but not limited to: organisational culture, legal climate, trust, rater training, and appraisal documentation. Their long list of variables highlighted the complexity of the performance appraisal system that goes far beyond the psychometric properties of the rating instruments.

Source: adapted from Mulvaney *et al.* (2008)

Review questions

From your knowledge of the processes involved, what factors do you think are relevant to the Elmhurst case study?

Do you think it matters that only full-time employees were included in the process?

How do you think the chosen method could relate back to overall organisational objectives?

What other advantages and disadvantages can be associated with the approach taken at Elmhurst?

Of course the Elmhurst case study, in common with the vast majority of PA systems, relates only to individual performance. However, particularly in the sports environment, the team performance is often the key arbiter of how overall success is measured and subsequently valued. In this context Kline and Sulsky (2009:166) argue:

The search to find a standardised set of items that assesses team performance across organisations is rather futile. Instead, it is suggested that a standardised process to design an assessment system for each team makes more sense (Jones and Schilling, 2000). This process includes identifying the role of the team in the organisation and analysing the tasks of the team.

In other words the process engaged in by Elmhurst should be replicated within team environments and should include considerations of 'black box' processes such as team decision-making, communication, feedback, leadership and internal relations (Kline and Sulsky, 2009:166). Clearly it is necessary to first have a reasonable understanding of such processes, all covered at different points within this textbook, before attempting to move this forward. However, there are both similarities and differences here. For example, it is self-evident that engaging in PA at team versus individual level is likely to be more complex and, therefore, difficult to manage due to the increased number of variables and interrelationships at play. Not surprisingly, therefore, the number of organisations who evaluate and reward in this way tends to be in the minority, despite the evidence suggesting the efficacy of this approach (Geber, 1995 in Kline and Sulsky, 2009).

Professional team sports share some of the characteristics found in the process of individual performance review. For example, sports teams can often be promoted and financially remunerated on the basis of league position. Typically, this is not the case with more generic interpretations of team performance within organisations. However, all sports teams are made up of individuals who, normally, have either standard or individually negotiated employment contracts. Typically, these will be for between one and five years. If these include elements related to PIs such as number of games played, number of goals scored etc., and these are linked directly to remuneration, it is easy to see how such issues can create a tension between individual and team agendas. Leonard (2005:34) argues that such discussions should be kept confidential for exactly this reason. However, when details are released this can lead to player disaffection and a pressure to review the equity of overall wage structures. There are also consequences in terms of overall organisational performance. For example, during the 2003/2004 season Barcelona FC had a newly elected executive board whose primary agenda was to restore the club's rapidly declining performance both on and off the pitch. The reality for Barcelona was that if they won the league they would still be in financial deficit by triggering large bonus payments to its players. If they didn't win the league, they would be much closer to the financial break-even point and in line with their election manifesto promises to over 100,000 Barcelona members! Which is preferable and to whom? Fast-forward to 2010 and the next Barcelona Board are reported to be negotiating a €150 million bank loan in order to pay the wages of the players and coaches, despite recording world record revenues following two of the greatest seasons in the clubs history. According to Domingues (2010): 'Newly-elected president Sandro Rosell, who recently replaced Joan Laporta, said he took over a club full of debts and cash flow problems: "Our members can be reassured. The club is not bankrupt." '

Player's wages seem to be dominating the cost structures of professional football clubs across Europe. However, with the exception of the top and bottom performers, there appears to be no direct correlation between wages and team performance (Deloitte, 2010:7). For example, Blackpool FC secured their return to England's top division during 2010, despite the fact that they had one of the lowest expenditures in the football championship. Similarly, the unfancied FC Porto rose to the pinnacle of club football during the 2003/2004 season by winning the European Champions League, having progressed from winning the UEFA Cup during the previous year. Clearly the team 'black box' alchemy engaged in both by Ian Holloway (Blackpool's manager) and by Jose Mourinho (Porto's manager) has much to do with this, although cynics could argue that the promise of future riches had a little to do with it also!

In many ways some professional sports, such as football, are idiosyncratic in the sense that they may be financed by rich benefactors who are not looking for a traditional return on their investment. For example, Roman Abramovich, at Chelsea Football Club, is reported to have spent £725 million in six years at the club (Deloitte, 2010:9). Furthermore, Deloitte (2010:2) argues that:

the range of funding models appears to be contracting. A model of profit maximisation is now pursued by a very limited number of clubs and, whilst some clubs seek to break-even on a consistent basis, the emerging norm for many Premier League and Championship clubs appears to require significant ongoing benefactor support. As such we appear to be seeing a continuing shift from a sustainable 'not for profit' model towards one with potentially calamitous consistent and significant loss making characteristics.

If the above assertions are accurate, then this can create large divisions between the haves and the have-nots. Ultimately, it has the potential to undermine the competitive balance and financial stability of both club and league structures. Unsurprisingly, in order to respond to such challenges, UEFA, the governing body which represents football in Europe, is discussing the implementation of a financial 'fair play' policy where clubs will not be allowed to spend more than they earn through their differing revenue streams (from the 2013/2014 season). Clearly, this has the potential to affect the pay and bonus payments paid to staff and particularly players throughout all European leagues. It could also be argued that this represents a back-door salary cap; something that has been previously resisted by the majority of European leagues and clubs. However, things change and timing is everything as an increasing number of football clubs face financial administration and possible bankruptcy! If such proposals become reality, the leagues that benefit will be those with the largest revenue streams. These will be able to justifiably maintain their operating licences, under UEFA regulations, whilst paying their staff and players higher gross wages relative to their competition; both in domestic and international leagues. This has wider implications for the labour market and the international flow of players from one league to another through the current player transfer system (also see Chapter 2).

Of course, the working assumption, up to this point in the chapter, has been that any performance evaluations will take place between one appraiser and one individual or team. Both in traditional organisational structures and in those associated with professional sports, this is not always the case.

8.7 Stakeholder analysis

The above term is used extensively in the literature surrounding organisational strategy, particularly with respect to the partnership arrangements found within many sport and leisure organisations. It exists to account for the fact that there are a number of organisations that have a vested interest in how another organisation is managed. Sometimes, this will extend to decisions about individual or team performance within a given organisation; for example, who really takes the decision, in professional sport, when players are transferred and/or released from their contract to go to another competitor? In business, this would often be the individual's decision based on a number of personal motivations. In professional sport, however, it could be the individual, the manager, the other players, the chief executive, the chairman and/or the fans who prove instrumental in such moves. In other words, there are a number of internal and external stakeholders (or customers) who may have a vested interest in the PA process. How is this accounted for?

Multi-source, or the more commonly termed 360° appraisal, represents a PA process that considers the views of a range of stakeholders in the assessment of individual or team performance. This is not without its detractors, but generally it is seen to be a positive and more accurate process, particularly in relation to enhancing the judgements formed by the appraiser. Moreover, it is seen to be more effective when used in a more developmental and not purely evaluative context (Kline and Sulsky, 2009:167). This must also be placed in the context of individual perceptions and the other factors at play within organisations. As we have seen with the previously reviewed Elmhurst Case Study, a much more relevant issue is the perceived quality and usefulness of the ratings by employees. This issue is not amenable to simply improving the measure of performance – it calls for an understanding of the motivations of the stakeholders and of the system context.

(Kline and Sulsky, 2009:167–168)

Exhibit 8.3

Fabio's fantasy football

Just before the 2010 World Cup in South Africa, the personal standing of the England manager, Fabio Capello, could not have been much higher. He had seen the England team through a virtually unblemished World Cup qualification stage and had handled some difficult personal issues with players with much-needed personal assurance and integrity. Through a more traditional style of leadership, he had also managed to reinvigorate the team with a respect for the manager and a more overtly professional approach to their international preparation. This had manifested itself very positively in terms of team performance. He had not put a foot wrong!

However, even great managers can get it wrong, particularly where there may be a perceived conflict between personal gain and team performance. According to Burt (2010:S3), 'Capello appeared to score a public relations own goal … in launching a private venture by which he will effectively rate the performance of his players on the internet" This would be done immediately after the conclusion of a World Cup game, as part of an alleged new fantasy football game. Unsurprisingly, Fabio withdrew from the venture just before the World Cup and just after the story broke in the English press.

Review questions

Having read the chapter to this point, what do you think may have been the consequences both for Fabio and the for England team if Fabio's fantasy football venture had continued?

Do you think this impacted, in any way, on the relatively poor performance of the England team in the 2010 World Cup in South Africa?

What other factors could have affected the performance of the England team?

Chief amongst such stakeholders is the external customer. These rarely reflect an homogeneous group with similar needs, priorities and opinions. However, one of the main purposes of most organisations is to better meet customer needs, wants and requirements. It seems sensible, therefore, to suggest that this should be considered when reviewing the PA process within sports and leisure organisations. Customer feedback can help improve performance by better understanding and targeting the most important behaviours that are perceived to enhance customer experience and value. Warman (2010) points out that 'Nike+' technology can now track the behaviour of users (the most popular time to go for a run is Sunday at 5 p.m.!). Similarly, the Royal Shakespeare Company can now better target its marketing effort through their analysis of seven years of ticket data, whilst the Royal Opera House sends reminders out to customers as part of its customer relationship management operation. With regards to professional sport, AC Milan are well known, in football circles, for looking after their players; they 'collect 50,000 individual pieces of data about their top players and uses it to encourage these prized assets to modify their techniques so that injury is less likely' (Warman, 2010:33). Of course, such factors may also influence player decisions. David Beckham is alleged to have chosen AC Milan on the recommendation of Fabio Capello, the England manager and Beckham's previous boss at Real Madrid. One of Beckham's primary goals was to play for England in the 2010 World Cup in South Africa. However, even the best laid plans can be frustrated as David Beckham suffered an injury just before the start of the World Cup which would effectively end his international career!

Rial *et al.* (2008) discusses the application of importance-performance analysis (IPA) to the management of sports centres in Spain. Chapter 1 argues the importance of establishing organisational priorities around an understanding of customer needs. If PA is based largely around organisational objectives, then an understanding of customer needs is also pivotal to this process. IPA seeks to do this through a relatively simple process of establishing the strong, weak and improvement aspects of any given service. The technique seeks to establish the perceived importance of all factors contributing to the service provided. It does this by researching customer views in a two-dimensional matrix containing both an x axis (perceived importance of factor) and y axis (perceived performance of factor), as demonstrated by Figure 8.1.

Interestingly, the most important components of customer perceptions of service quality related to staff issues, are below:

1   Kindness and treat[ment] from staff
2   Professionalism of instructors
3   Efficacy of instructors

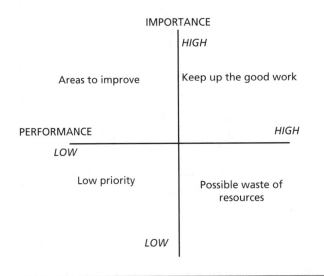

Figure 8.1 Classical representation of IPA.

Source: Martilla and James, 1977, taken from Rial *et al.* (2008).

4 Personalized service
5 Interest showed by staff for your comeback
6 Physical environment
7 Sport areas
8 Hygiene and cleanliness
9 Equipment
10 Dressing rooms, toilets and showers

(Rial *et al.*, 2008:184)

If organisations are genuinely serious about providing effective systems of PA, for both measurement and development purposes, this must include the views of customers, staff and management. As previously established, this entails the establishment and subsequent understanding of relevant performance data. It also requires the buy-in of staff and should consider such aspects as an integral part of its conception, development and subsequent implementation.

8.8 Summary and conclusion

This chapter has sought to provide a framework for the development and integration of a performance evaluation system within sport and leisure organisations. Performance evaluation and rewards should take place within a strategic approach to HRM. This needs to take account of the open systems context in which most organisations operate. External factors influence the internal dynamics of the organisation and managers must ensure that performance and reward systems are flexible enough to respond to such challenges. The chapter has reviewed many factors that contribute to a wider and deeper understanding of the performance evaluation within sport and leisure organisations. Performance evaluation should not be considered an end in itself, but merely a means to an end. It should not be concerned with inputs or outputs in isolation, but must take a more eclectic look at what, why and how related products and services are provided. It requires a range of value judgements to be made with respect both to interpersonal relationships and to resource allocation. Targets should not simply be imposed without prior discussion, but should be consultative in nature. Performance appraisal allows interested parties to monitor direction and establish trade-offs between competing and often contradictory demands for limited resources.

What is clear is that there is no one best way of organising this and that there are a number of different stakeholders to account for within this process. As a consequence, each organisation, each team and each individual represents a unique set of motivations and associated implications, both positive and negative. It is only when all such factors are combined do the inputs both of capital and of human resources transform into outputs that can be measured against the *raison d'être* of the organisation(s) in question. A variety of specialist, general and front of house staff are likely to be involved in this process. It is only by better understanding such interrelationships and developing complementary systems, procedures, training and personal skills that the PA process can be more effectively used both for appraisal and for developmental purposes.

Chapter 9

Organisational development and the management of change

Learning outcomes

By the end of this chapter you will be able to:

- understand the philosophy and principles of organisational development as this applies to sport and leisure organisations;
- identify and apply organisational development methods and applications to appropriate sport and leisure management contexts;
- critically evaluate the theories and models of change as applied to sport organisations;
- review the key aspects of change management relating to sport organisations.

9.1 Introduction

Sport and leisure organisations, like most present day organisations, are complex. As we have outlined so far in the book there are no easy, quick fix solutions with regard to effective human resource management (HRM). What is clear is that in order for sport organisations to be effective there needs to be effective human resource strategies deployed at an individual, group, unit and organisational level. Moreover, as discussed in Chapter 1, sport and leisure organisations often have to deal with multiple stakeholders in their approach to organisational development and associated change management strategies.

9.2 Organisational development

Organisational development, hereafter termed OD, is one way to address these important HRM concerns. This chapter has two purposes: first, to explore the potential of OD as both a philosophy and a set of practical operational methods to help address the issues of managerial effectiveness, leadership and human resource strategy within sport and leisure organisations. Clearly this is a tall order, but it is important to make the connection between these important and interrelated variables. Second, the chapter will critically examine the theories and approaches to the analysis and management of change with regard to sport organisations, including a critical analysis of OD in this context.

There have been a number of studies which have examined the effectiveness of change management approaches within sport and leisure organisations but few have explicitly applied the concept of OD to sport. A key aim of this chapter will be to discuss how OD could be beneficial to sport organisations, and how this can be juxtaposed with related concepts of organisational change.

OD is not a new concept in itself and its popularity has waxed and waned over the last half century. However, in the last decade it has flourished within UK organisations, particularly in the public and third sector; including related sport and leisure provision.

Concept check

Organisational development

Organisational development relates to improving the overall efficiency, effectiveness and performance of an organisation through the involvement of people.

A key issue with OD is its eclectic nature, which is illustrated by the range of, at times, conflicting definitions, some of which are listed below:

> a system-wide process of planned change aimed at improving overall effectiveness by way of enhanced congruence of such organisational dimensions as external environment, mission, strategy, leadership, culture, structure, information and reward system, and work policies and procedures.
>
> (Bradford and Burke, 2005:12)

Organisational development is a long-term effort, led and supported by top management, to improve an organisation's visioning, empowerment, learning and problem solving processes through an ongoing, collaborative management of organisational culture – with special emphasis on the culture of intact work teams and other configurations – utilising the consultant-facilitator role and the theory and technology of applied behavioural science, including action research.

(French and Bell, 1999:25–26)

A system wide process of data collection, diagnosis, action planning, intervention, and evaluation aimed at (1) enhancing congruence among organisational structure, process, strategy, people and culture; (2) developing new and creative organisational solutions; and (3) developing the organisation's self-renewing capacity. It occurs through the collaboration of organisational members working with a change agent using behavioural science theory, research and technology.

(Beer, 1980:10)

A consequence of the diverse nature of OD is the perception of it being a 'scavenger discipline', that borrows from other disciplines such as systems thinking and the behavioural sciences including psychology, anthropology, sociology and organisation theory (Holbech and Cheung-Judge, 2009:6). Thus, it is also seen as homeless, with many HR practitioners lacking an understanding of its true meaning and potential. As a result, according both to Holbech and Cheung-Judge (2009) and to Garrow (2009), it is often not utilised and applied to its optimum capability within organisations.

OD aims to institutionalise the processes of change and development within organisations. This, in turn, makes a positive contribution to organisational tasks, targets and strategies, which are accomplished more efficiently and/or effectively, whilst also seeking to maximise human satisfaction. This seems sensible and links some of the early thinking in HRM, based on the work of Blake and Mouton (1964), with some of the early writers on human motivation and leadership such Herzberg, Maslow, and John Adair (see Chapter 4). A theme common to both areas is that effective performance requires managers to have a high degree of concern for both the task and the needs of the people who will be carrying out such tasks. OD reinforces this philosophy but also adds the ingredient of organisational health.

Organisational health is a key ingredient to the successful implementation of organisational development techniques. In organisational development terms, organisational health is about the state of internal collaboration, openness and trust that exists within the organisation. High degrees of trust and openness are a prerequisite for effective implementation of OD techniques and principles. As we have seen, in previous chapters, this is not as easy as it sounds, particularly when there are multiple constituencies and interests groups who are not always moving in the same direction; a common feature of sport and leisure organisations.

Robbins identifies the philosophy and values that underline organisation development approaches and activities:

- The individual should be treated with respect and dignity.
- The organisation climate should be characterised by trust, openness and support.
- Hierarchical authority and control are de-emphasised.
- Problems and conflicts should be confronted, not disguised or avoided.
- People affected by change should be involved in its implementation.

(2001:553)

In order to fully understand OD, a brief historical overview will be provided followed by an examination of the place of OD in contemporary HRM within sport organisations.

The history of OD can be traced to the late 1940s and the development of management thinking as a response to more traditional and instrumental approaches to management. As

155

discussed in Chapter 1, the classical approach to management thinking placed little regard on individual and group needs; often leaving individuals and groups feeling isolated and alienated. A core value of OD, which is shared by all of the definitions identified earlier, is its humanistic approach which recognises that individual and organisational needs can be aligned. Thus the dehumanising 'machine' metaphors, related to the concept of scientific management, were replaced by natural images of the organisation as a healthy body where 'people, systems and technology could be organised in a more effective and humane way' (Garrow 2009:2). Central to this was the contribution of individual effort to the achievement of higher level organisational performance. However, this early 'individual' focus gradually shifted to a consideration of group dynamics. According to Garrow (2009) this was known as the T-group movement and was led by Kurt Lewin. T groups involve unstructured group activities which focus on processes rather than content; the communication of feelings rather than information and opinions. The aim is to allow individuals to learn about themselves and their impact on others (for a discussion of the importance of self-awareness see Chapter 5).

The 1960s and 1970s were the highpoint of OD in terms of its rapid spread within American and then into UK organisations such as ICI, where it was often used in helping to change management styles in order to improve organisational performance (Cannell and Daniels, 2010). However, the use of OD began to decline in the late 1970s and 1980s as increasing doubts surfaced relating to its validity. An over reliance upon the importance of the individual, relative to the organisation, was seen to be both simplistic and naive (Armstrong, 2006; Cannell and Daniels, 2010). Consequently, in the 1980s and 1990s, OD was replaced by other approaches such as total quality management and business process re-engineering, which built upon earlier OD approaches to change management and organisational culture.

In the last ten years, within the UK, OD has seen somewhat of a resurgence, albeit with more of an emphasis on change management (Garrow and Varney, 2009). The Chartered Institute of Personnel and Development (CIPD) have stated that they see OD as having considerable importance within HRM and argue that it should be seen as a continuous review process rather than just a one-off change intervention. They identify the following underlying characteristics that mean that OD is of value to organisations in the present day:

- OD work contributes to the sustained health and effectiveness of the organisation;
- OD work is based upon robust diagnosis that uses real data from organisational, behavioural and psychological sources;
- OD work is planned and systematic in its focus, that is taking account of the whole organisation;
- OD practitioners help to create alignment between different activities, projects and initiatives;
- OD work involves groups of people in the organisation to maximise engagement, ownership and contribution.

(Cannell and Daniels, 2010)

One of the reasons for the resurgence of OD in the UK has been the changes in the public sector which have led to OD being embraced by the NHS and local authorities. This is particularly true when many economies are subject to massive reductions in government spending in response to the general world economic crisis which originated in 2008. Interestingly, the concept of OD can be resurrected and modified to suit the political and economic realities of the time. For example, in 2005, the Office for the Deputy Prime Minister, in the UK, produced a position paper which argues that:

> The demands on local government are constantly shifting, driven by user expectations and government initiatives such as CPA and efficiency targets. Councils have learned to

cope with and to embrace continuous change to maintain their relevance and quality of service but the changes now facing the public sector are more complex still and will need different solutions and different thinking. Using OD techniques, councils can explore more transformational approaches to change and ready themselves for a new era of networked local governance and greater user choice and involvement.

(Office of the Deputy Prime Minister, 2005:2)

According to the paper, OD is concerned with 'planned interventions to bring about significant improvements in organizational effectiveness' (Office of the Deputy Prime Minister, 2005:2). However, given the massive UK public sector spending cuts, announced during 2010, its difficult to see how OD can deliver improvements in service delivery in the sport and leisure sector, i.e. improvements in effectiveness. More likely, it will simply look to preserve as many existing services as possible, whilst significantly reducing associated costs, i.e. improvements in efficiency but not necessarily effectiveness measures (see Chapter 8). It is also interesting to note that OD is defined purely in terms of 'significant improvements' rather than planned and incremental changes embedded within developing organisational cultures.

Review question

With specific reference to sport and recreation (see policy updates at http://www.sportandrecreation.org.uk), to what extent is the UK government's rhetoric surrounding OD realistic?

More specifically, Sport England, England Hockey and the Football Foundation have all used organisational development consultants (Pharos) to address organisational issues. The testimonial in Exhibit 9.1 illustrates that type of approach involved in OD.

Exhibit 9.1

Sport England OD programme: restructuring and re-engineering

Our business objectives were to realign our systems, processes and people with the expectations and purpose of Sport England. In essence, we were delivering an efficiencies programme and addressing a significant amount of HR issues in particular employee relations, consultation, performance management and total pay. We had gone through change programmes before but they were done to us – not with us. Pharos introduced consensus and consultation which enabled engagement and commitment, top down.

The executive was fully involved in decision-making and we were committed to making it happen. Colleagues have commented positively about the quality of communication because they knew where they stood and felt the process was transparent and authentic. Whenever we got bogged down in the detail, Pharos made us take a step back to generate realistic solutions.

Source: testimonial from Baddeley and Harlow on behalf of Sport England (in Pharos, 2010)

A challenge in the implementation of OD is that its philosophy and values tend to run against the grain in most organisations, particularly with regard to issues of hierarchy, power and control. Implicit in its values is the need for senior people in organisations to relinquish some power and control, to enable the focus to be on the needs of individuals and groups in an environment of trust and openness. An acid test of this is how information is shared within the organisation. If information is withheld or distorted then it is likely there will be trouble down the line and trust and openness will be difficult to achieve. Conversely, if information is open and shared then the potential for trust and openness is much greater.

Another crucial feature of OD is that it is organisation wide. This requires quite a lot of effort to achieve in practice. Change is often seen to be driven in the interest of senior people within the organisation leaving others to feel less well connected to the need to change and develop. Clearly this is problematic because without real commitment, at all levels, change and organisation development will be limited. Moreover, resistance to change will be more likely if there is a lack of understanding, or buy-in, across organisational levels. The important feature is that OD is a planned process not an ad hoc one. This requires a clearly defined, systematic and thoughtful approach to the process of OD that identifies the issues to be addressed and accounts for the current state of play. Given this approach OD includes the key elements of development, self-knowledge, diagnosis and learning and intervention. Each will be discussed in turn.

Development. As OD emphasises trust, openness and organisational health it is important that its focus is developmental at all levels (the individual, unit, group, inter-group and organisational wide levels).

Self-knowledge. This requires that the organisation is self-critical and open to a diverse range of views when faced with change. This could be instigated internally by senior managers or others with the requisite skill set or through the use of change agents in the form of external consultants.

Diagnosis and learning. It is implied here that organisations have the ability to diagnose the relevant change management issues and are also able to learn from previous experience how best to address such issues. A technique developed by Lewin (1947a) is action research. According to Arnold *et al.* (2005), this involves the systematic collection of data from key groups: the organisation (i.e. senior managers), the subject (people in the area of change) and the change agent. This data is used to diagnose problems and then survey feedback techniques are used to analyse and interpret data within the groups. This work is then used to form the basis of action plans.

This, as we have seen, is not as straightforward as it might appear. It will really depend on the extent to which the sport organisation has the capacity to be self-critical and open in order to facilitate learning. This relates to the notion of the learning organisation which Garrow (2009) sees as a crucial element of OD. Learning organisations are discussed in more detail in the next chapter, but a useful explanation of them is provided by Rowden (2001:117): 'a model of strategic change in which everyone is engaged in identifying and solving problems so that the organisation is continuously changing, experimenting and improving, thus increasing its capacity to grow and achieve its purpose'.

Intervention. The pattern of intervention underlying OD is also systematic and based on a diagnosis of the appropriate choice of action. So, for example, if the problem is perceived to be about aligning organisational objectives to individual performance, the choice of action may be over a longer term and is likely to include performance review, appraisal or a form of management by objectives. Conversely, if the sport organisation is in danger of not surviving then the implementation of the choice of action may have to be quick with little time for consultation. However, the process also requires a degree of assessment and evaluation of how well the process worked and what lessons have been learned.

There is a range of intervention techniques available to sport managers under the broad heading of OD. As discussed, this choice of action will depend on the nature of the problem, the organisational context and culture, time scales and the skill set of the managers who are leading the change process. Some of the available techniques for individual and group performance are highlighted below.

9.3 Techniques to improve individual and group performance

9.3.1 Managerial grid training

This functions at all levels, including individual, group, and organisation wide levels. It is based on the managerial grid developed by Blake and Mouton (1964), which focuses on the approach taken by managers with regard to leadership and management. The essence of the model is that all managers should strive to achieve the ideal balance between a strong emphasis on the task, at the same time having a high regard both for individual and group needs. The training associated with the model is intended to help managers reflect on their own managerial style, with the intention of helping managers move closer to the ideal style and type of management where there is an equal focus on task and human development needs. It attempts to develop a balanced approach to management focusing on what is most important, i.e. people and their ability to perform in an environment of support, trust and openness. There is also a connection here to the development of higher order needs identified in many important motivation theories such Herzberg, Maslow, Argyris and Macgregor (see Chapter 4).

9.3.2 Life and career planning

This is something that would be appropriate to consider during performance review and appraisal meetings. The approach here is trying to gain a balance between work and other important aspects of an individual's life. This is important at a number of levels. First to keep individuals motivated through a wider consideration of their individual interests, ambitions and personal interests. This will, in turn, help to create an atmosphere of trust and openness. If an individual genuinely feels that his/her line managers care about their development, both at a personal and professional level, then there is more potential for a positive and healthy relationship to develop. This, in turn, can pay dividends in terms of individual performance and well-being.

9.3.3 Behaviour modelling

Behaviour modelling is a psychological term that simply means learning by *copying* or *mimicking* the behaviour that we are exposed to. In managerial terms this means modelling the behaviours that are considered to be appropriate within the organisation. This is closely aligned to the concepts of organisation culture developed by Chapter 3. We often learn behaviours based on our observations of others; particularly the leaders in an organisation. So, for example, if our leaders are open and willing to both listen and act on the views of others then we may also take on this approach in our behaviours with others. This sits well within the organisational development framework. If, on the other hand, our leaders distort or withhold information we may not trust their behaviour and equally may demonstrate some of these same behaviours as a means of survival or even progress.

9.3.4 Training: skills, knowledge, problem solving

This is directly related to individual needs development and links to processes of staff appraisal and performance review (see Chapter 8). If undertaken with a mature problem solving approach the potential for individual growth and autonomy is enhanced. This again requires trust and a focus on development rather than control. There needs to be a genuine concern for individual development aligned to the potential resources required to support training and knowledge development.

9.3.5 Job design

This includes such job developments as job rotation and job enlargement – in other words, trying to make work more meaningful and interesting for employees. It attempts to match the design of work to the needs of employees with the aim of enhancing satisfaction and productivity

9.3.6 Job stress analysis

Increasingly employers have to account for the stress related factors that are evident in the workplace, which relates to employers having a duty of care to protect the health and safety of workers in the workplace. Professional sport is highly dependent upon its athletes in both the production and subsequent sale of the sporting experience. However, unlike machines, which can be worked harder and easily 'fixed' when broken, this is not such an easy option with both the psychological and physical welfare of professional athletes. As Fran Cotton, former professional RFU player argues of the UK's top professional league: 'The Premiership is just a war now. ... No wonder there are so many injuries. A third of the Premiership squads are unavailable every weekend. In any other business it would be totally unacceptable' (quoted in Reason, 2009). As a consequence, there comes a point where professional sport cannot simply continue to increase the supply of games and tournaments in response to the temptations of increasing demand and profitability. This tipping point was reached in 2009 and 2010 for the women's and men's professional tennis tours, respectively. They have both now taken the decision to reduce their seasons by two to three weeks in response to continuing worries and mounting evidence about player burn-out and injuries.

9.3.7 Team building

It is becoming increasingly accepted that teams are the basic building blocks for organisational performance and satisfaction. How well teams work together and how they are structured and led are also critical ingredients in this process. Team building can be carried out within the organisation led by management or human resource professionals with the appropriate skill set. Alternatively, this can be led by external consultants with expertise in team building and task accomplishment. However, if this is the case any resultant changes and/or lessons need to be structured in such as a way as to be embedded within a more progressive and developmentally orientated organisational culture that is more likely to be self-correcting in the future.

As with all approaches to management there are pros and cons to each of the above approaches. Using internal expertise can save on time and money and has the added benefit of local knowledge and context. The drawback here is that sometimes in order to deal with difficult interpersonal conflicts it is problematic for internal facilitators to be seen to be impartial. On the other hand external consultants can bring both a degree of expertise and impartiality to the situation. They can act as honest brokers or third party peacemakers in a way that internal facilitators may find difficult. The disadvantage is that they will not have the local and contextual knowledge and may be seen to reinforce decisions already taken by senior managers in their interests. This is called post-rationalisation of decisions already taken and is often highlighted as a negative aspect of using external consultants.

9.3.8 Survey feedback

This is a technique where surveys are carried out with regard to staff attitudes and expectations. This information is then fed back anonymously to senior managers for their consideration and action. This is becoming a common practice and, for example, is seen as good practice by the health and safety executive in the UK who encourage a strong dialogue between employers, employees and trade unions. In this case respondents may even be invited to identify themes that are important for wider consideration; for example, the relationship between managers and managed in a form of upward appraisal. This is where employees have a chance to discuss and feed back on their manager's performance and behaviour.

9.3.9 Process consultation

This approach requires either an internal or external consultant to work with the organisation to identify and deal with the problems that have been identified. The consultant uses his/her expertise to facilitate this discussion and fits well with the key themes of OD where the organisation takes a mature and open stance when addressing and solving problems. It is important that the consultant genuinely facilitates mutually agreed and informed solutions to organisational problems. If not then this may be seen as an example of a hit and run approach to consultancy where the problems are left behind after the consultant has long gone.

9.4 OD and sport organisations

The discussion of OD within the first part of this chapter has highlighted how OD can, and is, being applied to sport organisations. The actual need for the approach that OD offers is illustrated in Exhibit 5.3 'The hardest job in leisure' (Chapter 5), which highlights the unhealthy situation that exists within some sport and leisure organisations. Sport organisations are under constant pressure to improve their effectiveness and achieve the highest level of performance and OD may offer the way of developing effective leaders and motivated teams that create agile structures and processes (Garrow, 2009).

Exhibit 9.2

A case study of organisational development and leadership

Phil Jackson was a member of the New York Knicks basketball team during their most successful period in the late 1960s and early 1970s. What was unique about the New York Knicks was their emphasis on team play, hard work and effective communication. They had a talented team but they were not the most talented players in the NBA. Phil Jackson was a substitute player and by no means a star player. He is, what is described in the NBA as a role player, or someone who concentrates on particular aspects of the game rather then being the main play maker. Watching the Knicks during this period was a pleasure. They worked for each other, played to their strengths and were clearly well prepared for their matches. There was an emphasis on the fundamentals of the game, on team work, on shared responsibility and on playing hard defence; often considered the most difficult aspect of the game.

Phil Jackson turned his hand to coaching basketball in the NBA for the Chicago Bulls in the 1980s. Prior to Phil Jackson joining the Chicago Bulls they had limited post-season success even with the efforts of the great Michael Jordon as their floor leader. They lacked a sense of balance on the court and relied very heavily on the skills of Michael Jordon. This was always going to be limited in a team sport such as basketball. Phil Jackson had to work not only on the mechanics of the game but also on the philosophy of team play and leadership with elite highly paid professional sportsmen. In essence his job was closely aligned to OD and leadership in a professional sporting context. He was extremely successful as a coach with the Chicago Bulls winning six NBA championships during his time with the Bulls. Much like the great American college basketball coach John Wooden, he emphasised the need for personal responsibility on the court and in so doing created the potential for players to act as coaches on the court. This would then require less intervention on the part the coach giving players more responsibility for what happens on the court. What was interesting, watching the final game of the Bulls' first NBA championship, was the importance of role players in the final and crucial moments of the game. It was John Paxon, a shooting guard, who scored most of the final points and not Michael Jordon. This was replicated in many of the final moments of key games leading to the Bulls' successive wins and was not a feature of the less successful Bulls even with Michael Jordon.

Phil Jackson retired from his role of head coach with Chicago after winning six NBA championships; an exceptional achievement by any standards. However, he came out of retirement to join the Los Angeles Lakers; again a team with many great players but limited recent success. The Lakers had a long history of success but prior to Phil Jackson joining the team their recent form was less impressive. The problem here was how to get a group of exceptionally talented players to play together. In both cases Phil Jackson used an approach where he diagnosed the issues and identified a course of action underpinned by a strong sense of philosophy and personal commitment to the players, the team and the team's performance. This was no easy agenda; it took skill, patience, clarity of thought and the intense training and development of his players.

An important feature of Phil Jackson's approach to management and coaching is highlighted by Ullman (2010:1)

> Team leaders often diminish their impact despite their intention to do the opposite. By encouraging too much dependence on their own interventions, they risk being fractional leaders. By contrast, team leaders who carefully develop the ability of their team members to adapt to change and challenge can increase their leadership impact so that it is felt even in their absence. They can become leaders and a half, rather than half-leaders.

Phil Jackson's approach was based on deep levels of understanding, managerial and technical skill and explains his exceptional performance as a coach, mentor and leader. As stated previously some of these very same features can be observed in another great American basketball coach, John Wooden. In both cases, Phil Jackson and John Wooden emphasised a strong commitment to the personal growth and development of their players, a clear understanding of the context and problems they were facing and understanding that they needed players to take more responsibility for the success, or otherwise, of the their teams. In the case of John Wooden, it was his attention to detail and preparation, based on what he described as a triangle of success that meant that his players would step up during matches and require less of his intervention. You could often see him sitting calmly on the bench when his team was playing in contrast to most other coaches who felt the need to be more interventionist during matches. In the case of Phil Jackson he would let his players play through bad patches during matches to allow them to work through problems for themselves rather than calling a time out to intervene in the situation. This is also exceptional and not the way professional coaches normally tend to operate.

> ### Review question
>
> Discuss the extent to which Jackson and Wooden are taking an OD approach; include specific examples of the activities they undertook to support your discussion.

9.5 The management of change

As has been identified in the earlier part of this chapter, a key part of OD is the management of change. The rest of the chapter will explore the location of OD within the main and alternative approaches to the management of change.

All sport organisations experience day-to-day fluctuations; however, the discussion in this chapter generally relates to the view of change expressed by Slack and Parent (2006), i.e. change that an organisation systematically develops. They identify that change can occur in four different areas of a sport organisation:

- The introduction or removal of **products** and **services** offered by the organisation.
- **Technological** change in terms of production processes and the skills and methods used to deliver its services.
- **Structural and systemic** change, for example staffing structures.
- **People**, with regard to how people think and behave.

(Slack and Parent, 2006:239–240)

These changes are caused by external factors, such as economic and political conditions, and to some extent internal factors such as the ageing of material resources and human resources, in terms of people and their skills and abilities (Mullins, 2007). A key task for sport managers is to identify the most appropriate changes and implement them. There are two main approaches to organisational change. This chapter will review them both in relation to sport.

9.5.1 Planned change

Burnes (2009:600) distinguishes planned change from other approaches in terms of being 'consciously embarked on and planned by an organisation as opposed to types of change that might come by accident, impulse or forced on the organization'. Planned change is most closely aligned with OD. Accordingly, planned change focuses on change at a group level and factors such as group norms, roles, interactions and socialisation processes and how they create disequilibrium and change (Burnes, 2009). As with OD, Lewin (1947b) was a key architect in developing models of planned change of which his Three Step Model of change lies at the core.

Step 1. The belief underpinning this model is that human behaviour is in a quasi stable equilibrium that is supported by a complexity of driving and restraining forces.

For change to occur this equilibrium needs to be destabilised by reducing the restraining or driving forces that maintain current behaviour so that current behaviour becomes redundant and new behaviour is able to be adopted. This enabling process takes into account the threats people may feel so that psychological safety is created in the new state of equilibrium (Schein, 1996).

Step 2. *Moving* involves the implementation of the change through the development of new attitudes and behaviour. However, due to the complexity of the forces at work it is

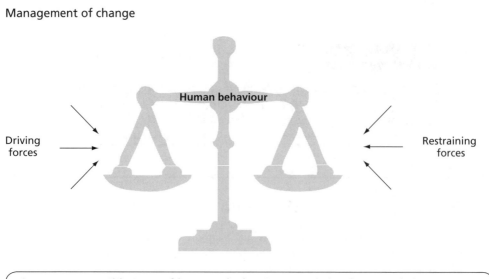

Driving forces

Human behaviour

Restraining forces

Figure 9.1 Equilibrium of human behaviour and the forces of change.

difficult to control the direction of change. Therefore it is important to undertake a learning approach, inherent in action research, that takes an 'iterative approach of research, action and more research that enables groups and individuals to move from a less acceptable to a more acceptable set of behaviours' (Burnes, 2009:339).

Step 3. Refreezing – aims to stabilise the new behaviours and lock in the changes so a new equilibrium is attained. This may need to be supported through changes in organisational policies, structures and norms (Mullins, 2007:736).

An example of how Lewin's model could be applied to sport organisations is increasing diversity within the workforce. According to Sport England (2010) this is perceived to be a key issue for sport organisations. The freezing stage would require both individuals and groups to identifying possible diversity issues within the organisation. This would need to be supplemented by a moral and business justification for ensuring the workforce is diverse. Positive movement forward would involve diversity training and education, including addressing any individual concerns people may have. Refreezing would ensure that policies and procedures, in addition to training, would support a change in organisational culture with regard to diversity.

A key issue that Cameron and Green (2004:99) warn against is using the model purely as a tool for planning change, rather than an organisational development process.

> The unfreeze becomes a planning session. The move translates to implementation. The refreeze is a post-implementation review. This approach ignores the fundamental assumption of the organism metaphor that groups of people will change only if there is a felt need to do so. The change process can then turn into an ill-thought-out plan that does not tackle resistance and fails to harness the energy of the key players.

A criticism of Lewin's model has been that the three steps are relatively broad. Consequently, a number of authors have built on his model by expanding the numbers of steps or phases (Arnold *et al.*, 2005). These include Bullock and Batton's (1985) four phase model and Cummings and Huse's (1989) eight phase model. However, a major criticism is that planned change models are not appropriate for change situations where there is complex, dynamic and coercive change (Arnold *et al.*, 2005). Moreover, the models tend to oversimplify the decisions and choices managers make during a period of change (Carnall, 2007). An alternative to planned change is the emergent approach to change.

9.5.2 Emergent approach to change

The emergent change approach does not involve an agreed set of methods and techniques and does not form a coherent group of theories and models. Instead, 'it tends to be distinguished by a common disbelief in the efficacy of planned change' (Burnes, 2009:366). However, Burnes does identify the key themes of the emergent change approaches which are outlined below:

- Stresses the developing and unpredictable nature of change;
- Change is a process that unfolds through the interplay of multiple variables (context, political process and consultation) within an organisation.
- Processional approach – views organisation's members as shifting coalitions.

(2009:368)

Emergent change has been the main approach used in the study of sport organisations. However, as already identified, the concept of emergent change utilises a range of models and theories which will now be further developed within the chapter.

9.5.3 Processual/contextual theory

These theoretical approaches to change have dominated since the 1990s. They contrast with the more linear and planned approaches to change by, instead, suggesting that far from logical and predictable, change can be much more messy. Huczynski and Buchanan (2007:606) use a cocktail analogy to describe how more emergent approaches to change are seen as: 'rational decisions, mixed with competing individual perceptions, stimulated by visionary leadership, spiced with "power plays" and attempts to recruit support and build coalition behind particular ideas'.

Two key theorists are Andrew Pettigrew and Patrick Dawson. Dawson (2003) argues that although it is useful to identify the tasks and decision-making underpinning the change process, it is important not to treat those as sequential stages as exemplified by Lewin's Three Step Model. Dawson (2003:42) argues that those stages interlock and overlap in that 'organisations continuously move in and out of different states, often concurrently'. In developing his framework for analysing change he has attempted to develop an approach that can cope with the complexity but is still uncluttered and practical. Consequently his three categories are:

1 the initial conception of a need to change caused either by forces internal or external to the organisation;
2 the process of organisational change, which Dawson (2003:42) describes as a 'complex non-linear and "black box" process of organizational change' which will include a range of tasks, activities and decisions;
3 operation of new work practices and procedures. It is during these early stages where conflict and uncertainty may emerge as employees adapt or redefine their positions in relation to new practices and new patterns of relationships. Moreover, relatively stable systems may begin to emerge and at this point the outcomes of the change can be reviewed against the former operating system. Although Dawson warns against seeing this as an endpoint as the change process is ongoing.

Dawson also advocates that the 'black box' of the process of change should be analysed as it happens in terms of three groups of determinants:

1 politics of change – an understanding of organisational politics is crucial in analysing change;

2 context of change – an understanding of the historical context of past and present external and internal operating environments and organisational culture may explain why certain change options are promoted whilst others are devalued;

3 substance of change – which takes into account:

- the scale and scope of the change
- defining characteristics of the change
- timescale
- perceived centrality – how central is the change to the survival of the organisation.

The notion of the historical content of change combined with an understanding of organisational politics is highlighted in Gilmore and Gilson's (2007) research into change management at Bolton Wanderers Football Club. Bolton is one of the oldest football clubs in Britain but it had experienced decline, falling into what is now the second division (formerly the fourth division) in the late 1980s. It then emerged from this 'relative obscurity to become a Premiership side capable of challenging the elite English clubs within the Premier League' (Gilmore and Gilson, 2007:410); consequently it provided an opportunity to examine how that change occurred.

A key finding of the case study was the centrality of history in the management of change at Bolton. In 1999 the club appointed Sam Allardyce as manager to lead the club's return to higher league football, i.e. the Premiership. Allardyce was a former player and it was felt that he provided a link between the past, present and future. The importance of this with regard to change is explained by Gilmore and Gilson (2007:417):

> Crucially, however, the manager and club chairman were also adept at respecting the club's historic way of working. This manifested itself in the important principle of autonomy and responsibility between administration and the football side of the business. In many football clubs, chairmen are notorious for their interference in all aspects of the game, from team selection and tactics to transfer decisions. The continued tradition of autonomy of operation that exists at Bolton was and remains a critical factor in the club's ability to thrive in an overtly hostile environment:
>
> Bolton's always believed … that you don't interfere in the football. You let the manager manage – give him a budget and you try and work within that budget, but you don't interfere with the running of the football. And I've never seen any success come out of operating in another way.
>
> (Vice Chairman, Brett Warburton)

The Bolton case also illustrates Pettigrew (1985) and Dawson's (2003) view that organisations experience change and continuity concurrently, as Gilmore and Gilson (2007:412) state: 'even when major change events occur the ongoing nature of organizational life is still largely evident creating a simultaneous sense of connectedness through time'. This was manifested at Bolton by its short-term reaction to inflated transfer markets by signing players in the twilight of their careers, plus their focus on ensuring that staff continue to promote innovation through their application of sport science. Alongside this Bolton employed a long-term approach through the development of young players in the academy. This served the joint purpose of servicing the first team squad whilst generating additional revenue through the sale of players to other clubs.

Huczynski and Buchanan (2007) have identified that the strengths of the processual/contextual approach to change are its recognition of the complexity of change and that it is a process with a past, present and future. However, they also identify three limitations, the second of which obviously contrasts with the values of OD:

1 Change may be presented as over-complex and overwhelmingly confusing and therefore unmanageable.

2 The people involved within the change process are sometimes portrayed as minor characters in a broad sequence of events, relegated to the role of pawns controlled by social and organisational forces rather than proactive 'movers and shakers'.

3 There is a lack of practical recommendations beyond generalised advice such as 'recognise complexity' and 'think processually'.

(Huczynski and Buchanan, 2007:609)

9.5.4 Other approaches to change

Two other approaches to change that have been applied to sport organisations are 'Institutional Theory' and the 'Evolution and Revolution' approach. Institutional theorists, such as Meyer and Scott (1983) suggest that organisations 'change their formal structure to conform with expectations within their institutional environment about appropriate organisational design' (cited by Slack and Parent, 2006:242). This approach has been used to examine the structural features and institutionalised pressures for change in Canadian National Sports Organisations (Smith *et al.*, 2005).

The Canadian studies also used the Evolution and Revolution approach to examine sport organisations. Theorists using this approach assume that organisations resist change and will continue as they are, even when there is a possibility of failure (Slack and Parent, 2006). Slack and Parent explain that a consequence is that the prevailing organisational condition is momentum, which is the organisation's propensity to continue with its existing structure. Where organisations make incremental changes to their structures, strategy or processes this is termed evolutionary change. Where a major upheaval or crisis is experienced then revolutionary change occurs, in that an organisation will change from one structure to another.

In their investigation of competing change management theories in relation to sport organisations in Australia, Smith *et al.* (2005:116) found that evolutionary models provided a significant explanation of incremental change at an industry level but did not acknowledge 'internal management initiatives as catalysts for change'. Moreover they found that Revolution theories 'clarify the consequences of quantum, industry-wide change, but do so at the expense of elucidating the role of individual organisations'.

The previous discussion of key change management approaches and theories serves to illustrate a variety of views on the area. Both Smith *et al.* and Slack and Parent view this as a positive, with Slack and Parent (2006:253) suggesting that the diversity of change theories provides 'considerable potential for the study of sport organisations', whilst Smith *et al.* (2005:117) reject the notion of 'uni-dimensional or one-model explanations as comprehensive change theories'.

9.5.5 Resistance to change

It is important to recognise that change is viewed by people both positively and negatively. For some it provides an opportunity to be challenged, develop themselves and create new systems, processes and services. For others, change means a loss of familiarity and a movement into the unknown. The latter creates resistance to change, where individuals or groups may engage in behaviours that are aimed at disrupting or even blocking the change.

Concept check

Resistance to change

Resistance to change: 'an inability, or an unwillingness to accept changes that are perceived to be damaging or threatening to an individual' (Huczynski and Buchanan, 2007:598).

Daniels (2010:2) identifies two broad types of resistance:

1   Resistance to the content of the change – for example, the introduction of a new technology, such as FIFA's resistance to goal line technology.
2   Resistance to the process of change, which relates to concerns about how change is being introduced, for example, an organisational restructure which has not involved consultation with employees. Again FIFA provide a useful example of this with their attitude towards the bidding and decision making process of allocating the World Cup tournament to host countries.

Bedeian (1980) has proposed four common causes of resistance to change:

1   **Parochial self-interest.** Change may threaten an individual's or group's interests in terms of power, status, security or may simply be inconvenient. In this situation people think of their own self-interest rather than that of the organisation. An example is horse racing in the UK, where race courses are considering selling the television rights to the sport's biggest events as a single, maximum-value package from 2013 (Wood, 2010). The notion of self-interest is reflected in Wood's (2010:9) comment below and the piece also reflects the multiple stakeholders in sport organisations and their impact on change.

   What everyone will ask, of course, if this plan ever reaches the stage of a yes-or-no decision, is: what's my slice? Owners, for instance, will want guarantees about the amount of the television money to be returned to them in prize money. Tracks outside the elite will want to know how – or whether – their revenues will be protected. Jockeys who will be the public face of a 'premier league' sport may decide that they deserve 'premier league' wages.

2   **Misunderstanding and lack of trust.** If there has not been a clear explanation of the reason for the change, how it is to be carried out and its consequences, then this will create uncertainty. Additionally, if there is a lack of trust between managers and employees then managers may withhold/distort information and/or employees may not believe managers.

3   **Contradictory assessments.** People's personal values will impact on whether they perceive change positively or negatively. Hence it may be seen as a challenge or as a threat. However, having different views on change may actually create constructive criticism which may lead to the change and its implementation being more effective (Huczynski and Buchanan, 2007).

4   **Low tolerance for change.** Individuals have different levels of tolerance for uncertainty and ambiguity. Huczynski and Buchanan (2007) suggest that a response to change may be self-doubt, in terms of an individual's belief in whether they can develop a new skill or the behaviour that may be required with the change.

Exhibit 9.3

Change at the Amateur Athletics Association of England

In 1880, the Amateur Athletic Association (AAA) came into being as the controlling power of track and field in England. At this time, there was significant resistance to change with regard to the fight to keep athletics as the sole preserve of the so-called 'gentleman amateur'. Ultimately, however, the rule precluding 'mechanics, artisans and labourers' from open competition was rescinded. In 2006, a century and a quarter later, the AAA of England have relinquished their jurisdiction in the face of opposition from a group of clubs fighting against a perceived lack of 'democracy and accountability' in the proposed new English association, under the umbrella of UK Athletics, the overall governing body of athletics in Britain.

The creation of England Athletics has resulted from the review into the modernisation of the sport in the UK (the Foster Report). The project to implement the recommendations has been led by Jack Buckner, former European 5,000 m champion and double AAA champion. Adoption of the modernising proposals was a condition for the release of £41 million of government funding.

The 1,400 athletics clubs in Britain had until 25 October 2005 to respond to a poll about the proposals and an automatic transference of power was on the agenda of an extraordinary meeting of the AAA of England that was scheduled for 29 October.

The Association of Great Britain Athletic Clubs (ABAC) attempted to affect a turning of the tide. Formed in April 2005, specifically to oppose the changes, its 120 plus members were unhappy about the direction of UK Athletics, the planned displacement of the AAA of England and about several aspects of the proposals, chiefly the introduction of regional councils in which elected club officials would have 'a majority' but also include paid officers of England Athletics who are answerable to a national council and, in turn, to UK Athletics.

'We do accept the need to change', one ABAC committee member said,

> but that doesn't have to involve so much sacrifice of democratic control and such a leap into the financial unknown. We don't feel the new body is sufficiently accountable to the clubs, who at the current time are the guardians of the sport, the custodians. We're not resistant to change. We're resistant to this change being imposed on us by a body that's got so little credibility in what it has achieved in the time it's been at the helm. Under UK Athletics, the sport has deteriorated alarmingly in standard of performance and in numbers.

Buckner spent 12 months travelling the country consulting with those involved in grass roots athletics and has found 'a huge level of frustration' among clubs about the 'managerial-driven' approach of UK Athletics. He states that 'What we've tried to do is strike a balance and we've ended up with proposals similar to those made by the AAA two or three years ago. It's nothing revolutionary'.

Source: summarised from Turnball (2005:86)

Review questions

Using both Daniel's (2010) two broad types of resistance and Bedeian's (1980) framework, what were the possible causes of resistance to change within English athletics at that time?

9.6 Managing resistance

One of the most cited approaches for managing resistance to change in sport organisations is Kotter and Schlesinger's (2008) framework (Slack and Parent, 2006). They identify six techniques that can be used:

1 **Education and commitment**: where resistance to change is based on misunderstanding then this can be addressed by providing more information through the use of training, group meetings and written communication. However this approach is only effective if there is trust between those involved.

2   **Participation and involvement:** if those who potentially could resist change are involved in aspects of the planning and implementation of change then their resistance could not only avoid conflict but has the potential to foster future commitment. Participation could be a benefit where the change initiator does not feel that they have complete information in order to make appropriate changes. However, it is a time consuming approach.

3   **Facilitation and support:** this could include training, allowing time off after a period of hard work due to the change or just providing emotional support. This is particularly effective where the resistance to change is due to fear and anxiety. However, this can be time consuming and expensive.

4   **Negotiation and agreement:** is where incentives are offered, particularly where it is clear that some people are going to lose out due to the change and that they have the power to derail the change. Obviously this may be an expensive option.

5   **Manipulation and co-option:** involves 'the very selective use of information and the conscious structuring of events' (Kotter and Schlesinger, 2008:136). An example of manipulation is co-option where one of the key leaders of resistance is given a key role in the change process. This differs from participation as it is about endorsement from that individual rather than advice. Although it is a quick solution it can lead to problems further down the line if that person realises that they have been manipulated.

6   **Explicit and implicit coercion:** change is forced through explicitly or implicitly threatening people, e.g. through potential job losses. This is a risky approach as people will resent being coerced. However, it is sometimes the only option where speed is required and it is likely that the change will not be popular however it is presented.

In deciding which is the best strategy to use, change initiators must take into account the speed of change needed and key situational variables such as:

- Amount and kind of resistance anticipated
- The position of the initiator vis-à-vis the resisters, especially with regard to power
- The person who has the relevant data for designing the change and the energy for implementing it;
- The stakes involved.

(Kotter and Schleslinger, 2008:138–139)

9.7 Summary and conclusion

This chapter has provided an overview of OD and how it may be relevant to sport organisations. It has also examined organisational change and the key theories that have been used to manage change within sport organisations, including selected approaches to managing resistance to change. Within this section it noted that OD has traditionally been associated with planned approaches to change, although it is important to acknowledge that OD has developed over the last half century to recognise the complexity of organisations. As Garrow and Varney (2009:30) state, OD practitioners are now, 'talking about working with emergent (some call it "improvisational") change; this means establishing a direction for change and working in a way that is responsive and adapts to fluctuations in the real world'.

However, a key feature of OD continues to be its underpinning humanistic values. This is important to sport organisations who should respond to the impetus to change by thinking through the consequences with respect both to the internal staff and to external stakeholders.

Chapter 10

Coaching, mentorship and the learning organisation

Learning outcomes

By the end of this chapter you will be able to:

- compare, contrast and critique the benefits of coaching and mentorship;
- appreciate the potential benefits of a culture of learning within the organisation;
- understand the links between coaching, mentorship and the concept of the learning organisation;
- develop your own conceptual model of how best to manage people in sport and leisure organisations.

10.1 Introduction

This book has explored many of the human resource management (HRM) and development issues facing the contemporary sport and leisure industry. It has reviewed a number of inter-related factors that cumulatively affect individual, group and, ultimately, the overall performance of a diverse range of sport and leisure organisations. Above all, it has demonstrated both the positive and negative contributions that employees at all levels can have on the past, present and future success of their respective sport and leisure organisations.

Given the complexity of the issues and the variety of organisations covered by the book, it is difficult, and some might say impossible, to establish an holistic model that can be easily applied to all HR situations. What is clear, however, is that organisations must learn from their collective experiences and shape the future in a way that has a resonance with the majority of its key stakeholders; in particular the 'people' most affected by its decisions and actions.

In the new millennium the efficiency mantras of doing more with less, puts intense pressures on managers to get the best both out of themselves and their staff. In this sense today's managers need to constantly rationalise and balance a complex multiplicity of competing demands, whilst being measured against both internal and external performance yardsticks. They need to think about appropriate ways of managing the business, managing their staff, managing their own bosses and, perhaps, most importantly, managing themselves. This raises a series of difficult questions. How can managers continue to balance the range of competing priorities in a world where accountability is often measured in short-term wins rather than longer-term strategic development? How can managers be motivated to find the time and wisdom to take a more active interest in their staff? How can organisational strategy seek to support related HR developments and what evidence exists to support such initiatives? Above all, how do managers get the best out of their staff relative to the expressed needs of the organisation?

There can be no question that such issues are complex and it is not surprising that there is no universally agreed answer to the conundrum of how best to manage organisations and the people within them. By their very nature each sport and leisure organisation represents an idiosyncratic balance of both internal and external drivers at any given moment in time. Gilson *et al.* (2000:xv) have attempted to understand what it takes for sports organisations to produce continued success and, unsurprisingly, argue 'we have observed passing trends in organizational theory and attempted to apply them. And we have found them wanting'. However, their research into successful internationally recognised sporting organisations does result in the development of an holistic model that attempts to rationalise why sports organisations succeed in the longer term. Their model of Peak Performing Organisations (PPOs) is founded upon three main and interrelated principles that they argue are equally applicable to a wide range of sports organisations. These are (Gilson *et al.*, 2000:241):

1 Peak purpose: provides meaning and direction within organizations.
2 Peak practices: creates the necessary organizational context for peak performance.
3 Peak flow: how people work together to achieve optimal performance.

In many ways the previous nine chapters of this book have covered all of the above principles. For example, organisational structure and culture should provide both meaning and direction (see Chapter 3), whilst also underpinning the foundations of individual and group performance (Chapter 4). Similarly, how people work together should be informed by the training, learning and development strategies of the organisation (Chapters 5, 7, 9 and 10). What is clear, however, is that there is an evolving management discourse in which organizations are beginning to embrace a new management culture based on inclusion, involvement and participation, rather than on the traditional command, control and compliance paradigm. ... This new management paradigm calls for facilitative behaviours that focus on employee empowerment, learning and development; in other words, coaching (Beattie, 2002a, 2006a, 2006b; Ellinger, 2003; McGill and Slocum, 1998). Over a decade ago Evered and Selman argued that good coaching was the essential feature of really effective management. They advocated a paradigm in which 'the process of creating an organizational culture for coaching becomes the core managerial activity', and where coaching is viewed 'not as a subset of the field of management but rather as the heart of management' (1989, pp. 2–3). Since that time many other writers have argued that coaching is an essential and critically important role that most managers, managerial leaders and organizational leaders need to develop and perform as an integral part of their everyday management practice.

(Hamlin *et al.*, 2006:306)

Most advice offered with regards to managing people will allude to the need to better understand the individual motivations of staff and manage them accordingly. However, this takes time, effort and an in-depth understanding of the prevailing socio-psychological/political issues (...amongst many other things!). This is an increasingly unrealistic expectation of managers. What is needed is an acceptance that this is becoming more and more difficult to achieve in practice. What is needed, perhaps, is for managers to work with staff in the facilitation of more appropriate work boundaries, targets and helpful frameworks within which they can collectively explore a way of working that provides an appropriate balance between individual, group and organisational needs. This is not to abrogate management responsibility, but recognition of the key role(s) and contributions that all people have to play in this endeavour. Coaching provides one potential ingredient to a more effective conceptualisation of how this could work in practice.

10.2 The rise and potential significance of coaching

Hamlin *et al.* (2008), in a study looking to compare different understandings of 'coaching' and 'HRD' (human resource development) found a very strong fit between the two concepts. Meanwhile, back in the real world, interesting but often semantic theoretical discussions have to be balanced against a backdrop of structural rationalisation and a downsizing of all staff, particularly although not exclusively, at middle management level. This, in turn, impacts the number of managers left who have the time and wisdom to engage in organisational coaching and mentorship programmes. Paradoxically, the de-layering of organisations, in this way, makes it much more of an organisational imperative that staff are made to feel both engaged and empowered to operate more autonomously in the continual pursuit of appropriate organisational objectives. In this instance, faced with a lack of funds to develop a more holistic and inclusive programme, organisations may choose to target their efforts and investment towards those with the highest potential. As a consequence, talent development programmes are becoming more and more common within organisations.

Chapter 1 discusses the many stakeholders found within sports and leisure organisations and the 'wicked problems' this creates when attempting to manage within a 'systems' context. Unsurprisingly, when faced with the need to instantly deal with a variety of day-to-day problems, Hardingham (2004) argues that most managers favour action over reflection. However, by creating a little more time and space to reflect on the issues and their antecedents, it is more likely that a variety of alternative and, potentially, more appropriate actions will emerge.

> Reflection enables us to see the interconnectedness of things. We are less likely after reflecting to suffer from 'unintended consequences' of our actions. We are more likely to identify the points of leverage, the actions that will yield the best return for least effort. It takes time to explore and understand the nature of the social and organizational systems around us. Reflection gives us that time.
>
> (Hardingham, 2004:121)

The encouragement of such deeper levels of systems thinking should improve decisions. It also has the added benefit of reducing the stressors in the system by better understanding the prevailing issues and, thus, potential consequences of proposed actions. This minimises the likelihood of poor decisions and the consequences thereof. This applies equally to paid staff and volunteers, to shareholders or to the many external stakeholders that are so prevalent in sport and leisure organisations.

Against this backdrop both coaching and mentorship have gained an increasing prominence in the literature relating to HRD. The Work Foundation (2004, cited in Grant and Cavanagh, 2007:752) found that 20 per cent of UK managers had received 'coaching' training. Similarly, Hamlin *et al.* (2008:288) cites the Chartered Institute of Personnel and Development (CIPD, 2005) who found that 90 per cent of surveyed organisations adopted an internal coaching approach, whilst two-thirds employed external practitioners. Moreover, Orenstein (2006) reports an American coaching market worth $1 billion that is expected to increase exponentially during the years to come. Indeed, Executive Coaching, in particular, is said to be provided within 'corporate, governmental and non-profit sectors by ... over 10,000 practitioners in the United States (Riveara, 2002) and 15,000 worldwide (Greco, 2001)' (Orenstein, 2006:106).

Unsurprisingly, against this backdrop, Ledgerwood (2003:46) argues, 'Coaching ... may be a key mode of management development.'

10.3 Coach or mentor or both?

As with most attempts to agree definitions, within the HR literature, there are a number of competing interpretations and considerable overlap between their conceptual foundations and their practical applications. Business coaching in a sports context is not the same as sports coaching, although they do share some common traits. Similarly, both business coaching and mentoring are often used interchangeably despite some very fundamental differences. Moreover, it would be disingenuous to claim that much of what passes as business coaching, within organisations, can be justifiably regarded as a profession (Bennet, 2006). More relating to this later in the chapter.

Broadly speaking business coaching is seen as a relatively short-term relationship designed to improve performance by facilitating learning that is individually defined and context specific. Typically, this occurs within a one:one relationship although this may also, occasionally, take the form of team based coaching interventions. Business coaches work with clients to achieve appropriate levels of self-reflection, self-diagnosis and above all to facilitate both an action- and goal-oriented agenda. This helps individuals and sometimes teams resolve prevailing work and/or personal challenges.

Generally, coaches are seen to be non-directive, although this does depend upon the background of the coach and whether they are deployed to fulfil this function or offer a more consultancy based or therapeutic service. Of course, counselling and therapy services tend to deal with deeper psychological issues which require expert help from 'professional' and appropriately qualified practitioners. These issues, therefore, should lie outside the scope of a typical business coach. Unfortunately, however, this is not always the case!

Concept check

Coaching typologies and definitions

According to McMahon (in Blinkhorn, 2008:12), Vice President of the Association for Coaching, there are three main areas of coaching, as below:

1 Executive coaching

- Performance recovery after promotion or following a performance dip.
- Excellence, make the best even better.
- Team coaching, relationships, communication, and performance.

2 Life coaching

- Career development.
- Parenting skills etc.

3 Speciality coaching

- Stress.
- Confidence etc.

Each of the above coaching areas represents a specialist area in its own right. It is by no means an exhaustive or, indeed, inclusive list as it fails to cover the coaching needs of all staff that work within sport and leisure organisations. Typically, this responsibility is fulfilled by a line manager who is sometimes ill equipped to offer the level of time and skill required to benefit her/his staff in this regard. According to Whitmore (1992:2, cited in Palmer and Whybrow, 2007b:1)

> In too many cases they [coaches] have not fully understood the performance-related psychological principles on which coaching is based. Without this understanding they may go through the motions of coaching, or use the behaviours associated with coaching, such as questioning, but fail to achieve the intended results.

Similarly, Grant (2007:34) argues that much of the coaching services that are commercially available are atheoretical and largely based upon corporate health and wellness literature. He posits that coaching definitions often vary between the 'ask' and 'tell' dimensions: 'The skillful and experienced coach knows when to move across the ask–tell dimension, and knows when to promote self-discovery and when to give expert-based authoritative or specialized information.' As a consequence a relatively new area of academic literature has emerged during the last decade. Coaching psychology, according to Grant (2007:23) draws upon 'sport, counseling, clinical, and organizational and health psychology'. Unlike more traditional forms of clinical psychology that tend to concentrate upon dysfunction, the focus here is on how to make something that is not broken even better. This, in turn, can be related to the complementary explosion in the literature surrounding positive psychology or, to put it another way, the art and science of positivity and happiness. This is inextricably linked with aspects of emotional intelligence, previously reviewed during Chapter 5.

In this context, it is easy to see that a dose of perpetual optimism provides a welcome antidote to the sometimes stifling complexities and contradictions found within the contemporary sports management arena. Having a positive helping hand to guide you through the idiosyncratic vagaries of how success is both recognised and rewarded is also of considerable value. We are now moving our focus towards the more paternal and directive role adopted by the mentor. This moves the relationship more to the right of the ask–tell continuum found in Figure 10.1 and is often regarded as fundamental to the career transition and development of individuals within the organisation and, indeed, wider industry (Rekar Munroe, 2009).

Business coaching facilitates self-diagnosis and learning through self-discovery, whereas consultancy, counselling, therapy and mentorship are all likely to offer the same, but through a more directive approach. Often mentoring requires no formal qualifications, whilst counselling and therapy, in particular, are likely to require professional accreditation and, often, a sustained period of advanced education and training.

Concept check

Mentoring mythology

Mentoring, as a concept, has been around for around 300 years following the publication of the book *Les Aventures de Telemaque*, by François Fénelon. In it, the main character was named 'Mentor', based on the Greek myth of Odysseus who placed his son in the charge of his trusted friend Mentor when he left to fight in the Trojan Wars.

In life in general and sports in particular, parental influence is often fundamental to harnessing the full potential of the individual. In tennis, where would the Williams sisters be without their father to help direct, guide and support them? Where would Louis Hamilton be without his father and Ron Dennis at McClaren to help encourage and promote his undoubted driving talents? What about Mike Tyson, who without the positive influence of his trainer, friend, father figure and mentor Cus D'Amato is very unlikely to have become the youngest ever undisputed world heavyweight boxing champion.

Young (1990, cited in Pastore, 2003:1) argues that both athletic administrators and sports managers in the United States should engage in mentoring as an integral part of their professional training and development. According to Allen *et al.* (2004:127) it was not 'until the publication of Kram's (1985) seminal work on mentoring relationships at work has empirical research on the topic proliferated'. Kram identified two main functions of mentors in an organisational setting. The first relates to career advancement where the mentor provides guidance and sometimes more tangible help to open doors and suggest appropriate actions based upon a greater experience of the organisational

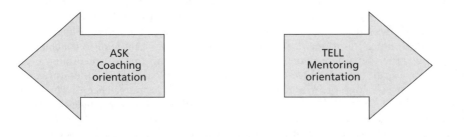

Figure 10.1 The ask–tell continuum of coaching and mentorship.

norms, culture and key stakeholders. The second is classified as psychosocial support and deals with the development of appropriate interpersonal skills and feelings of self-efficacy. It is likely that each individual will require a mixture of both coaching and mentorship during her/his lifetime. Sometimes this will be formal, through structured programmes, whilst most of the time and for most people this will be much more informal in nature.

For Andre Agassi, the American tennis player, this resulted in the need for several people, both in terms of tennis coaching, fitness coaching but more generally coaching in sports psychology and the finer points of achieving the necessary balance in his life. He asserts, 'these people around me aren't an entourage, they're a team. I need them for company, for counsel, and for a kind of rolling education. They're my crew, but also my gurus, my blue-ribbon panel' (Agassi, 2009:141). Whilst tennis coaches such as Brad Gilbert were relatively temporary and designed to fix perceived and specific weaknesses in Agassi's tennis performance, others formed lasting and respectful friendships and were trusted to provide wise counsel.

Whether we are talking about coaching and mentoring in either a sport, business or an overall life context, there can be no doubt that its perceived usefulness has a lot to do with the qualities of the coach or mentor (Allen et al., 2006; Coatsworth and Conroy, 2009; Dubois et al., 2002; Vergeer and Lyle, 2009) and the associated strength of the relationship developed between the two parties (de Haan, 2008; Dubois et al., 2002; Jones and Spooner, 2006; Lowman, 2007; Potrac et al., 2002). Often those that have the benefit of such help, support and guidance then reciprocate at some point in the future. Andre Agassi, for example, developed a good friendship with singer and entertainer Barbara Streisand and claims, in his autobiography, to have advised her around issues such as confidence and stage fright. Similarly, Tim Henman (2009:2), the UK based tennis player, has informally mentored Andy Murray:

> when he first came on the tour I suppose I acted as something of a surrogate big brother to him. He repeatedly asked me for advice and I'd regularly give it on matters such as travel schedules, dealing with the press or simply which hotel to use. ... We'd practice together a lot of the time and share dinner tables several times a week. We had something of an affinity and I was more than happy to pass things on, though he was never one to impose.

Mentorship represents a longer-term relationship that is no less important than the coaching conversations that have been previously reviewed. As with all other aspects of personal development, they must be regarded as an integral part of a systems tapestry that contains training, learning, development and performance elements. It may also require staff to assume greater responsibility for their own development as, typically, line managers are not well equipped to fulfil this role. In this context, Megginson (2004:93) argues that using mentors as alternatives to line managers is, 'proving a useful adjunct in the development process, but they are often too peripheral to take the central role. Inexorably, the responsibility for development has moved to individuals themselves.'

However, it could be argued that to simply leave staff to plan and often fight for their own development is an abrogation of management and organisational responsibility. If organisations are fundamentally measured by the quality of people who work for and with them, it would be folly to leave the development of both the individual and teams of staff to happenstance. Instead, a supportive culture is needed, that taps into the motivations of staff at all levels. Both individual and organisational development requires several HR components, such as training, coaching, mentoring and performance appraisal to operate synergistically. This, in turn, provides the necessary guidance and support to better motivate individuals to achieve success for themselves, their team, their organisation and sometimes beyond!

10.4 Coaching and mentoring for individual success and performance improvement

Klemash (2006) provides an interesting insight into the perceptions of some of the world's top sports coaches. When asked 'How would you define success?' many referred to setting challenges and incremental goals and having fun. Red Auerbach, one of the most successful coach/executives in NBA history puts it like this:

> There are two kinds of success. There's success in your own eyes and there's success in the eyes of other people. If you want to feel successful in your own eyes, you gotta feel satisfied with your life, satisfied with your accomplishments. That's success.
>
> (Klemash, 2006:3)

The British cyclist Victoria Pendleton has credited her sports psychologist with instilling a strong self-belief and a change from extrinsic motivators, such as family, to a more powerful inner drive that propelled her from an Olympic silver medal in Sydney to a Gold in Beijing (see Chapter 4 for a more detailed discussion of such concepts). Similarly, Paula Radcliffe, the British world record marathon runner, credits her grandmother with instilling the need for patience, perseverance and above all the need to 'Stand outside yourself and ask yourself if you like what you see. If the answer is yes then that's all that matters' (cited in Hewett, 2007:2).

Clearly, there are many opportunities for the general concept of HRM and more specific notions of coaching and mentoring to be related to the sporting context. Ironically, given the early origins of business coaching through practitioners of sports psychology, an interesting and recent development has been an increasing tendency for organisations to be interested in the transferrable business lessons from sports performance and coaching. This is particularly appropriate in relation to similarities between elite level sport and executive coaching (Loehr and Schwartz, 2001). With this in mind Whitrod Brown (2010:3) argues:

> Graham Jones (2002) concludes from his experiences as a sports psychologist to elite athletes and business consultant to executives that 'the principles in elite performance in sport are easily transferrable to the business context, and also that sport has a considerable amount to learn from excellence in business' (Jones, 2002:268). He notes five major themes within which several commonalities and links can be drawn: Organisational issues, stress, leadership, high performing teams, and one-to-one coaching/consulting. A study by Jones and Spooner (2006) into high achievers in sport and business found that a 'one-size-fits-all' approach common in business coaching will not suit high achievers in either context.

Furthermore, the evidence suggests that a general approach to developing people in such ways will be less effective than one that is tailored to the particular context. By definition, individuals are all different and are likely to need very different kinds of help at different times in their lives and careers. For example, Lewis Hamilton, the 2008 Formula One World Champion, split from his business manager in 2009. This also happened to be his father who, like many young athletes, has their parent(s) as trusted mentor(s) and, occasionally, business managers. Around the same time Hamilton also became more detached from his McClaren based mentor Ron Dennis, who moved from hands-on 'Team Principal' to act in a more detached and strategic capacity as 'Executive Chairman' within McLaren Automotive. In 2010, Hamilton appeared to enter a phase of his life and career when he was keen to take control and make more of his own decisions. Indeed, McKenzie (2010:73) reports that Lewis is looking for a manager who can fulfil a very different role from that of his father; someone who can 'help me grow as a brand'. A sign of the sporting and commercially orientated times in which we live perhaps!

The concepts of coaching and mentorship, if applied appropriately to sport and leisure organisations, can provide a possible antidote to the 'wicked problems' experienced within day-to-day operations. In Chapter 1 we reviewed the concept of the 'black box', which represented the site of exchange between organisational inputs and their subsequent outputs. The black box in an aeroplane records all the actions that occur during the process of a flight. However, they are rarely consulted unless difficulties are experienced. Unfortunately, the decision to only review information and processes in this way can be fatal! Encouraging both individuals and organisations to better justify, implement and review their decisions will help improve performance based on a better understanding of the processes involved. In the 'quality' lexicon this is termed Kaizan. This refers to the continual review and improvement of all processes by all individuals at all levels. As Grey and Antonacopoulou (2004:5) argue:

> to understand individual learning one must understand the social nature of learning with and from others ... this provides us with a much wider spectrum for exploring the black box of individual learning, particularly in the context of managing and organizing.

Abraham *et al.* (2006:549) have previously argued that sports 'coaching is predominantly a decision-making process'. This is no less true for managers in sport and leisure organisations. If better decisions are made, at every level, and these are both captured and combined to create an evolving organisational consciousness, this is likely to have a tangible and positive effect upon business performance. If, however, as with many other initiatives before it, there is only limited organisational commitment, then personal coaching is likely to become little more than the latest management fad.

Review questions

Panacea or placebo

Outline five of the main advantages of coaching and mentorship and provide a justification for each.

Does this vary between the individual and the group?

What barriers may prevent this from being effectively conceptualised, structured and implemented?

Compare, contrast and critique the issues/themes/key words and concepts.

Discuss how structures and roles could be modified to better facilitate both individual and group development.

Organisations are complex entities that are in a constant state of internal flux. The extent of such fluidity is really a function of the dynamic interplay between the human, structural and customer capital experienced by the organisation at any moment in time. As Storey (2005:200) explains:

> Horibe (1999) follows other writers in distinguishing between 'human capital' (brainpower) and 'structural capital' (in part database systems but also the wider infrastructure that supports and allows optimal use of human capital). The HR aspects relating to both, however, amount to largely the same agenda – namely encouraging learning and use of the available knowledge.

Table 10.1 Summary of implications for coaches and high achievers

Characteristics of high achievers (HAs)	Implications for coaches of high achievers (CHAs)
Self-focused	Ensure that the HA's personal performance and development is the primary focus of the coaching
Goal driven	Ensure that the HA's goals are a clear and central focus of the coaching process
	Have a thorough knowledge of the process of setting and achieving goals
Totally committed	Understand the world of high achievement, and what it takes to become an HA
Demanding	Expect to be challenged
Continually striving for improvement	Help them to identify the different possibilities and options for improvement
A sponge for information	Provide them with a steady supply of relevant information (e.g. latest thinking etc.) that will stimulate their thinking around continual improvement
Confident	Be self-assured in the presence of HAs
(sometimes) isolated and lonely	Establish the nature of the coaching relationship in terms of the frequency and method of contact outside formal coaching sessions
Needs of HAs	*Implications for CHAs*
Ultimate trust in the coaching relationship	Continually emphasise the confidential nature of the coaching relationship
A coach with credibility	The coach does not necessarily have to have achieved what the HA has achieved, but a detailed and informed knowledge of and empathy for the HA's situation is essential

A coach confident in own ability	Have genuine confidence in your own ability
A lack of ego in the coach	Explore own motives for coaching HAs
Feedback	Be ready to provide (developmental) feedback at all times
Confidence boosting	Remember that the coach is a valuable source of positive reinforcement. Provide positive (motivational) feedback as appropriate
To feel continually at the cutting edge	Keep up to date with relevant theories, literature, methods, etc.
Rapid results	Have a continual focus on helping the HA to identify specific actions that will deliver short-term, as well as longer-term results

Coaching HAs — *Implications for CHAs*

Do not try to be his/her friend	Work hard at maintaining a professional relationship
Find out how you can add value – quickly	Establish a 'contract' as soon as possible
Find the right pace	Recognise when to dwell on something and when to move on quickly
Be flexible	Expect the coaching agenda to change and respond accordingly
Be challenging	Ensure that the coach provides a level of stretch that challenges the HA's current thoughts and behaviours

Source: Jones and Spooner (2006:48).

As explained in Chapter 1, the organisation of human resource systems has to be placed in the context of its customers and/or wider stakeholders. Cegarra-Navarro and Dewhurst (2007) refer to this as 'customer capital', i.e. the extent to which the cultivation and understanding of customer relationships makes a contribution to revenue generation. This is regarded as a key source of competitive advantage in the knowledge economy.

For sports organisations in particular, such relationships are often complicated by the many idiosyncratic and contextual factors outlined by Chapter 1. According to Gibb (1977:17), the complex interplay of a variety of overlapping factors now means that: 'The organization is no longer a production function seeking internal efficiency. It is more of a node in a complex network of economic relationships, dependencies and mutual obligations.' This is particularly true of many sport and leisure organisations who work in partnership with a number of stakeholders. However, what is clear is that organisational development runs concurrently with that of its people. Notions of the organisation as an organic repository of knowledge have led to an attempt to reify such abstractions around the notion of the 'learning organisation'. As Pesavento *et al.* (2001:26) contends: 'Leisure service managers need to commit resources to create "learning organizations" so that an environment of commitment, dedication and care will lead to professionalism.'

This is an issue for most sport and leisure organisations as we search for more appropriate ways of getting the best out of management systems and the people who operate within them. However, this is far from straightforward and often proves difficult both to conceptualise and to apply to the real world (Metaxiotis *et al.*, 2005).

10.5 Embedding a coaching philosophy into a learning organisation

In order to understand how sports and leisure organisations can move things forward there needs to be a more critical understanding of the issues (Grey and Mitev, 2004); both in conceptual terms and how they impact upon the day-to-day realities of managing within such organisations. If knowledge is power and Alvin Toffler's notion of a 'knowledge-based society' is now upon us, then it is important to develop a deeper understanding of the nature of knowledge.

According to Metaxiotis *et al.* (2005:6),

> There is growing recognition in the business community about the importance of knowledge as a critical resource for organizations (Foucault, 1980; Winter, 1987; Leonard, 1999). The new, knowledge-based economy places great importance on the diffusion and use of information and knowledge, as well as on its creation. In this new economy, individuals and companies are obliged to focus on maintaining and enhancing their knowledge capital in order to innovate. Their ability to learn, adapt and change, becomes a core competency for survival.

Broadly, knowledge can be subdivided into two basic elements. In an HR context 'explicit' knowledge represents that which is known by individuals, groups and the wider organisation. 'Tacit' or 'informal' knowledge, however, is much more difficult to access by the individual and, therefore, by the wider organisation. This represents the hidden, intuitive knowledge that we all hold deep in our subconscious and is influenced by our experiences, values and emotions. Ask anyone how they accomplish a particular task and they will, often, find it difficult to accurately articulate the processes involved ... it just kinda happens!

Nonaka *et al.* (2005:42) argue that organisations are not merely engaged in processing information, but it is also incumbent upon them to generate knowledge. Typically this is accomplished through social interaction and teamwork. They propose that the creation of new knowledge has four interrelated (SECI) components, as below:

1 **Socialisation**: knowledge becomes embedded (or tacit) through shared experiences within the prevailing culture and/or micro cultures of the organisation (also see Chapter 3).
2 **Externalisation**: where hidden (tacit) understandings are revealed, i.e. made explicit; for example, through team meetings (also see Chapter 4).
3 **Combination**: where knowledge that is now explicit (externalised) is combined to create new ways of understanding.
4 **Internalisation**: where newly created knowledge is shared and internalised to become 'the way that things are done around here'. In other words new knowledge is embedded in the evolving culture/micro cultures of the organisation and internalised by those that work within it.

Furthermore, Storey (2005:199) argues that:

> Capabilities and competencies (underpinned by knowledge) are regarded as the most strategic assets (Prahalad and Hamel, 1990: Stalk et al., 1992). Within this same strategic framework, the creation and sharing of knowledge are thus regarded as major contributors to organizational advantage (Hahapiet and Ghoshal, 1998).

However, there is a paucity of research in this area, particularly relating to sport and leisure organisations. Exhibit 10.1 illustrates how knowledge management systems were used by the Sydney Olympics of 2000 to improve knowledge retrieval, communication and development.

Exhibit 10.1

The 2000 Sydney Olympic Games and knowledge management

Growth in staff numbers in the run up and during the 2000 Sydney Olympic Games:

- originally 16 employees in 1993
- July 1995, 54 employees
- January 1996, 97 employees
- January 1997, 200 employees
- January 1998, 521 employees
- January 1999, 870 employees
- January 2000, 1,424 employees
- Summer 2000 Games, 2,971 employees, 46,967 volunteers and a huge number of external contractors.

The 2000 Sydney Olympics represented the first time that there was a serious attempt to learn and transfer the lessons from one Olympic games to another. Indeed 'there was a formal agreement between the IOC and SOCOG, which formalized SOCOG's selling of explicit and tacit knowledge' (Halbwirth and Toohey, 2001:91). This is representative of the 'combination' phase identified by Nonaka *et al.* (2005) where the real lessons of organising an Olympic games have both implicit value to the host nation/organising committee and, also, a real world capital value. Indeed, the International Olympic Committee (IOC) paid a reported $5 million (Australian) to the Sydney Organising Committee for the Olympic Games (SOCOG) for the production of a related report that reviewed the lessons learnt. This would then be used by the organising committees of the next two

Olympic Games, in Athens and Salt Lake City, to further improve systems, processes and understandings.

Overall, this took the form of an information system (Athena), which acted as a knowledge repository to aid the coordination of data and information. This is then used to generate tangible knowledge that, in turn, can be transferred across relevant functional areas within the overall organisation.

The 1996 Atlanta Olympic Games had illustrated that there was a need for a unified information management structure where key information could be accessed and updated by relevant stakeholders. SOCOG heeded this lesson and instigated a professionally staffed information unit. This was renamed 'Knowledge Management Services' in January 2000 to reflect its prominent role within SOCOG. Amongst other things, it included responsibility for a record library, public information, corporate intranet and a public call centre.

This leads to a number of related issues that need to be recognised and effectively managed. Organisation culture is one such issue. This needs to be sensitively handled during dramatic increases in staff (both employed and voluntary) and the increasing exposure of the games to the local, national and world media. As a consequence, SOCOG found it challenging to retain a positive organisational culture when faced with such pressures. There was also an acknowledgment from Sandy Holloway, SOCOG's CEO, that the rapid growth of the organisation had created a 'silo' culture and it was important for departments to act cooperatively towards the overarching goal of creating the best ever Olympic Games.

> In large organizations it is not unusual for individuals and/or departments to hoard information. Individuals value 'their' information. Knowledge is perceived to be power and some equate this to job security ... a problem for the KM team was that functional area staff did not necessarily appreciate the breadth of interrelationships between functional areas within the organizations. It was not so much the attitude of not wanting to share information but of not understanding the benefits of sharing.
>
> *Source*: Halbwirth and Toohey (2001:99)

In this context it was important for senior managers to both talk the talk and walk the walk. That is to say they needed to be seen to be supportive whilst ensuring that communication was clear, consistent and inclusive. In order to help mitigate such issues, social events were organised in an effort to ensure the effective integration of staff teams within a more informal and unthreatening environment. In addition, the Sydney 2000 Games Information System was publicly endorsed by senior management and introduced to all staff at the same time. At the time of the games the traditional and functionally orientated line management structures were superseded by a venue based reporting structure. This further reinforces the integrative and systemic nature of the work being undertaken.

Clearly, there is a large technological component to the way that information is organised and databases are seamlessly integrated to produce an overarching information portal. However, the real value of the information is in the ability to filter, prioritise, combine and translate the 120,000 records into knowledge that has practical value. Broadly, this was accomplished through the Transfer of Knowledge (TOK) and Post Games Report (PGR). Both of these reports used the Games Information System in their compilation. The TOK involved evidence from a variety of SOCOG managers and in excess of 90 individual guides were produced. These are a matter of public record and can be accessed at http://gamesinfo.com.au/.

Source: adapted from Halbwirth and Toohey (2001)

The previously reviewed work of Chris Argyris (Chapters 3, 4 and 5) and that of Donald Schön are pivotal in developing a deeper understanding of the issues involved in knowledge acquisition and development. Argyris and Schön (1978, cited in Smith 2001a) argue that learning involves both the detection and correction of error based on individual perceptions of what should happen in any given situation. The quality management literature refers to these as 'corrective actions'. Where the correction of that error is made within an existing understanding of the issues this is termed 'single-loop learning'. In this circumstance relatively small adjustments are made within existing systems and procedures. However, where significant changes are identified which critique and thus transcend traditional understandings and procedures, this is termed 'double-loop learning'. In other words there is a fundamental shift in the ways that both individuals and, sometimes, organisations conceptualise the issues involved; an epiphany or eureka moment if you will! The difficulty is that it is much more typical for both individuals and organisations to engage in single-loop learning. This is often influenced by perceived time constraints that limit the extent to which creative and systems thinking is deployed within the 'black box' of organisational decisions. What is sometimes needed is for organisations to be able to think outside the box. Charles Handy (1993:99) called this the 'helicopter factor', i.e. an ability to be able to rise above the day-to-day issues in order to see the bigger, more strategic picture. That said, there are a number of barriers to a more fundamental reimaging of existing orthodoxies, i.e. ways of thinking and doing things. These may prevent the wider team and organisation from changing direction and improving culturally embedded practices.

Lawrence *et al.* (2005:180) point out: 'that any theory of organizational learning without an understanding of its political dynamics will always be incomplete; organizations are inherently political and, consequently, so are the processes of organizational learning'. In this context, there are two main distinctions. 'Episodic' power represents its application at certain moments in time. For example, in times of crisis where there is a lack of time it may be very justifiable to exercise executive authority over the actions of others, i.e. the manager asserts his/her legitimate authority and directs people towards specific actions. Of course, this assumes that appropriate circumstances are initially identified and that the manager has the personal skills, e.g. assertiveness, to carry this through. It also assumes that the organisation has an appropriate action plan, with adequate communication systems to ensure that plans are understood and systems are in place for its effective implementation. Of course, power is not only used to stop fires; it may also be used to start them!

Review questions

Think of a team situation in which you have been involved where there were a number of different views and actions.

Which view prevailed?

Was this the most appropriate action?

Why did this view prevail?

What were the consequences?

Would it have been better to go with an alternative view?

What would have been the consequence of this?

What are the barriers to the best ideas being heard and then effectively implemented?

Whilst episodic power is more typically associated with managers asserting their authority at particular moments in time, 'systemic' power represents the processes and procedures embedded within the organisation. However, this may stifle the efficient and effective communication of new ideas. As such systemic power is diffused throughout the structure and culture of organisations and can, therefore, act as an agent for either positive or more negative actions. It is, therefore, important to consider such factors when making decisions about structural issues and attempting to influence the organisational culture (see Chapter 3). Moreover, as we have argued that organisations represent a system of interrelated parts, it is also possible to imbue appropriate messages with respect to the requisite use of power within HR systems; for example, within induction, training and performance review processes (see Chapters 7 and 8).

Similarly, Nissley and Casey (2002) argue that there is a distinction between 'episodic memory' and 'semantic memory' in terms of how corporate memories are constructed. This has clear implications for the perpetuation of prevailing organisational cultures/ hegemony. As previously reviewed, the use of the term 'episodic' to denote a particular use of power is very similar to that when it is used to describe organisational memory. Episodic memory is context and outcome specific and is often deliberately shared and externally imposed (Nissley and Casey, 2002); no doubt to inculcate certain messages and promote specific behaviours. Semantic memory is more closely aligned to the concept of systematic power and relates to the handbooks, procedures and shared interpretation of significant events that may not have been personally experienced (Nissley and Casey, 2002). However, it is simply not possible to retain control and manipulate all organisational memories. Think of Jesse Owen winning four gold medals at the 1936 Berlin Olympics; a sporting event deliberately designed by the Nazis to showcase their worldview of the superiority of the Aryan race. However, it is also true to say that history is normally written by those who maintain power. This usually involves winning several battles along the way!

So, what are the messages here? Perhaps, yet again, that organisations need to think about the importance and interconnectiveness of such concepts and build this into their strategic and operational planning. It also suggests, at the level of the individual, that a degree of political understanding and behaviour is necessary in order to get messages heard by the right people at the right time in the right way!

Exhibit 10.2

The fall of an England cricket captain: a question of personality and politics

In January 2009, the England cricket captain, Kevin Pietersen, was effectively sacked by the English Cricket Board (ECB) after differences emerged between himself and Peter Moores, who was the team coach at the time. Pietersen is known as a highly talented player, but also as somewhat of an individual and maverick. To hand Pietersen the leadership role of the England cricket captaincy was, arguably, a calculated risk by the ECB. The role is a significant one and involves a variety of skills; not just with the bat and ball. Pietersen's personality and relative inexperience in leadership roles emerged when he is reported to have issued a 'him or me' ultimatum to the ECB. This is something that could not be tolerated by his employers, who needed to consider the longer-term consequences of agreeing to Pietersen's demands. In Pietersen's own words 'everyone was saying I got the politics wrong. I'm not a politician' (Kimmage 2009).

Peter Moores also left as England's cricket coach to be replaced by Andy Flowers. The importance of the relationship between the coach and the coachee, whether in business or in sport, is critical. As Adams (2009:9) reports, Andy Flowers was head-hunted by a specialist recruitment consultant after conducting 360 degree feedback (also see Chapter 6). The consultant comments: 'Top coaches are not necessarily people with big personalities who are effervescent and avuncular. It's more important they have a skill-set that can be respected by all the stakeholders.'

The same can be said for the England cricket captaincy!

What is needed is a way of actively promoting a deeper, more meaningful way of examining the complexity of issues facing sport and leisure organisations. Or, to put it another way, promoting the notion of double-loop learning within the organisation. Heavily influenced by such work, Peter Senge is widely regarded as one of the original and key thinkers in the area of organisational learning. In 1990 he published his seminal book *The Fifth Discipline*. In it he defines a learning organisation as: 'where people continually expand their capacity to create the results they truly desire, where new and expansive patterns of thinking are nurtured, where collective aspiration is set free, and where people are continually learning to see the whole together' (Senge, 1990:3, cited in Smith, 2001a). He goes on to identify five disciplines that he argues are central to organisations wishing to cultivate a learning culture, as below:

1 **Systems thinking**. This forms the cornerstone of the model. It views the organisation as a whole, with a plethora of constituent parts. These, in turn, generate a multiplicity of interrelationships. It is necessary to better understand how the whole is constructed in order to better facilitate a deeper notion of learning within organisations.
2 **Personal mastery**. This relates to the importance of individual learning within the system. In a sense this is recognition of the need for individuals to engage in continual lifelong learning. It implies self-confidence but also a clear recognition that there is always more to learn. It does not imply complacency.
3 **Mental models**. This is characterised as the embedded mental programs that help us make sense of the world. Such generalised assumptions may be difficult to recognise and articulate. It is, therefore, important to question experiences both during and after they have occurred.
4 **Building shared vision**. This is required to ensure that the organisation moves forward as one. It is not something that can be imposed from above; instead it is something that taps into the common motivations of staff who, in turn, feel a sense of ownership over the mission ahead.
5 **Team learning**. This recognises learning as an overtly social process, where shared vision is translated into appropriate actions.

All five areas are seen to be symbiotic and provide a systemically driven way of conceptualising a learning organisation. To some, such elements remain abstract and thus difficult to practically apply. This is where, potentially, the role of training in conjunction with a coach and/or mentor may prove instrumental in teasing out such fundamental distinctions and promoting deeper levels of reflection, i.e. double-loop learning. Senge recommends the use of systems maps to illustrate the key factors and their interconnectivity within the overall organisational system. The more perceptive amongst you will have already realised that each chapter has asked you to create your very own 'system map' for each area of HR practice. However, a systems approach dictates that viewing each element in its discrete form does not adequately represent the interconnectivity of the whole, both in terms of the positive synergy and negative barriers that may be generated as a result. This is where deeper levels of learning can help, facilitated by effective training and reinforced by complementary coaching and/or mentoring. This idea is perhaps best illustrated by the words of Peter Senge himself (1990:182–183, cited in Smith 2001a) commenting on an informal workshop presented by Chris Argyris:

> Within a matter of minutes, I watched the level of alertness and 'presentness' of the entire group rise ten notches – thanks not so much to Argyris's personal charisma, but to his skilful practice of drawing out … generalizations. As the afternoon moved on, all of us were led to see (sometimes for he first time in our lives) subtle patterns of reasoning which underlay our behaviour; and how those patterns continually got us into trouble. I had never had such a dramatic demonstration of own mental models in action. … But even more interesting, it became clear that, with proper training, I could become much more aware of my mental models and how they operated. This was exciting.

Of course, there will be a need for some sport and leisure organisations to adapt and identify new ways of thinking more than others. The local golf club, sustained by a bulging membership list is not the same as one where there is an economic imperative to maximise renewals and aggressively promote new custom. Where business models are delivering the desired results, incremental change based on existing structures and ways of thinking may be entirely appropriate. This has been termed 'survival' or 'adaptive' learning, often driven by knowledge that is explicitly known to organisational members. If it isn't broke don't fix it! That said, in an ideal world this should be enhanced through 'generative learning', which promotes the ability to create new ways of thinking and managing the business (Senge, 1990:14, quoted in Smith, 2001). In order to accomplish this, however, it is necessary to access and creatively repackage existing knowledge. For obvious reasons, this is easier to accomplish in practice when knowledge is largely explicit. However, it is often in the tacit knowledge of individuals that more innovative insights can be found. This can be much more difficult to access and exploit.

Leonard and Swap (2005) refer to this holy grail of organisational learning and development as 'deep smarts'. These represent an ability to offer profound and often intuitive insights by establishing connections between a specific issue and the bigger organisational picture. Clearly, the more organisations can cultivate such systemic insights, at individual, team and organisational levels, the increased likelihood that performance will be enhanced through a deeper understanding of the 'black box' processes at play. This in turn helps to mitigate the 'wicked problems' experienced by most organisations, as related and often problematic issues are accounted for in advance.

Despite the view that this concept is not managed well by organisations, Leonard and Swap (2005) contend that it is possible to facilitate their development; although off the shelf programmes are unlikely to offer the most productive way forward. They argue for several methods of more bespoke development but, interestingly, appear very supportive of the concept of the 'knowledge coach'. Paradoxically, on one level, this perhaps has more in common with previously reviewed definitions of mentorship. Knowledge coaches are seen as

> experts who were motivated to share some of their deep smarts with protégés. While some played the traditional mentor role of helping their protégés navigate organizations or providing personal advice, the coaches primarily served as teachers transmitting experience-based expertise.
>
> (Leonard and Swap, 2005:163)

However, this belies the fact that it is often considered better to learn through first hand experience rather than to simply be told how to do things. This represents a more didactic and uni-dimensional way of developing an appropriate learning culture. You can learn the lessons from others but in order to create new ways of thinking you need to be able to join the dots for yourself. Practical experience tends to intensify learning and encourages key lessons to be identified. Better still if such personal and/or group insight is facilitated through appropriately supported reflection that is likely to lead to improvements in organisational performance. This is, in part, recognised by Leonard and Swap (2005:163) who argue 'the novice needs to discover the expert's know-how through practice, observation, problem solving and experimentation – all under the direction of the knowledge coach. In the process, the smarts of both the expert and the novice are deepened'. This represents a real opportunity for organisations. Individual staff and/or teams are encouraged to learn from others, but also develop their own insights. In the same way, their 'knowledge coaches' could assume the role of both facilitator and learner as they work with their protégé(s) to develop their own understanding of contemporary practice. Given that most mentor relationships will typically occur with more senior colleagues, this allows them to become better informed about the day-to-day realities of organisational life. This, in turn, allows both learners and their mentors to develop a better understanding of how this should translate into subsequent discussions about strategic and operational directions. This should be seen as a true learning partnership. However, despite the potential benefits, Leonard and Swap argue that the costs of such schemes are often seen as prohibitive. The alternative could be a perpetuation of existing levels of non-practice in this area, i.e. a sink or swim attitude to both individual and organisational development. However, Leonard and Swap recognise that it is much more profitable, in the longer term, to provide an appropriate framework in which such development can flourish. Gilson *et al.*'s (2000) previously reviewed notion of peak performing organisations provides such a framework. However, it is incumbent upon sport and leisure organisations to provide a customised version of this that meets the needs of all stakeholders and operates throughout all levels of the organisation. Adidas provide an example of an organisation that have been working with their staff, facilitated by management consultants Dale Carnegie, to cultivate such an environment.

Halbwirth and Toohey (2000:109) assert that:

> Sport management in the coming years will be subject to two obligations: first, producing knowledge that is appropriate to the special needs of the sports organisations; and efficient management personnel ... secondly, training effective and efficient management personnel (Loret, 1996, p.133).

Exhibit 10.3

The adidas Group, UK division

Partnership working: embedding a development culture in the organisation

The adidas Group is committed to developing its people so that they continue to operate ahead of the pace of constant change, ensuring it is well-placed to respond to new consumer demands, innovation in technology and the expanding global market. Sport is at the heart and soul of the adidas Group. It is what links their past and present. It is what points their way forward. They are committed to the positive values found in sport – performance, passion, integrity and diversity.

In 2002 when Dale Carnegie and the adidas Group began their partnership, the objective was to initiate and sustain a development culture where employees thought in the same way as athletes by having an end goal, a game plan of how to get there and were committed to improving and having the best in their field.

A structured development approach was introduced which took on a multi-tier approach at different levels within the organization. By offering programmes which could cut across all sections of the organization, the outcome would be that all employees would be operating in a consistent way.

In 2003, the first 'People Mania' programme was launched – an innovative and creative management and leadership skills programme for Senior Managers. The following year saw the introduction of 'Forever People' – a programme for team leaders to develop and enhance their leadership skills so that they can get the very best out of the people in their teams. The final piece in the people development strategy was the launch of 'Tomorrows People' – aimed at people at entry level who are not yet in a management position but have been identified as up and coming people within the business and who are likely to be the managers of tomorrow.

Demand for development within the business became infectious, as people recognized the benefits to themselves and to the business. Everyone understood the clear people development strategy and the business started to see departments and individuals working together to achieve business goals rather than working in isolation, and a culture of ongoing continuous development was in place.

In this fast-paced industry the needs of the organization are continually evolving. The flexible and creative approach of the Dale Carnegie Team has created additional programmes to meet the ever changing needs of the organization and the people within it, thereby helping to sustain a competitive edge.

Research and discussions amongst current and potential employees reveal that a training and development strategy is very much a pre-requisite as far as 'Employer of Choice' criteria are concerned. The adidas Group appreciates and understands this and over the last 7 years, people development has been a prominent feature on the agenda. The key point of difference that Dale Carnegie delivered to our Group, that has now been sustained into its 7th year, is the tangible, relevant learning outcomes that are regularly achieved and transferred creatively back into the workplace. Since 2002 when the first 'People Mania' course was successfully delivered, Dale Carnegie Training have touched and developed 367 people across the adidas Group … 117 of whom have achieved promotion in that time. You have truly helped to lead, embed and reinforce the people development culture that exists here.

Throughout these 7 years we have been particularly proud of the success that we have enjoyed and we will continue this approach by offering continuous learning opportunities to all employees – after all, the success of our business depends on the performance of our people.

Source: Simon Turner, HR and Training Manager,
Sales and Marketing at the adidas Group

We have already seen how such issues have been addressed at the Sydney Olympics and within the UK base for the German sports company adidas. There is also a need to consider how much change is a good thing. This is often an issue of both luck and judgement. The trick is to minimise the former and maintain a requisite degree of control over the latter. March (1991, cited in Cegarra-Nevarro and Dewhurst, 2007) develops this thinking by arguing that there is a balance needed between knowledge 'exploration' and 'exploitation' within organisations. The latter has similarities with the concept of single-loop and generative learning, previously reviewed. It represents the ability of the firm to leverage its existing competencies. Conversely, the concept of exploration is more closely aligned to notions of double-loop and generative learning through the promotion of creative ways of conceptualising systems, related skills and processes. The trick is to get an appropriate balance between the two concepts. This, in turn, is dependent upon the prevailing internal and external environmental conditions. Tushman and

O'Reilly (1996, cited in Cegarra-Nevarro and Dewhurst, 2007:1,721) refer to the balancing of such tendencies as the 'ambidexterity context'. Levinthal and March (1993) argue that it is important to have an appropriate balance between the two in order to ensure that existing competencies, perhaps core to the business, can be applied and improved upon, whilst more expansive thinking and skills development is needed to grow the business. Interestingly:

> Organizations with the highest levels of customer capital appear able to explore and exploit knowledge simultaneously through an ambidexterity context. These findings have important implications for general organizational learning theory. In the literature is often stated that firms more often converge (exploit) rather than reorient (explore) due to a variety of reasons such as organizational inertia (e.g. Hannan and Freeman, 1984; Milliken and Lant, 1991).
>
> (Cegarra-Nevarro and Dewhurst, 2007:1721)

In this context, Harper and Glew (2008:29) identify several issues, based on their research, that conspire against the facilitation of learning within organisations:

- Leadership does not set the example of learning
- Insular management
- Management arrogance, ignorance or complacency
- Poor top-down communication
- Not soliciting ideas
- Lack of upward communication
- Lack of empowerment to learn and change
- Ineffective mental models
- Preoccupation with the short term and bottom line
- Lack of holistic approach to change
- Lack of communication about change
- Fear and anxiety about change
- Change in leadership
- Inadequate training
- Inadequate system for knowledge acquisition and sharing
- Unwillingness to use the appropriate technology
- Lack of multidirectional communication
- Lack of performance measurement and accountability for poor performance.

Hopefully you will be able to recognise the significance of many of the above factors both in the content of this chapter and also throughout the book in general. Indeed, faced with so many potential barriers it is not surprising that there is an inbuilt organisational inertia to change and seeking out new methods of thinking, organising and managing. Equally, it is not surprising that external pressure from customers and competitors often proves to be the catalyst for innovation in most companies. Arguably, given the dynamic external environment of most sport and leisure organisations, it is now incumbent upon them to engage in activities that continually challenge existing ways of thinking, operating and thus performing. This is particularly appropriate for those organisations operating within a more competitive and commercially orientated environment. However, this is not something that is the exclusive domain of such organisations. Many public and voluntary sector sport and leisure organisations work within a dynamic and complex environment with a number of partners and a multiplicity of additional stakeholders. Albert Einstein defined insanity as repeating the same mistakes and expecting things to miraculously improve. Only those that are able to adapt and learn quickly will develop and prosper over the longer term. According to Senge (1990:4; cited in Smith, 2001b) if this is the goal then it is necessary to 'tap people's commitment and capacity to learn at all levels'. Developing a coaching culture could be one possible answer. However, that is not to underestimate the difficulty of this task as it is littered with the many obstacles previously reviewed by Harper and Glew (2008). Similarly, Gregory *et al.* (2008:42) argue:

> Pick up any current article regarding executive coaching and you are guaranteed to read a reiteration of the need for a more thorough understanding of the actual *process* of coaching. Researchers are quick to point out the lack of empirical research surrounding the field of coaching, yet few have made attempts to fill in that gap.

Clearly there are a number of complex and interrelated factors that can either work for or against an organisation looking to develop a coaching culture. One organisation that appears to be getting it largely right is Lane 4.

Exhibit 10.4

Lane 4: building a coaching culture

Lane 4 are a management consultancy firm that employs approximately 75 full-time staff and 50 associate consultants. They offer consultancy services aimed at improving individual, team and organisational performance. They have a background in elite sport and business performance and work with organisations in a variety of ways, but particularly in relation to helping staff to develop an internal coaching culture.

The Managing Director is Adrian Moorhouse, who won an Olympic Gold medal in Seoul (1988) and currently doubles as a swimming commentator for the BBC. Given his background, he considers himself to be fully committed to the philosophy of coaching that, in turn, is embedded into the culture and systems of Lane 4. Moorhouse recognises the fact that most people in business develop their career and organisations without formal coaching; unlike sport where the opposite is true.

Unsurprisingly, therefore, he has developed the business by recruiting many of his staff from a sports psychology background. However, as has been illustrated within Chapters 4 and 8, it is often difficult for individuals and organisations to maintain congruence between words (espoused theory) and actions (theories in use). What is said by managers and HR representatives may not reflect the lived reality for its staff on the ground. No doubt, at least in part, this represents the very real difficulties that organisations face when attempting to develop staff and systems within an overtly complex and political environment. Lane 4 have several advantages in this regard. Employees are recruited because of their commitment to the key principles of coaching. This not only implies a particular skill set, but deliberately recruiting staff who share the prevailing values and beliefs is much more likely to reinforce a culture based upon effective coaching interventions and related personal/organisational development. This predisposition, however, has to be carefully managed, as expectations may be raised within an organisation with such an overtly coaching orientation. Moorhouse (in Hardingham, 2004:187–188) argues that this is achieved through the following actions:

- the large number of cross-company teams, whose composition is based on individual interest and passions as much as on expertise;
- the leadership of those teams: the person with the most energy is the person who leads, irrespective of company position;

- the atmosphere of those teams, an atmosphere of openness and respect for an interest in everyone's views;
- a lot of coaching of staff by other members of staff; a 'Lane 4 does Lane 4' philosophy;
- a habit of constant goal-setting, about all aspects of the organisation's life, from individual performance goals to goals of meetings to goals of conversations;
- the prevalence of strong relationships with a great deal of mutual recognition and respect;
- there are only team bonuses, no individual ones;
- a lot of reviews with clients, exploring not just the overall delivery of a piece of work but also individuals' performance.

That is not to say, however, that Lane 4 represent an entirely utopian view of organisations. Developing a coaching culture involves the careful cultivation of a series of relationships. This can be tricky as Lane 4 wrestle with the issue of providing effective feedback within a mutually supporting environment. As Hardingham (2004:190) explains:

> A coaching culture is not the same as a cosy culture. In fact, it demands a high level of self-awareness and self-belief in the people who are part of it. It also demands the skills to have 'difficult conversations' with each other.

Lane 4, no doubt, are continuing to have difficult but ultimately productive internal conversations that deliver individual, team and organisational improvements. Clearly, this will not always be straightforward, but it is possible to see that by setting the correct conditions, a culture of development can be actively promoted within organisations.

Source: adapted from Hardingham (2004)

10.6 Summary and conclusion

The chapter has argued the case for coaching and mentoring within sports and leisure organisations. Whilst it is not always clear how best this can be accomplished, there is a growing body of evidence that concurs with the efficacy of this approach and the potential benefits in terms of individual, group and organisational learning and development. Hardingham (2004:191) presents the case succinctly, as below:

> When a Gallup organization conducted a piece of research with over a million employees in a broad range of companies, industries and countries into the core characteristics an organization needs to attract, focus, and keep the most talented employees (*First Break All the Rules* by Buckingham and Coffman, 1999), they discovered that what those talented employees wanted was to do what they do best, to be cared about as a person, to have their development encouraged, and to have opportunities to learn and grow. All these things are natural outcomes of effective coaching.

However, this is not just about well-resourced talent development programmes and the executive coaching of senior managers. It must also have a much greater reach in order to get the very best out of all staff; particularly as they are much more likely to understand the needs of the customer. This relates as much to part-time, casual and voluntary staff as it does to full-time employees; arguably more so dependent upon the sector under consideration. The chapter has reviewed examples of where a more inclusive approach has been adopted during the Sydney 2000 Olympics and at adidas and Lane 4.

The nature of management is changing. It is neither possible nor desirable to retain the same levels of command and control over staff. In order to get the best out of employees, organisations need to think differently. They need to listen to staff and allow them to work with managers to better define both individual and organisational requirements going forward. Given the early origins of business coaching in sports psychology, it is interesting that organisations are becoming interested in the lessons from the sports world. In this context, the challenge for organisations can be demonstrated through the words of Brian Ashton, former coach to the 2007 English Rugby World Cup squad:

> It's up to them now ... I've always said that, ultimately, the players are the ones who must back their judgment and react to events as they unfold ... I've said my piece; from now on, I'll be keeping out of the way. In my experience, the longer a coach stays with his team in the build up to a match, the more the anxiety levels tend to rise. The players are more than capable of looking after themselves, so I'm leaving them to get on with it.
>
> (Hewett, 2007:78)

Bibliography

Abraham, A., Collins, D. and Martindale, R. (2006) The coaching schematic: Validation through expert coach consensus. *Journal of Sports Sciences*; 24(6): 549–564.

Abrams, J. (2001) The management of change in the leisure and sport management sector. In Wolsey, C. and Abrams, J. (eds) *Understanding the Leisure and Sport Industry*. London: Longman, pp. 174–187.

Abrams, J., Long, J., Talbot, M. and Welch, M. (1995) Organisational change in National Governing Bodies of Sport: Report to the Sports Council. Carnegie National Sports Development Centre, Leeds Metropolitan University, UK.

Adair, J. (1973) *Action-Centred Leadership*. London: McGraw-Hill.

Adams, T. (2009) Manager of the month No. 16 Andy Flower. *Observer Sport Monthly*; July 2009, p. 9.

Adcroft, A. (2009) Taking sport seriously. *Management Decisions*; 47(1): 5–13.

Adcroft, A. and Teckman, J. (2008) Theories, concepts and the Rugby World Cup: Using management to understand sport. *Management Decisions*; 46(4): 600–625.

Addleson, M. (2000) What is good organization? Learning organizations, community and the rhetoric of the 'bottom line'. *European Journal of Work and Organizational Psychology*; 9(2): 233–252.

Agassi, A. (2009) *Open: An Autobiography*. London: HarperCollins.

Alexander, B. (2010, 20 May) What makes Mourinho tick? Online, available at: http://news.bbc.co.uk/sport1/hi/football/europe/8693118.stm (accessed 28 December 2010).

Allen, J.B. and Shaw, S. (2009) 'Everyone rolls up their sleeves and mucks in': Exploring volunteers' motivation and experiences of the motivational climate of a sporting event. *Sport Management Review*; 12(2): 79–90.

Allen, T.A., Eby, L.T., Poteet, M.L., Lentz, E. and Lima, L. (2004) Career benefits associated with mentoring for protégés: A meta-analysis. *Journal of Applied Psychology*; 89(1): 127–136.

Allen, T.D., Eby, L.T. and Lentz, E. (2006) Mentorship behaviors and mentorship quality associated with formal mentoring programs: Closing the gap between research and practice. *Journal of Applied Psychology*; 96(3): 567–578.

Andreff, W. (2009) The economic effects of 'muscle drain' in sport. In Walters, G. and Rossi, G. (eds) *Labour Market Migration in European Football: Key Issues and Challenges: Vol. 2, No. 2*, Birkbeck Sport Business Centre Research Paper Series. London: Birbeck Sport Business Centre, pp. 9–31.

Antonio, R., Javier, R., Varela, J. and Real, E. (2008) An application of importance analysis (IPA) to the management of sport centres. *Managing Leisure*; 13(3/4): 179–188.

Argyres, N., Kyle, K.J. and Mayer, J. (2007) Contract design as a firm capability: An integration of learning and transaction cost perspectives. *Academy of Management Review*; 32(4): 1,060–1,077.

Argyris, C. (1957) *Personality and Organization*. New York, NY: HarperCollins.

Argyris, C. (1962) *Interpersonal Competence and Organizational Effectiveness*. Homewood, IL: Dorsey Press.

Argyris, C. (1964) *Integrating the Individual and the Organization*. New York: John Wiley & Sons.

Argyris, C. (1977) Double loop learning in organizations. *Harvard Business Review*; 55(5): 115–125.

Argyris, C. (1982) *Reasoning, Learning, and Action: Individual and Organizational*. San Francisco, CA: Jossey-Bass.

Argyris, C. (1991) Teaching smart people how to learn. *Harvard Business Review*; 69(3): 99–109.

Argyris, C. (1993) *Knowledge for Action: A Guide to Overcoming Barriers to Organizational Change*. San Francisco, CA: Jossey-Bass.

Argyris, M. and Schön, D. (1974) *Theory in Practice: Increasing Professional Effectiveness*. San Francisco, CA: Jossey-Bass.

Argyris, C. and Schön, D. (1978) *Organizational Learning: A Theory of Action Perspective*. Reading, MA: Addison Wesley.

Argyris, C. and Schön, D. (1996) *Organizational Learning II: Theory, Method and Practice*. Reading, MA: Addison Wesley.

Argyris, C., Putnam, R. and McLain Smith, D. (1985) *Action Science, Concepts, Methods, and Skills for Research and Intervention*. San Francisco, CA: Jossey-Bass.

Armstrong, M. (1992) *Management Processes and Functions*. London: Institute of Personnel and Development.

Armstrong, M. (2006) *A Handbook of Human Resource Management Practice*. London: Kogan Page.

Armstrong, M. (2009) *Armstrong's Handbook of Human Resource Management Practice*. London: Kogan Page.

Arnold, J., Silvester, J., Patterson, F., Robertson, I., Cooper, C. and Burnes, B. (2005) *Work Psychology: Understanding Human Behaviour in the Workplace*, 4th edn. Harlow: Prentice Hall.

ASA (2009) The ASA Strategy 2009–2013: More than a governing body. Loughborough, ASA. Online, available at: http://tblp.localknowledge.co.uk/Assets/3646/swimming%20 0,,5157–1–1–149369–0-file,00%5B1%5D.pdf (accessed 30 December 2010).

Audit Commission (2006) Public sports and recreation services: Making them fit for the future. Local Government Summary, June 2006, p. 4.

Bach, S. (2005) *Managing Human Resources: Personnel in Transition*. Oxford: Blackwell.

Bacon, B. (1990) Gatekeeper of public leisure: A case study of executive managers in the UK. *Leisure Studies*; 9(1): 71–87.

Bacon, W. (1996) Accredit to the industry. *Leisure Manager*, Febuary/March.

Bale, S. (2009, 3 June) Edwards leans on his defence. *Daily Express*, p. 73.

Bandura, A. (1986) *Social Foundations of Thought and Action: A Social Cognitive Theory*. Englewood Cliffs, NJ: Prentice Hall.

Bandura, A. (1997) *Self-efficacy: The Exercise of Control*. New York, NY: Freeman.

Baptiste, N.R. (2008) Tightening the link between employee wellbeing at work and performance: A new dimension for HRM. *Management Decisions*; 46(2): 284–309.

Baraldi, E., Brennan, R., Harrison, D., Tunisini, A. and Zolkiewski, J. (2007) Strategic thinking and the IMP approach: A comparative analysis. *Industrial Marketing Management*; 36: 879–894. Online, available at: http://www3.uma.pt/filipejmsousa/ge/ Baraldi%20et%20al.%202007.pdf (accessed 28 December 2010).

Barber, A.E. (1998) *Recruiting Employees: Individual and Organization Perspectives*. Thousand Oaks, CA: Sage.

Barnard, C.I. (1938) *The Functions of the Executive (Thirtieth Anniversary Edn)*. Cambridge, MA: Harvard University Press.

Bar-On, R. (1997) *The Emotional Quotient Inventory (EQ-i): Technical Manual*. Toronto, ON: Multi-Health Systems.

Baum, T. (2006) *Human Resource Management for the Leisure and Tourism Industries: An International Perspective*. London: Thomson.

BBC (2010) UEFA recruitment manager. Online, available at: http://www.bbc.co.uk/wales/ raiseyourgame/sites/concentration/getyourkiton/pages/florian_python.shtml (accessed 3 February 2010).

Beckford, M. (2009, 28 January) Sport and leisure services for teens are a dogs breakfast. Online, available at: http://www.telegraph.co.uk/news/newstopics/politics/4358465/ Sport-and-leisure-services-for-teens-are-a-dogs-breakfast-Audit-Commission-claims.html (accessed 1 June 2010).

Bedeian, A.G. (1980) *Organizational Theory and Analysis*. Homewood, IL: Dryden Press.

Beech, J. and Chadwick, S. (eds) (2004) *The Business of Sport Management*. Harlow: Prentice Hall.

Beer, M. (1980) *Organization Change and Development: A Systems View*. Santa Monica, CA: Goodyear Publishing Company.

Belbin, R.M. (2010) *Management Teams: Why They Succeed or Fail*, 3rd edn. London: Butterworth-Heinemann.

Bennett, J.L. (2006) An agenda for coaching-related research: A challenge for researchers. *Consulting Psychology Journal: Practice and Research*; 58(4): 240–249.

Berschied, E. (1994) Interpersonal relationships. *Annual Review of Psychology*; 45: 79–129.

Bills, P. (2007, 14 October) Pichot full of pampas passion. *Independent on Sunday*, p. 90.

Billsberry, J. (2007) *Experiencing Recruitment and Selection*. Hobeken, NJ: John Wiley & Sons.

Blake, R.R. and Mouton, J.S. (1964) *The Managerial Grid: Key Orientations for Achieving Production through People*. Houston, TX: Gulf Publishing.

Blake, R.R. and Mouton, J.S. (1969) *Building a Dynamic Organisation through Grid Organisation Development*. Reading, MA: Addison Wesley.

Blinkhorn, A. (2008, 17 February) Bosses let coach take the strain. *Sunday Times* (Appointments Section), p. 12.

Böhlke, N. and Robinson, L. (2009) Benchmarking of elite sport systems. *Management Decisions*; 47(1): 67–84.

Booth, L. (2009, 21 June) The world at their feet. *Sunday Times* (Sport Section), p. 13.

Borrett, N. (ed.) (1991) *Leisure Services UK: An Introduction to Leisure, Entertainment and Tourism Services*. Basingstoke: Macmillan.

Boselie, P., Dietz, G. and Boon, C. (2005) Commonalities and contradictions in HRM and performance research. *Human Resource Management Journal*; 15(3): 67–94.

Bourne, M. and Franco-Santos, M. (2010) *Investors in People, Managerial Capabilities and Performance*. Cranfield: Cranfield University.

Bowles, S.V., Reed, W. and Picano, J.J. (2006) Dimensions of coaching related to productivity and quality of life. *Consulting Psychology Journal: Practice and Research*; 58(4): 232–239.

Boyatzis, R.E. (1982) *The Competent Manager*. New York, NY: John Wiley & Sons.

Bradford, D.L. and Burke, W. (2005) *Reinventing Organization Development: New Approaches to Change in Organisations*. San Francisco, CA: John Wiley & Sons.

Braham, P. and Henry, I. (1985) Political ideology and leisure policy in the United Kingdom. *Leisure Studies*; 4(1): 1–19.

Braid, M. (2008, 2 November) Sports officials raise their game. *Sunday Times*. Online, available at: http://business.timesonline.co.uk/tol/business/career_and_jobs/recruiter_ forum/article5062415.ece (accessed 24 February 24 2010).

Branson, R. (2009) *Losing My Virginity: The Autobiography*. London: Virgin Books Ltd.

Bratton, J. and Gold, J. (2007) *Human Resource Management: Theory and Practice*. Basingstoke: Palgrave Macmillan.

Breaugh, J.A. (2008) Employee recruitment: Current knowledge and important areas for future research. *Human Resource Management Review*; 18(3): 103–118.

Breaugh, J.A. (2009) The use of biodata for employee selection: Past research and future directions. *Human Resource Management Review*; 19(3): 219–231.

British Swimming (2007) *A Vision for Swimming*. Loughborough: British Swimming.

Brown, M., Metz, I., Cregan, C. and Kulik, C.T. (2009) Irreconcilable differences? Strategic human resource management and employee well-being. *Asia Pacific Journal of Human Resources*; 47(3): 270–293.

Buchanan, D. and Huczynski, A. (2001) *Organisation Behaviour*, 4th edn. Harlow: Prentice Hall.

Budhwar, P.S. (2000) Evaluating levels of strategic integration and devolvement of human resource management in the UK. *Personnel Review*; 29(2): 141–161.

Bullock, R.J. and Batten, D. (1985) It's just a phase we're going through: A review and synthesis of OD phase analysis. *Group and Organizational Studies*; 10(4): 383–412.

Burnes, B. (2005) *Work Psychology: Understanding Human Behaviour in the Workplace*, 4th edn. Harlow: Prentice Hall.

Burnes, B. (2009) *Managing Change*. Harlow: Prentice Hall.

Burns, T. (2005) FA structural review. London: The Football Association. Presented to the English Football Association Board of Directors, 12 August 2005, pp. 1–7. Online, available at: http://www.thefa.com/TheFA/WhoWeAre/NewsAndFeatures/2005/~/media/Files/PDF/TheFA/BurnsReview/StructuralReviewConclusions.ashx/StructuralReviewConclusions.pdf (accessed 23 July 2010).

Burt, J. (2010, 11 May) Manager risks own goal with web player ratings. *Daily Telegraph* (Sport Section), p. S3.

Burt, J. (2011) Carlo Ancelotti: Ray Wilkins was sacked as assistant manager by Chelsea, not me. *Telegraph*, 12 November 2010. Online, available at: http://www.telegraph.co.uk/sport/football/teams/chelsea/8130102/Carlo-Ancelotti-Ray-Wilkins-was-sacked-as-assistant-manager-by-Chelsea-not-me.html (accessed 28 December 2010).

Busser, J.A. and Carruthers, C.P. (2010) Youth sport volunteer coach motivation. *Managing Leisure*; 15(1/2): 128–139.

Cameron, E. and Green, M. (2004) *Making Sense of Change Management: A Complete Guide to the Tools and Techniques of Organisational Change*. London: Kogan Page.

Campbell Quick, J. and Macik-Frey, M. (2004) Behind the mask: Coaching through deep interpersonal communication. *Consulting Psychology Journal: Practice and Research*; 56(2): 67–74.

Cannell, M. (2009) Emotional intelligence. Chartered Institute for Personnel Management, November. Online, available at: http://www.cipd.co.uk/subjects/lrnanddev/selfdev/emotintel.htm (accessed 1 March 2010).

Cannell, M. and Daniels, K. (2010) *Organisation Development*. London: CIPD. Online, available at: http://www.cipd.co.uk/subjects/corpstrtgy/orgdevelmt/orgdev.htm (accessed 25 November 2010).

Carnall, C. (2007) *Managing Change in Organisations*, 5th edn. Harlow: Prentice Hall.

Carter, N. (2006) *The Football Manager: A History*. Oxford: Routledge.

Cartlidge, D. (2009, April) The hardest job in leisure. *Recreation*, p. 24.

Cartwright, S. and Pappas, C. (2008) Emotional intelligence, its measurement and implications for the workplace. *International Journal of Management Reviews*; 10(2): 149–171.

Castles, D. (2007, 16 February) Ramos turns into supercoach. *Observer* (Sport Section), p. 2.

Cegarra-Navarro, J.G. and Dewhurst, F. (2007) Linking organizational learning and customer capital through an ambidexterity context: an empirical investigation in SMEs. *International Journal of Human Resource Management*; 18(10): 1,720–1,735.

Chandler, A.D. (1962) *Strategy and Structure: Chapters in the History of the Industrial Enterprise*. Cambridge, MA: MIT Press.

Chang, D.-S. and Sun, K.-L. (2007) Exploring the correspondence between total quality management and Peter Senge's disciplines of a learning organization: A Taiwan perspective. *Total Quality Management*; 18(7): 807–822.

Chartered Institute of Personnel and Development (2009a) *Learning and Development*. London: CIPD.

Chartered Institute of Personnel and Development (2009b) *Annual Survey Report: Recruitment, Retention and Turnover*. London: CIPD.

Chartered Institute of Personnel and Development (2009c). Working hours in the UK. October. Online, available at: http://www.cipd.co.uk/subjects/hrpract/hoursandholidays/ukworkhrs (accessed 1 December 2009).

Chartered Institute of Personnel and Development (2010a) *Annual Survey Report 2010: Resourcing and Talent Planning*. London: CIPD.

Chartered Institute of Personnel and Development (2010b) What is CPD? Online, available at: http://www.cipd.co.uk/cpd/aboutcpd/whatiscpd.htm (accessed 24 March 2010).

Chartered Institute of Personnel and Development (2010c) The Skills Agenda in the UK. February. Online, available at: http://cipd.co.uk/subjects/lrnanddev/general/ukskillsagenda.htm (accessed 18 March 2010).

Chartered Institute of Personnel and Development (2010d) Continued professional development. Online, available at: http://www.cipd.co.uk/NR/rdonlyres/9F59E085-A459–4EEC-8F8C-A749EF05C95B/0/CPDPractitionerlevelstandards.pdf (accessed 18 March 2010).

Chartered Institute of Sport Project Working Group (2009) Chartered Institute of Sport Project Update. March. Online, available at: http://www.isrm.co.uk/resources/mem_consult120509.pdf (accessed 4 March 2011).

Checkland, P. and Holwell, S. (2004) 'Classic' OR and 'soft' OR: An asymmetric complementarity. In Pidd, M. (ed.) *Systems Modelling: Theory and Practice*. Chichester: John Wiley & Sons, pp. 45–60.

Chelladurai, P. (2006) *Human Resource Management in Sport and Recreation*. Champaign, IL: Human Kinetics.

Chermack, T.J. and Kasshanna, B.K. (2007) The use and misuse of SWOT analysis and implications for HRD professionals. *Human Resource Development International*; 10(4): 383–399. Online, available at: https://www.indiana.edu/~istr621/cho10fall/PDF%20Readings/Chermack%20&%20Kasshanna%20(2007).pdf (accessed 23 July 2010).

Cherniss, C., Extein, M., Goleman, D. and Weissberg, R.P. (2006) Emotional intelligence: What does the research really indicate? *Educational Psychologist*; 41(4): 239–245.

Clegg, S.R., Kornberger, M. and Rhodes, C. (2005) Learning/becoming/organizing. *Organization*; 12(2): 147–167.

Coahen, N. (2008, 23 November) Let Brown be our best-paid employee. *Observer*, p. 36.

Coakley, J. (2003) *Sports in Society: Issues and Controversies*, 8th edn. Boston, MA: McGraw-Hill.

Coalter, F. (1990) The politics of professionalism: Consumers or citizens? *Leisure Studies*; 9(2): 107–119.

Coalter, F. (2005) The social benefits of sport. Research Report No. 98. Edinburgh: Sport Scotland.

Coalter, F. and Potter, J. (1990) *A Study of 1985 Graduates from Sport, Recreation and Leisure Studies*. London: Sports Council.

Coalter, F., Long, J. and Duffield, B. (1986) *Rationale for Public Sector Investment in Leisure*. London: Sports Council/ESRC.

Coatsworth, J.D. and Conroy, D.E. (2009) The effects of autonomy-supportive coaching, need satisfaction, and self-perceptions on initiative and identity in youth swimmers. *Developmental Psychology*; 45(2): 320–328.

Collins, M.F. and Buller, J.R. (2000) Bridging the post-school institutional gap in sport: Evaluating champion coaching in Nottinghamshire. *Managing Leisure: An International Journal*; 5(4): 200–221.

Conway, N. and Briner, R. (2005) *Understanding Psychological Contracts at Work: A Critical Evaluation of Theory and Research*. Oxford: Oxford University Press.

Cook, M. (2004) *Personnel Selection: Adding Value Through People*, 4th edn. Chichester: John Wiley & Sons.

Couzins, M. and Beagrie, S. (2005, 17 May) How to develop your self awareness. *Personnel Today*, p. 31.

Crilley, G. and Sharp, C. (2006) Managerial qualities and operational performance: A proposed model of relationships at Australian sports and leisure centres. *Measuring Business Excellence*; 10(2): 4–18.

Cummings, T. and Huse, E.F. (1989) *Organisational Development and Change*. St Paul, MN: West Publishing.

Cuskelly, G., Hoye, R. and Auld, C. (2006) *Working with Volunteers in Sport*. London: Routledge.

Daniels, K. (2010) *Change management*. London: CIPD. Online, available at: http://www.cipd.co.uk/subjects/corpstrtgy/changemmt/changgmgmt.htm (accessed 25 November 2010).

Darcy, S., Taylor, T., Cuskelly, G. and Hoye, R. (2008) Professional rugby, community rugby clubs and volunteers: Creating advantage through better volunteer management. In Chadwick, S. and Arthur, D. (eds) *International Cases in the Business of Sport*. London: Butterworth-Heinemann Elsevier, pp. 404–422.

Dawson, P. (2003) *Understanding Organizational Change: The Contemporary Experience of People at Work*. London: Sage.

Dawson, P., Dobson, S. and Gerrard, B. (2000) Estimating coaching efficiency in professional team sports: Evidence from English association football. *Scottish Journal of Political Economy*; 47(4): 399–421.

de Haan, E. (2008) I doubt therefore I coach: Critical moments in coaching practice. *Consulting Psychology Journal: Practice and Research*; 60(1): 91–105.

Dee, K. and Hatton, A. (2006) How to face training evaluation head-on. *People Management*; 12(6): 40–41.

Dehler, G.E., Welsh, M.A. and Lewis, M.W. (2004) Critical pedagogy in the 'new paradigm'. In Grey, C. and Antonacopoulou, E. (eds) *Essential Readings in Management Learning*. London, Sage Publications Ltd, pp. 167–186.

Deloitte (2010) *Annual Review of Football Finance 2010*. Manchester: Sports Business Group/Deloitte.

Department for Business, Innovation and Skills (2009) *Skills For Growth: The National Skills Strategy*. London: BIS.

Department for Business, Innovation and Skills (n.d.) *Direct Discrimination*. Online, available at: http://www.bis.gov.uk/policies/higher-education/access-to-professions/prg/legal-issues/direct-discrimination (accessed February 22nd, 2010).

Department for Business, Innovation and Skills (n.d.) *Indirect Discrimination*. Online, available at: http://www.bis.gov.uk/policies/higher-education/access-to-professions/prg/legal-issues/indirect-discrimination (accessed February 22nd, 2010).

Department for Culture, Media and Sport (2002) *The Coaching Task Force: Final Report*. London: DCMS.

Department for Culture, Media and Sport (2003) *The Government's Plan for Sport Review 2003*. London: DCMS.

Department of the Environment (1975) *Sport and Recreation*. London: HMSO.

Dineen, R. (2010, 27 December) New coach has to get Britain out of a jam, *The Times*, p. 63.

Doherty, A. (2006) Sport volunteerism: An introduction to the special issue. *Sport Management Review*; 9(2): 105–109.

Domingues, B.P. (2010) Barcelona looks for loan to pay delayed player wages. Online, available at: http://www.sportbusiness.com/news/178702/barcelona-looks-for-loan-to-pay-delayed-players-wages (accessed 7 July 2010).

Douglas Coatsworth, J. and Conroy, D.E. (2009) The effects of autonomy-supportive coaching, need satisfaction, and self-perceptions on initiative and identity in youth swimmers. *Developmental Psychology*; 45(2): 320–328.

Downward, P. and Dawson, A. (2000) *The Economics of Professional Team Sports*. London: Routledge.

Downward, P. and Ralston, R. (2005) Volunteer motivation and expectations prior to the XV commonwealth games in Manchester, UK. *Tourism and Hospitality: Planning and Development*; 2(1): 17–26.

Draper, R. (2010, 24 October) How Wayne Rooney used Yaya Toure's wages to convince the Glazers he is worth £10m a year. Online, available at: http://www.dailymail.co.uk/sport/football/article-1323219/How-Wayne-Rooney-used-Yaya-Toures-wages-convince-Glazers-worth-10m-year.html (accessed 5 March 2011).

Drucker, P.F. (1990) *Managing the Non-profit Organization: Practices and Principles*. New York, NY: HarperCollins.

DuBois, D.L., Holloway, B.E., Valentine, J.C. and Cooper, H. (2002) Effectiveness of mentoring programs for youth: A meta-analytic review. *American Journal of Community Psychology*; 30(2): 157–197.

Dunphy, D.C. and Stace, D.A. (1988) Transformational and coercive strategies for planned organizational change: Organization studies. *Journal of Management Studies*; July: 317–334.

Edgar, F. and Geare, A. (2009) Inside the 'black box' and 'HRM'. *International Journal of Manpower*; 30(3): 220–236.

Edwards, A. (1999) Reflective practice in sport management. *Sport Management Review*; 2(1): 67–81.

Elkjaer, B. (2004) The learning organization: An undelivered promise. In Grey, C. and Antonacopoulou, E. (eds) *Essential Readings in Management Learning*. London: Sage, pp. 71–87.

Ellis-Worthington, J. (2009) Bringing along a new generation: Daryl Owen enjoys mentoring future wrestling officials. *Ontario Wrestler*, Spring, p. 14.

Erickson, K., Côté, J. and Fraser-Thomas, J. (2007) Sport experiences, milestones, and educational activities associated with high-performance coaches' development. *Sport Psychologist*; 21(3): 302–316.

Erickson, K., Bruner, M.W., MacDonald, D.J. and Côté, J. (2008) Gaining insight into actual and preferred sources of coaching knowledge. *International Journal of Sports Science and Coaching*; 3(4): 527–538.

Etizioni, A. (1959) Authority structure and organizational effectiveness. *Administrative Science Quarterly*; 4(1): 43–67.

Evers, W.J.G., Brouwers, A. and Tomic, W. (2006) A quasi-experimental study on management coaching effectiveness. *Consulting Psychology Journal: Practice and Research*; 58(3): 174–182.

Fayol, H. (1916) *Administration industrielle et générale; prévoyance, organisation, commandement, coordination, controle*. Paris: H. Dunod et E. Pinat

Feather, K. (2008) Helping HR to measure up: Arming the 'soft' function with hard metrics. *Strategic HR Review*; 7(1): 28–33.

Fee, C.E., Hadlock, C.J. and Pierce, J.R. (2006) Promotions in the internal and external labor market: Evidence from professional football coaching careers. *Journal of Business*; 79(2): 821–850.

Ferkins, L., Shilbury, D. and McDonald, G. (2005) The role of the board in building strategic capability: Towards an integrated model of sport governance research. *Sport Management Review*, 8(3), pp. 195–225.

Festinger, L. (1957) *A Theory of Cognitive Dissonance*. Evanston, IL; Row, Peterson

Fielding, L.W. and Pitts, B. (2003) Historical sketches: The development of the sport business industry. In Quarterman, J.B. and Parks, J. (eds) *Contemporary Sport Management*. Champaign, IL: Human Kinetics, pp. 41–78.

Findlay, L.C. and Ste-Marie, D.M. (2004) A reputation bias in figure skating judging. *Journal of Sport and Exercise Psychology*; 26(1): 154–166.

Fleming, A. (2008) Learning styles. Chartered Institute for Personnel and Development, August. Online, available at: http://www.cipd.co.uk/subjects/lrnanddev/general/lrngstyles.htm (accessed 1 March 2010).

Fleming, I. (1996) The professionalisation of leisure management in Western Europe. *Managing Leisure*; 1(4), 248–251.

Fletcher, N. (2011, 17 February) Mike Ashley's Sports Direct benefits from problems at rival JJB Sports. Online, available at: http://www.guardian.co.uk/business/marketforces-live/2011/feb/17/sports-direct-benefits-from-jjb (accessed 4 March 2011).

Foot, M. and Hook, C. (2008) *Introducing Human Resource Management*. Harlow: Pearson Education.

Françoise, D., Guedri, Z. and Hatt, F. (2008) New insights into the link between HRM integration and organizational performance: The moderating role of influence distribution between HRM specialists and line managers. *International Journal of Human Resource Management*; 19(11): 2095–2112.

French, W.L. and Bell, C.H. (1999) *Organizational Development: Behavioural Science Interventions for Organizational Improvement*, 6th edn. Upper Saddle River, NJ: Pearson Education.

Gagne, M. and Deci, E.L. (2005) Self-determination theory and work motivation. *Journal of Organizational Behavior*, 26: 331–362. Online, available at: http://onlinelibrary.wiley.com/doi/10.1002/job.322/pdf (accessed).

Garman, A.N., Whiston, D.L. and Zlatoper, K.W. (2000) Media perceptions of executive coaching and the formal preparation of coaches. *Consulting Psychology Journal: Practice and Research*; 52(3): 201–205.

Garrow, V. (2009) OD: past, present and future. Brighton: Institute for Employment Studies, IES Working Paper: WP22.

Garrow, V. and Varney, S. (2009) What does OD do? *People Management*; 15(12): 28–30.

Garvin D.A., Edmonson, A.C. and Gino, F. (2008, March) Is yours a learning organisation? *Harvard Business Review*, pp. 1–16.

Giannoulakis, C., Wang, C.-H., Gray, D. and Harrah, W.F. (2007) Measuring volunteer motivation in mega-sporting events. *Event Management*; 11(4): 191–200.

Gibb, A. (1977) Small firms training and competitiveness: Building upon the small business as a learning organization. *International Small Business Journal*; 15(3): 13–29.

Gibson, O. (2010a, 22 March) Chief executive Ian Whatmore quits Football Association in frustration. *Guardian*. Online, available at: http://www.guardian.co.uk/football/2010/mar/22/ian-watmore-football-association-resignation (accessed 22 February 2010).

Gibson, O. (2010b, 2 December) How England's World Cup 2018 bid failed: A bid first scarred by infighting was taught a lesson in football's realpolitik by Fifa's powerbrokers. Online, available at: http://www.guardian.co.uk/football/2010/dec/02/how-england-world-cup-2018-bid-failed (accessed 11 October 2010).

Gilligan, C. and Wilson, R.M.S. (2003) *Strategic Marketing Planning*, 4th edn. Oxford: Butterworth-Heinemann.

Gilmore, S. and Gilson, C. (2007) Finding form: Elite sports and the business of change. *Journal of Organizational Change Management*; 20(3): 409–428.

Gilson, C., Pratt, M., Roberts, K. and Weymes, E. (2000) *Peak Performance: Business Lessons From The World's Top Sports Organizations*. London: HarperCollinsBusiness.

Girganov, V., Papadimitriou, D. and Lopez De D'amico, R. (2006) Cultural orientations of sport managers. *European Sport Management Quarterly*; 6(1): 35–66.

Gittus, B. (2007) *International Benchmarking UK-Australia-New Zealand*. London: SkillsActive.

Goleman, D. (1995) *Emotional Intelligence*. New York, NY: Bantam.

Grant, A.M. (2007) Past, present and future: The evolution of professional coaching and coaching psychology. In Palmer S. and Whybrow A. (eds) *Handbook of Coaching Psychology: A Guide for Practitioners*. London: Routledge, pp. 23–39.

Grant, A.M. and Cavanagh, M.J. (2007) The goal-focused coaching skills questionnaire: Preliminary findings. *Social Behavior and Personality*; 35(6): 751–760.

Grant, R.M. and Baden-Fuller, C. (2004) A knowledge accessing theory of strategic alliances. *Journal of Management Studies*; 41(1): 61–84.

Gratton, C. and Taylor, P. (1985) *Sport and Recreation: An Economic Analysis*. London: E. and F.N. Spon.

Gray, D.E. (2007) Facilitating management learning: Developing critical reflection through reflective tools. *Management Learning*; 38(5): 495–517.

Greater Manchester Sport (2007) *Workforce Development Plan: February 2007 – March 2008*. Manchester: Greater Sport.

Gregory, J.B., Levy, P.E. and Jeffers, M. (2008) Development of a model of the feedback process within executive coaching. *Consulting Psychology Journal: Practice and Research*; 60(1): 42–56.

Grey, C. and Antonacopoulou, E. (eds) (2004) *Essential Readings in Management Learning*. London: Sage.

Grey, C. and Mitev, N. (2004) Management education: A polemic. In Grey, C. and Antonacopoulou, E. (eds) *Essential Readings in Management Learning*. London: Sage, pp. 151–166.

Griffiths, S. (2008, 9 March) A cold, hard look at the numbers. *Sunday Times* (Outsourcing Supplement), p. 4.

Grugulis, I. (2009) Training and development. In Redman, T. and Wilkinson, A. (eds) *Contemporary Human Resource Management*, 3rd edn. Harlow: Pearson Education, pp. 117–134.

Haines, D.J., Kaiser, K. and Farrell, A.-M. (2009) How to develop and administer a college recreational sports graduate administrative assistant research program. *Recreational Sports Journal*; 33(1): 35–42.

Halbwirth, S. and Toohey, K. (2001) The Olympic Games and knowledge management: A case study of the Sydney organising committee of the Olympic Games. *European Sport Management Quarterly*; 1(2): 91–111.

Hamel, G. and Breen, B. (2007) *The Future of Management*. Stanford, CA: Harvard Business Press.

Hamilton, K.E.S., Coates, V., Kelly, B., Boore, J.R.P., Cundell, J.H., Gracey, J., Mcfetridge, B., Mcgonigle, M. and Sinclair, M. (2007) Performance assessment in health care providers: A critical review of evidence and current practice. *Journal of Nursing Management*; 15(8): 773–791.

Hamlin, R.G., Ellinger, A.D. and Beattie, R.S. (2006) Coaching at the heart of managerial effectiveness: A cross-cultural study of managerial behaviours. *Human Resource Development International*; 9(3): 305–331.

Hamlin, R.G., Ellinger, A.D. and Beattie, R.S. (2008) The emergent 'coaching industry': A wake-up call for HRD professionals. *Human Resource Development International*; 11(3): 287–305.

Handley, K., Sturdy, A., Fincham, R. and Clark, T. (2006) Within and beyond communities of practice: Making sense of learning through participation, identity and practice. *Journal of Management Studies*; 43(3): 641–653.

Handy, C. (1988) *Understanding Voluntary Organisations*. Harmondsworth: Penguin.

Handy, C.B. (1986) *Understanding Organisations*, 3rd edn. Harmondsworth: Penguin.

Handy, C.B. (1993) *Understanding Organizations*, 4th edn. London: Penguin.

Hanlon, C. and Jago, L.K. (2004) The challenge of retaining personnel in major sports events organisations. *Event Management*; 9(1): 39–49.

Hanlon, C. and Stewart, B. (2006) Managing people in major sporting event organizations: What strategies are required? *Event Management*; 10(1): 77–88.

Bibliography

Hanson, A., Minten, S. and Taylor, P. (1998) *Graduate Recruitment and Development in the Sport and Recreation Industry: Final Report*. London: Department for Employment/ SPRITO/Standing Conference on Leisure, Recreation and Sport.

Hardingham, A. (2004) *The Coach's Coach: Personal Development for Personal Developers*. London: CIPD.

Harman, N. (2010, 27 December) International exposure is essential, but funding issue casts dark shadow. *The Times*, p. 63.

Harney, B. and Dundon, T. (2006) Capturing complexity: Developing an integrated approach to analyzing HRM in SMEs. *Human Resource Management Journal*; 16(1): 48–73.

Harper, S. and Glew, D.J. (2008) Is your organization learning-impaired? *Industrial Management*; 50(2): 26–30.

Harrison, R. (2005) *Learning and Development*. London: CIPD.

Harrison, R. (2009) *Learning and Development*. London: CIPD.

Hart, S. (2009, 31 October) Radcliffe is streets ahead on form. *Daily Telegraph* (Sport Section), p. S28.

Harvey, C. (2009, 31 October) Pool winners. *Telegraph Magazine*, pp. 30–38.

Henman, T. (2009, 21 June) He's much better than I was. *Sunday Times* (Wimbledon 2009 supplement), p. 2.

Henry, I. (2001) *The Politics of Leisure Policy*. London: Macmillan.

Henry, I. and Spink, J. (1990) Planning for leisure: The commercial and public sectors. In Henry, I. (ed.) *Management and Planning in the Leisure Industries*. Basingstoke: Macmillan, pp. 33–69.

Henry, I.P. (1992) *Policy: The Politics of Leisure*. Basingstoke: Macmillan.

Hewett, C. (2007, 13 October) England's grand campaigners. *Independent*, p. 78.

Hoare, S. (2006, 23 February) Chasing promotion. *People Management*, pp. 36–38.

Hoch, D. (2007, April) Mentoring your coaches. *Coach and Athletic Director*, pp. 12–14.

Hogg, C. Competency and competency frameworks. Chartered Institute of Personnel and Development, June. Online, available at: http://www.cipd.co.uk/subjects/perfmangmt/ competnces/comptfrmwk.htm?IsSrchRes=1 (accessed 1 March 2010).

Holbech, L. and Cheung-Judge, M.Y. (2009) Organisational development: What's in a name? *Impact*, 26(26): 6–9.

Honey, P. and Mumford, A. (1996) *The Manual of Learning Styles*, 3rd edn. Maidenhead: Honey Publications.

Horne, J., Tomlinson, A. and Whannel, G. (1999) *Understanding Sport: An Introduction to the Sociological and Cultural*. London: E. and F.N. Spon.

Houlihan, B. and Green, M. (2009) Modernization and sport: The reform of Sport England and UK Sport. *Public Administration*; 87(3): 678–698.

Houlihan, B. and White, A. (2002) *The Politics of Sport Development: Development of Sport or Development through Sport*. London: Routledge.

Hoye, R. (2006) Leadership within Australian Voluntary Sport Organization Boards. *Non-Profit Management and Leadership*; 16(3): 297–313.

Hoye, R., Smith, A., Westerbeek, H., Stewart, B. and Nicholson, M. (2006) *Sport Management: Principles and Applications*. Oxford: Elsevier.

Hubbard, A. (2007, 14 October) Woodward punches his weight, say boxers. *Independent on Sunday*, p. 75.

Huczynski, A.A. and Buchanan, D.A. (2007) *Organizational Behaviour*, 6th edn. Harlow: Pearson Education.

Hunt, C. (2005) Reflective Practice. In Wilson, J.P. (ed.) *Human Resource Development*. London: Kogan Page, pp. 221–240.

Institute of Sport and Recreation Management (2009) *Continuous Professional Development*. Loughborough: ISRM.

Irvine, D. and Beard, C. (2005) Management training and development: Problems, paradoxes and perspectives. In Wilson, J. (ed.) *Human Resource Development: Learning and Training for Individuals and Organizations*. London: Kogan Page, pp. 351–374.

Janis, I.L. (1972) *Victims of Groupthink: A Psychological Study of Foreign Policy Decisions and Fiascos*. Boston, MA: Houghton Mifflin.

Janssens, M. and Steyaert, C. (2009) HRM and performance: A plea for reflexivity in HRM studies. *Journal of Management Studies*; 46(1): 143–155.

Jawahar, I.M. (2006) Correlates of satisfaction with performance appraisal feedback. *Journal of Labor Research*; XXVII(2): 213–236.

Jermier, J.M., Knights, D. and Nord, W.R. (1994) *Resistance and Power in Organizations*. London: Routledge.

Jones, G. (2002) Performance excellence: A personal perspective on the link between sport and business. *Journal of Applied Sport Psychology*; 14: 268–281.

Jones, G. and Spooner, K. (2006) Coaching high achievers. *Consulting Psychology Journal: Practice and Research*; 58(1): 40–50.

Jones, R.L. and Wallace, M. (2005) Another bad day at the training ground: Coping with ambiguity in the coaching context. *Sport, Education and Society*; 10(1): 119–134.

Kale, P. and Singh, H. (2007) Building firm capabilities through learning: The role of the alliance learning process in alliance capability and firm-level alliance success. *Strategic Management Journal*; 28(10): 981–1000.

Kampa-Kokesch, S. and Anderson, M.Z. (2001) Executive coaching: A comprehensive review of the literature. *Consulting Psychology Journal: Practice and Research*; 53(4): 205–228.

Kang, S.-C., Morris, S.S. and Snell, S.A. (2007) Relational archetypes, organizational learning, and value creation: Extending the human resource architecture. *Academy of Management Review*; 32(1): 236–256.

Kaplan, R.S. (2005) How the balanced scorecard complements the McKinsey 7-S model. *Strategy and Leadership*; 33(3): 41–46. Online, available at: http://academics.eckerd.edu/instructor/trasorrj/Consumer%20behavior/Consumer%20Behavior%20Articles/Value/How%20the%20Balanced%20Scorecard%20compliments%20the%20McKinsey%207-S%20model.pdf (accessed 20 January 2011).

Kaplan, R.S. and Norton, D.P. (1992, January/February) The balanced scorecard: Measures that drive performance. *Harvard Business Review*; 83(7): 172–180.

Kaplan, R.S. and Norton, D.P. (1996) *The Balanced Scorecard: Translating Strategy into action*. Boston, MA: Harvard Business School Press.

Kaplan, R.S. and Norton, D.P. (2001) *The Strategy-Focused Organization: How Balanced Scorecard Companies Thrive in the New Business Environment*. Boston, MA: Harvard Business School Press.

Kaplan, R.S. and Norton, D.P. (2004) *Strategy Maps: Converting Intangible Assets into Tangible Outcomes*. Boston, MA: Harvard Business School Press.

Keep, E. and Mayhew, K. (1999) The leisure sector, Skills Task Force Research Paper 6, Department for Education and Employment, Suffolk.

Kelleher, J. (2008, 5 October) A week in the life of Tony Hall: Chief executive of the Royal Opera House. *Sunday Times* (Appointments Section), p. 4.

Kelso, P. (2008, 31 May) Amaechi: True Olympian will stand up and speak out. *Guardian* (Sport Supplement), p. 8.

Kessel, A. (2009) Central Contract's for World's Best Athletes, *The Observer (Sport Section)*, 1.3.2009, p. 1.

Kilduff, G.J., Elfenbein, H.A. and Staw, B.M. (2010) The psychology of rivalry: A relationally dependent analysis of competition. *Academy of Management Journal*; 53(5): 943–969.

Kim, M., Zhang, J.J. and Connaughton, D.P. (2010) Comparison of volunteer motivations in different youth sport organizations. *European Sport Management Quarterly*; 10(3): 343–365.

Kimmage, P. (2009, 8 March) Kevin Pietersen: After the fall. *Sunday Times* (Sport Section), p. 12. Online, available at: http://www.timesonline.co.uk/tol/sport/cricket/article5864347.ece (accessed 3 December 2010).

Kitson, R. (2009, 7 March) Saracens face a backlash as lofty ambitions grate with player exodus. *Guardian* (Sport Section), p. 11.

Klemash, C. (2006) *How to Succeed in the Game of Life: 34 Interviews with the World's Greatest Coaches*: Kansas City, KS: Andrews McMeel Publishing.

Kline, T.J.B. and Sulsky, L.M. (2009) Measurement and assessment issues in performance appraisal. *Canadian Psychology*; 50(3): 161–171.

Knight, Kavanagh and Page (2009) Managing large scale recruitment. Online, available at: http://www.kkp.co.uk/case-studies/managing-large-scale-executive-recruitment (accessed 24 February 2010).

Knoppers, A. and Anthonissan, A. (2001) Meaning given to performance in Dutch Sport organizations: Gender and racial/ethnic subtext. *Sociology of Sport Journal*; 18: 302–316.

Kolb, D.A., Rubin, I.M. and McIntyre, J.M. (1974) *Organizational Psychology: An Experimental Approach*. Englewood Cliffs, NJ: Prentice-Hall.

Kombarakaran, F.A., Yang, J.A., Baker, M.N. and Fernandes, P.B. (2008) Executive coaching: It works! *Consulting Psychology Journal: Practice and Research*; 60(1): 78–90.

Kotter, J.P. and Schlesinger, L.A. (2008, July/August) Choosing strategies for change. *Harvard Business Review*, pp. 130–139.

Lane, P. (2008, 31 July) Local heroes. *The Economist*. Online, available at: http://www.economist.com/node/11825627 (accessed 16 June 2011).

Lashley, C. and Lee-Ross, D. (2003) *Organisational Behaviour for Leisure Services*. Oxford: Butterworth-Heinemann.

Latham, G.P., Budworth, M.-H., Yanar, B. and Whyte, G (2008) The influence of a manager's own performance appraisal on the evaluation of others. *International Journal of Selection and Assessment*; 16(3): 220–228.

Lawrence, T.B., Mauws, M.K., Dyck, B. and Kleysen, R.F. (2005) The politics of organizational learning: Integrating power into the 4i framework. *Academy of Management Review*; 30(1): 180–191.

Leary, M.R. and Hoyle, R.H. (2009) *Handbook of Individual Differences in Social Behaviour*. New York, NY: Guilford Press.

Ledgerwood, G. (2003) From strategic planning to strategic coaching: Evolving conceptual frameworks to enable changing business cultures. *International Journal of Evidence Based Coaching and Mentoring*; 1(1): 46–56.

Lee, J. and Beeler, C. (2009) An investigation of predictors of satisfaction and future intention: Links to motivation, involvement, and service quality in a local festival. *Event Management*; 13(1): 17–29.

Lee, S., Wagstaff, C.R.D., Fletcher, D. and Hanton, S. (2007) The psychosocial dynamics of organizational effectiveness: Common themes throughout the mainstream and sport literatures. *Journal of Sport and Exercise Psychology (Supplement)*; 29: S180.

Lee, S., Shaw, D.J., Chesterfield, G. and Woodward, C. (2009) Reflections from a world champion: An interview with Sir Clive Woodward, Director of Olympic Performance, the British Olympic Association. *Reflective Practice*; 10(3): 295–310.

Leisure Industries Research Centre (2003) *Sports Volunteering in England*. London: Sport England.

Leitch, S. (2006) *Prosperity for All in the Global Economy*. London: HM Treasury.

Leonard, D. and Swap, W. (2005) Deep smarts. In Little, S. and Ray, T. (eds) *Managing Knowledge: An Essential Reader*, 2nd edn. London: Open University in association with Sage Publications, pp. 157–170.

Leonard, R. (2005) *The Administrative Side of Coaching: A Handbook for Applying Business Concepts to Coaching Athletics*. Morgantown, WV: Fitness Information Technology.

Leonard, T. (2010, 15 May) Speed factory. *Daily Telegraph Magazine*, pp. 24–30.

Lepak, D.P. and Snell, S.C. (2005) The human resource architecture: Toward a theory of human capitial allocation and development. In Little, S. and Ray, T. (eds) *Managing*

Knowledge: An Essential Reader, 2nd edn. London: Open University in association with Sage Publications, pp. 273–298.

Levenson, A. (2009) Measuring and maximizing the business impact of executive coaching. *Consulting Psychology Journal: Practice and Research*; 61(2): 103–121.

Levine, H. (2009) Leadership, training, evaluation guide personnel decisions. *Street and Smith's Sportsbusiness Journal*; 12(3): 13.

Levinthal, D.A. and March, J.G. (1993) The myopia of learning. *Strategic Management Journal*; 14(S2): 95–112.

Lewin, K. (1947a) Frontiers in group dynamics: II. Channels of group life: Social planning and action research. *Human Relations*; 1(2): 143–153.

Lewin, K. (1947b) Quasi-stationary social equilibria and the problem of permanent change. In Warner Burke, W., Lake, D.G. and Waymire Paine, J. (eds) (2009) *Organization Change: A Comprehensive Reader*. San Francisco, CA: John Wiley & Sons.

Lillian, P., Pierre, J. and Burlot, F. (2009) Management practices in companies through sport. *Management Decisions*; 47(1): 137–150.

Little, S. and Ray, T. (eds) (2005) *Managing Knowledge: An Essential Reader*, 2nd edn. London: Open University in association with Sage Publications.

Lloyd, C. (2005a) Competitive strategy and skills: Working out the fit in the fitness industry. *Human Resource Management Journal*; 15(2): 15–34.

Lloyd, C. (2005b) The regulation of the fitness industry: Training standards as a policy option? *Industrial Relations Journal*; 36(5): 367–385.

Locke, E.A. (2005) Why emotional intelligence is an invalid concept. *Journal of Organizational Behavior*; 26(4): 425–431.

Lockstone, L.S., Smith, K. and Baum, T. (2010) Volunteering flexibility across the tourism sector. *Managing Leisure*; 15(1/2): 111–127.

Loehr, J. and Schwartz, T. (2001). The making of a corporate athlete. *Harvard Business Review*; 79(1): 120–128.

London 2012 (2009a, 14 January) Adecco announced as official recruitment services supplier to London 2012. Press Release. Online, available at: http://www.london2012.com/news/2009/01/adecco-announced-as-official-recruitment-services-supplier-to-london-2012.php (accessed 20 February 2010).

London 2012 (2009b, 1 March) The volunteer programme. Online, available at: http://www.london2012.com/get-involved/volunteering/the-volunteer-programme.php (accessed 1 March 2009).

London Organising Committee of the Olympic Games and Paralympic Games (2008, February) Diversity and Inclusion Strategy. London2012. Online, available at: http://www.london2012.com/documents/locog-publications/open-diversity-and-inclusion-strategy-document.pdf (accessed 25 February 2010).

Longmore, A. (2008, 9 November) The whole world in his hands. *Sunday Times* (Sport Section), pp. 14–15.

Longmore, A. (2009, 15 March) Ruby goes to town. *Sunday Times* (Sport Section), p. 19.

Loughborough University (2008) *Are we Missing the Coach for 2012?* London: SportNation.

Lowman, R.L. (2007) Coaching and consulting in multicultural contexts: Integrating themes and issues. *Consulting Psychology Journal: Practice and Research*; 59(4): 296–303.

Lussier, R.N. and Kimbal, D.C. (2009) *Applied Sport Management Skills*. Leeds: Human Kinetics.

Luthans, F. (1985) *Organizational Behavior*. New York, NY: McGraw-Hill.

Luthans, F. (1998) *Organisational Behaviour*, 8th edn. New York, NY: McGraw-Hill.

Lytras, M.D. and Sicilia, M.A. (2005) The knowledge society: A manifesto for knowledge and learning. *International Journal of Knowledge and Learning*; 1(1/2): 1.

McCormick, A. and Scholaris, D. (2009) Recruitment. In Wilkinson, T. and Redman, A. (eds) *Contemporary Human Resource Management: Text and Cases*. London: Prentice Hall, pp. 64–84.

McCormick, I. and Burch, G.S.J. (2008) Personality-focused coaching for leadership development. *Consulting Psychology Journal: Practice and Research*; 60(3): 267–278.

McGrath, R. (2009) A discourse analysis of Australian local government recreation and sport plans provision for people with disabilities. *Public Management Review*; 11(4): 477–497.

McGregor, D. (1960) *The Human Side of Enterprise*. New York, NY: McGraw-Hill.

McIlvanney, H. (2008, 19 October) Gerrard still splits opinions. *Sunday Times* (Sport Section), p. 24.

McKenzie, B. (2010, 7 May) Lewis ready to make up with his Dad. *Daily Express*, p. 73.

McLean, D.D., Hurd, A.R. and Jensen, R.R. (2005) Using Q-methodology in competency development for CEOs in public parks and recreation. *Managing Leisure*; 10(3): 156–165.

Macleod, D. and Clarke, N. (2009) Engaging for success: Enhancing performance through employee engagement. Department for Business, Innovation and Skills, London, July.

MacVicar, A. and Ogden, S.M. (2001) Flexible working practices in sport and recreation: Current practices in Scottish public, not-for-profit and private leisure facilities. *Managing Leisure*; 6(3): 125–140.

Madella, A. (2003) Methods for analysing sports employment in Europe. *Managing Leisure*; 8(2): 56–59.

Management Standards Centre (2008) National Occupational Standards for Management and Leadership. Management Standards Centre. Online, available at: http://www.management-standards.org/content_1.aspx?id=10:1917 (accessed 1 March 2010).

May, J. (2008, 29 October) Squires steps up to the plate to boost sports recruiter. *Recruiter*. Online, available at: http://www.recruiter.co.uk/news/squires-steps-up-to-plate-to-boost-sports-recruiter/338408.article (accessed 22 January 2010).

Mayer, J.D. and Salovey, P. (1997) What is emotional intelligence? In Sluyter, P. and Salovey, D. (eds) *Emotional Development and Emotional Intelligence: Implications for Educators*. New York, NY: Basic Books, pp. 3–31.

Mayer, J.D., Salovey, P. and Caruso, D.R. (2008) Emotional intelligence: New ability or eclectic traits. *American Psychologist*; 63(6): 503–517.

Megginson, D. (2004) Planned and emergent learning: Consequences for development. In Grey, C. and Antonacopoulou, E. (eds) *Essential Readings in Management Learning*. London: Sage, pp. 91–106.

Megginson, D. and Whitaker, V. (2007) *Continuing Professional Development*. London: CIPD.

Metaxiotis, K., Ergazakis, K. and Psarras, J. (2005) Exploring the world of knowledge management: Agreements and disagreements in the academic/practitioner community. *Journal of Knowledge Management*; 9(2): 6–18.

Milanovic, B. (2005) Globalization and goals: Does soccer show the way? *Review of International Political Economy*; 12(5): 829–850.

Millar, D. (2009, July) The view from the Peloton. *Observer Sport Magazine*, p. 23.

Miller, J.S. and Johnson, S.A. (2008) Double play: Creating the sport customer experience using an interdisciplinary framework for managing service employees. *Journal of Marketing Management*; 24(1–2): 87–112.

Mintel (2007) *Health and Fitness Clubs*. London: May.

Minten, S. (2007) Graduate employability in the sport and recreation industry: An analysis of the transition from higher education to the workplace. Unpublished PhD, University of Sheffield.

Minten, S. (2010) Use them or lose them: A study of the employability of sport graduates through their transition into the workplace. *Managing Leisure*; 15(1/2): 67–82.

Minten, S. and Foster, W. (2009) Human resource management. In Bill, K. (ed.) *Sport Management*. Exeter: Learning Matters Ltd, pp. 87–100.

Moore, B. (2008, 9 November) FA are hamstrung when it comes to imposing discipline on football. *Daily Telegraph* (Sport Section), p. 5.

Morrow, S. and Idle, C. (2008) The challenges of modernizing a professional sport: A case study of professional road cycling. In Chadwick, S. and Arthur, D. (eds) *International Cases in the Business of Sport*. London: Butterworth-Heinemann Elsevier, pp. 45–59.

Mullins, L. (2007) *Management and Organisational Behaviour*, 8th edn. Harlow: Pearson Education.

Mulvaney, M.A., McKinney, W.R. and Grodsky, R. (2008) The development of a pay-for-performance appraisal system for public park and recreation agencies: A case study. *Journal of Park and Recreation Administration*; 26(4): 126–156.

Nash, C.S. and Sproule, J. (2009) Career development of expert coaches. *International Journal of Sports Science and Coaching*; 4(1): 121–138.

National Society for the Prevention of Cruelty to Children (2009) Child protection in sport. CPSU Briefings. Online, available at: http://www.nspcc.org.uk/Inform/cpsu/Resources/Briefings/safe_recruitment_and_selection_procedures_wdf67399.pdf (accessed 25 February 2010).

Newell, S. (2006) Selection and assessment. In Wilkinson, T. and Redman, A. (eds) *Contemporary Human Resource Management: Text and Cases*. London: Prentice Hall, pp. 65–98.

Nichols, G. (2004) Pressures on volunteers in the UK. In Stebbins, R.A. and Graham, M. (eds) *Volunteering in Leisure: An International Assessment of Leisure and Volunteering*. Wallingford: CABI, pp. 197–208.

Nichols, G., Taylor, P., James, M., Garrett, R., Holmes, K., King, L., Gratton, C. and Kokolakakis, T. (2005) Voluntary activity in UK Sport. *Voluntary Action*; 6(2): 31–54.

Nieto, M.L. (2006) *Human Resource Management: An Integrated Approach*. London: Palgrave Macmillan.

Nike (2008) *Annual Report on Form 10K: The Fiscal Year ended May 31st*. Beaverton, OR: NIKE.

Nissley, N. and Casey, A. (2002) The politics of the exhibition: Viewing corporate museums through the paradigmatic lens of organizational memory. *British Journal of Management*; 13(S2): S35–S45.

Nonaka, I., Toyama, R. and Konno, N. (2005) SECI, Ba and leadership: A Unified Model of Dynamic Knowledge Creation. In Little, S. and Ray, T. (eds) *Managing Knowledge: An Essential Reader*, 2nd edn. London: Open University in association with Sage Publications, pp. 23–49.

Northcroft, J. (2008, 6 July) Samba stars on the way. *Sunday Times* (Sport Section), p. 18.

Northcroft, J. (2009, 19 July) Billion dollar team. *Sunday Times* (Sport Section), p. 12.

Office of the Deputy Prime Minister and Local Government Association (2005, July) Executive summary of the organisational development resource document for local government: Transforming your authority; creating real and lasting change. London: Office of the Deputy Prime Minister

Ogden, S. and MacVicar, A. (2001) Flexible working in sport and recreation: Current practices in Scottish public, not-for-profit and private leisure facilities. *Managing Leisure*, 6(3): 125–140.

Old, J. (2004) Organisational behaviour in sport organisations. In Beech, J. and Chadwick, S. (eds) *The Business of Sport Management*. London: Prentice Hall, pp. 69–92.

Orenstein, R.L. (2006) Measuring executive coaching efficacy? The answer was right here all the time. *Consulting Psychology Journal: Practice and Research*; 58(2): 106–116.

Owen, O. (2009, August) The 10 unbreakable records. *Observer Sport Magazine*, pp. 18–19.

Palmer, R. (2005) The identification of training needs. In Wilson, J. (ed.) *Human Resource Development: Learning and Training for Individuals and Organizations*. London: Kogan Page, pp. 117–135.

Palmer, S. and Whybrow, A. (2007a) Coaching psychology: An introduction. In Palmer S. and Whybrow, A. (eds) *Handbook of Coaching Psychology: A Guide for Practitioners*. London: Routledge, pp. 1–20.

Palmer, S. and Whybrow, A. (eds) (2007b) *Handbook of Coaching Psychology: A Guide for Practitioners*. London: Routledge.

Parent, M.M. and Harvey, J. (2009) Towards a management model for sport and physical activity community-based partnerships. *European Sport Management Quarterly*; 9(1): 23–45.

Parker, M. (2008, 30 November) If only business schools wouldn't teach business. *Observer* (Business and Media Section), p. 8.

Parkhouse, B. (2005) *The Management of Sport: Its Foundation and Application*. New York, NY: McGraw-Hill.

Parks, J.B. and Quarterman, J. (2003) Sport management: An overview. In Quarterman, J. and Parks, J.B. (eds) *Contemporary Sport Management*. Champaign, IL: Human Kinetics, pp. 5–22.

Passmore, J. (2008) An integrative model for executive coaching. *Consulting Psychology Journal: Practice and Research*; 59(1): 68–78.

Pastore, D.L. (2003) A different lens to view mentoring in sport management. *Journal of Sport Management*; 17: 1–12.

Payne, J. (2008) Sector skills councils and employer engagement: Delivering the 'employer-led' skills agenda in England. *Journal of Education and Work*; 21(2): 93–113.

Pearson, G. (2009) The Bosman case, EU law and the transfer system. University of Liverpool Football Industry Group Factsheet. Online, available at: http://www.liv.ac.uk/footballindustry/bosman.html (accessed 1 March 2009).

Percival, J. (2008, 27 December) FA to tackle homophobia with video featuring football stars. *Guardian*, p. 22.

Pesavento, L.C., Bator, M.G. and Ros, J.-E. (2001, June) Staff development practices: Is your organisation 'learning' for the 21st century? *Parks and Recreation*, pp. 24–30.

Peters, T.J. and Waterman, R.H. (1982) *In Search of Excellence*. New York, NY: Harper and Row.

Peterson, D.B. (2007) Executive coaching in a cross-cultural context. *Consulting Psychology Journal: Practice and Research*; 59(4): 261–271.

Pettigrew, A. (1985) *The Awakening Giant: Continuity and Change at ICI*. Oxford: Blackwell.

Pfeffer, J. (1981) *Power in Organizations*. London: Pitman.

Pfeffer, J. and Salancik, G.R. (1978) *The External Control of Organizations: A Resource Dependence View*. New York, NY: Harper and Row.

Pharos (2010) OD programming: Restructuring and re-engineering. Online, available at: http://www.pharospartners.com/simplifying-cs.html (accessed 1 December 2010).

Pheysey, D.C. (1993) *Organizational Cultures: Types and Transformations*. London: Routledge.

Pilbeam, S. and Corbridge, M. (2006) *People Resourcing: Contemporary Human Resource Management in Practice*. London: Prentice Hall.

Pitts, B. (2001) Sport management at the millennium: A defining moment. *Journal of Sport Management*, 15(1): 1–9.

Potrac, P., Jones, R. and Armour, K. (2002) 'It's all about getting respect': The coaching behaviors of an expert English soccer coach. *Sport, Education and Society*; 7(2): 183–202.

Price, A. (2007) *Human Resources Management in a Business Context*. London: Thomson Business Press.

Primault, D. (2006) Employment in sport. In Andreff, W. and Szymański, S. (eds) *Handbook on the Economics of Sport*. Cheltenham: Edward Elgar, pp. 153–167.

Pugh, S.D. (2001) Service with a smile: Emotional contagionin the service encouter. *Academy of Management Journal*; 44(5): 1,018–1,028.

Quality South West (n.d.) Investor in people case study: Skern Lodge, Quality South West. Online, available at: http://www.qualitysouthwest.co.uk/docs/Skern%20Lodge.pdf (accessed 5 March 2010).

Queensland Government Public Service Resources (2008) Recruitment and selection resources. Queensland Government Public Service Resources, November. Online, available at: http://www.psc.qld.gov.au/library/document/catalogue/recruitment-selection/recruitment-and-selection-resources.pdf (accessed 25 February 2010).

Radcliffe, P. (2008, 16 August) My mentors. *Guardian* (Work Section), p. 2.

Ravenscroft, N. and Gilchrist, P. (2005) Post-Fordist restructuring and vocational training in sport in the UK. *Managing Leisure*; 10(3): 166–183.

Reason, M. (2009, 27 October) I don't want my son to play rugby union: Its too violent. Online, available at: http://www.telegraph.co.uk/sport/rugbyunion/6440945/I-dont-want-my-son-to-play-rugby-union-...-its-too-violent.html (accessed 15 December 2010).

Register of Exercise Professionals (2009) What is REPs. Online, available at: http://www.exerciseregister.org/REPsWhatis.html (accessed 2 March 2009).

Rekar Munro, C. (2009) Mentoring needs and expectations of generation-Y human resources practitioners: Preparing the next wave of strategic business partners. *Journal of Management Research*; 1(2): 1–25.

Rial, A., Rial, J., Varela, J. and Real, E. (2008) An application of importance-performance analysis (IPA) to the management of sport centres. *Managing Leisure*; 13(3/4): 179–188.

Richards, J. and Hogg, C. (2009, December) Investors in people. Chartered Institute of Personnel and Development. Online, available at: http://www.cipd.co.uk/subjects/lrnanddev/general/iip.htm (accessed 2 March 2010).

Robbins, S.P. (2001) *Organisational Behavior: Concepts, Controversies and Applications.* Upper Saddle River, NJ: Pearson Education.

Roberts, G. (2005) *Recruitment and Selection.* London: CIPD.

Roberts, K. (2004) *The Leisure Industries.* Basingstoke: Palgrave/Macmillan.

Robinson, L. (2003) *Managing Public Sport and Leisure Services.* Oxford: Routledge.

Robinson, V. (2008) Is contemporary HR management strategic? *Strategic HR Review*; 7(1): 42–43.

Rowden, R.W. (2001) The learning organisation and strategic change. *S.A.M. Advanced Management Journal*; 66(3): 117pp.

Ruddick, G. (2009, 29 January) Sporting managers spot gap in the field: A sector that businessmen once ignored is suddenly proving attractive as revenues increase. *Daily Telegraph*. Online, available at: http://www.telegraph.co.uk/finance/newsbysector/retailandconsumer/leisure/4361962/Sporting-managers-spot-gap-in-the-field.html (accessed 24 February 2010).

Ruddock, G. (2010, 7 February) Francis Baron: a man not afraid to tackle rugby's problems. *Telegraph*. Online, available at: http://www.telegraph.co.uk/finance/financetopics/profiles/7182191/Francis-Baron-a-man-not-afraid-to-tackle-rugbys-problems.html (accessed 24 February 2010).

Ryan, R.M. and Deci, E.L. (2000) Self-determination theory and the facilitation of intrinsic motivation, social development, and well-being. *American Psychologist*; 55(1): 68–78.

Ryan, R.M. and Deci, E.L. (2008) Self-determination theory and the role of basic psychological needs in personality and the organization of behavior. In John, O.P., Robbins, R.W. and Pervin, L.A. (eds) *Handbook of Personality: Theory and Research.* New York, NY: Guilford Press, pp. 654–678.

Rynes, S.L., Gerhart, B. and Parks, L. (2005) Personnel psychology: Performance evaluation and pay for performance. *Annual Review of Psychology*; 56(571): 571–600.

Sadler-Smith, E. (2006) *Learning and Development for Managers: Perspectives from Research and Practice.* Oxford: Blackwell.

Sadler-Smith, E., Allinson, C.W. and Hayes, J. (2000) Learning preferences and cognitive style: Some implications for continuing professional development. *Management Learning*; 31(2): 239–256.

Saks, A.M. (2005) The impracticality of recruitment research. In Evers, A., Anderson, N. and Smit-Voskijl, O. (eds) *Blackwell Handbook of Selection.* London: Blackwell, pp. 47–72.

Salaman, G. (1981) *Class and the Corporation*. London: Fontana.

Sam, M.P. (2009) The public management of sport. *Public Management Review*; 11(4): 499–514.

Schein, E. (1987) *The Art of Managing Human Resources*. New York, NY: Oxford University Press.

Schein, E.J. (2007) *Process Consultation, Vol 2, Lessons for Managers and Consultants*. Reading, MA: Addison-Wesley.

Schein, Edgar H. (1996) Leadership and organizational culture. In Hesselbein, F., Goldsmith, M. and Beckhard, R. (eds) *The Leader of the Future*. San Francisco, CA: Jossey-Bass, pp. 59–69.

Schön, D. (1983) *The Reflective Practitioner: How Professionals Think in Action*. London: Temple-Smith.

Scott, M. (2011, 9 February) Lord Burns accuses FA of losing plot over regulation. *Guardian*. Online, available at: http://www.guardian.co.uk/football/2011/feb/09/lord-burns-fa (accessed 9 February 2011).

Silk, M.A., Andrews, M.L. and Cole, C.L. (2005) *Sport and Corporate Nationalisms*. Oxford: Berg.

Simon, H.A. (1982) *Models of Bounded* (3 vols). Cambridge, MA: MIT Press.

SkillsActive (2005) *Skills Needs Assessment for the Heath and Fitness Sector*. London: SkillsActive.

SkillsActive (2006a) *Analysis of Gaps and Weaknesses*. London: SkillsActive.

SkillsActive (2006b) Managing sport and active leisure national occupational standards. Online, available at: http://www.skillsactive.com/training/standards/level-4/Managing-Sport-and-Active-Leisure/ (accessed 1 March 2010).

SkillsActive (2008) *Working in Fitness Summary Report: 2008*. London: SkillsActive.

SkillsActive (2009a, Summer) Rising to the challenge. *Active Insight*, pp. 10–11.

SkillsActive (2009b) *Working in Fitness: Summary Report*. London: SkillsActive/REPs.

SkillsActive (2009c). *Skills Priorities for Active Leisure, Learning and Wellbeing*. London: SkillsActive.

Skills for Business (2010) About occupational standards. Online, available at: http://www.ukstandards.org.uk/About_occupational_standards/default.aspx (accessed 28 April 2010).

Slack, T. (1997) *Understanding Sport Organisations*. Leeds: Human Kinetics.

Slack, T. (2004) *The Commercialisation of Sport*. Oxford: Routledge.

Slack, T. and Hinings, B. (1987) Understanding change in national sports organizations: An integration of critical perspectives. *Journal of Sport Management*; 6: 114–132.

Slack, T. and Parent, M.M. (2006) *Understanding Sport Organizations: The Application of Organization Theory*, 2nd edn. Leeds: Human Kinetics.

Smith, A. (2006) *Grand Slam: Coach Your Mind to Win in Sports, Business, and Life*. Phoenix, AZ: Team Alf Books.

Smith, A. and Stewart, B. (1999) *Sports Management: A Guide to Professional Practice*. Crows Nest, NSW: Allen and Unwin.

Smith, A.C.T. and Stewart, B. (2010) The special features of sport: A critical revisit. *Sport Management Review*; 13(1): 1–13.

Smith, A.C.T., Evans, D.M. and Westerbeek, H.M. (2005) The examination of change management using qualitative methods: A case industry approach. *Qualitative Report*; 10(1): 96–121.

Smith, E. (2009, 2 August) She's got a one-track mind. *Sunday Times* (InGear section), p. 9.

Smith, M.K. (1996, 2005) Competence and competencies. *The encyclopaedia of informal education*. Online, available at: http://www.infed.org/biblio/b-comp.htm (accessed 3 March 2010).

Smith, M.K. (2001a) Chris Argyris: Theories of action, double-loop learning and organizational learning. *The encyclopedia of informal education*. Online, available at: http://www.infed.org/thinkers/argyris.htm (accessed 1 May 2010).

Smith, M.K. (2001b) Peter Senge and the learning organization. *The encyclopedia of informal education*. Online, available at: http://www.infed.org/thinkers/senge.htm (accessed 1 May 2010).

Smyth, R. (2009, July) The 10 unlikely Ashes heroes. *Observer Sport Monthly*, pp. 14–15.

Spender, J.C. (2004) Knowing, managing and learning: A dynamic managerial epistemology. In Grey, C. and Antonacopoulou, E. (eds) *Essential Readings in Management Learning*. London: Sage, pp. 107–129.

Sperry, L. (2008) Executive coaching: An intervention, role function, or profession? *Consulting Psychology Journal: Practice and Research*; 60(1): 33–37.

Sport England (2002) *Strategy for Sport for Young People*. London: Sport England.

Sport England (2004) *The Framework for Sport in England*. London: Sport England.

Sport England (2010) Equity and diversity. Online, available at: http://www.sportengland.org/support__advice/equality_and_diversity.aspx (accessed 11 December 2010).

Sport Industry Research Centre (2007) *The Economic Importance of Sport in England*. London: Sport England.

Sports Coach UK (2009) *Annual Report 2008–2009*. Leeds: Sports Coach UK.

Sports Council (1960) *Professional Training for Leisure Management*. London: Sports Council.

Sports Council (1969) *Professional Training for Leisure Management*. London: Sports Council.

Stacey, R.D. (2003) *Strategic Management and Organisational Dynamics: The Challenge of Complexity*. London: Prentice Hall.

Stafford, M. (2009, 18 February) McGeechan fears effect of exodus on Premiership. *Guardian* (Sport Section), p. 9.

Stone, A. (2008, 20 April) A mentor can tune your skills. *Sunday Times*, p. 3.11.

Stonehouse, G., Cambell, D.J., Hamill, J. and Purdie, A. (2004) *Global and Transnational Business: Management and Strategy*. Chichester: John Wiley & Sons.

Storey, J. (2005) Human resource policies for knowledge work. in Grey, C. and Antonacopoulou, E. (eds) *Essential Readings in Management Learning*. London: Sage, pp. 199–219.

Studd, S. (2008) Developing the workforce. ISPAL National Conference, Chesford Grange Hotel, Kenilworth, 3–4 June.

Sunday Times (2009, 8 March) Dallaglio: England must send for Woodward. *Sunday Times* (Sport Section), p. 1.

Swanson, R.A. and Holton, E.F. (2009) *Foundations of Human Resource Development*. San Francisco, CA: Berrett-Koehler.

Tamkin, P., Yarnall, J. and Kerrin, M. (2002) *Kirkpatrick and Beyond: A Review of Models of Training Evaluation, Report 392*. Brighton: Institute for Employment Studies.

Tannebaum, R. and Schmidt, W. (1973, May/June) How to choose a leadership pattern. *Harvard Business Review*; 36(2): 95–101.

Taylor, B. and Garrett, D. (2008) *The Professionalisation of Sports Coaching*. Leeds: Sports Coach UK.

Taylor, F. (1911) *Principles of Scientific Management*. New York, NY and London: Harper & Brothers.

Taylor, J. (2009, July) Identifying learning and development needs. Chartered Institute of Personnel and Development. Online, available at: http://www.cipd.co.uk/subjects/lrnanddev/trainingneeds/idtlneeds.htm (accessed 16 March 2010).

Taylor, L. (2008, 21 May) Barwick supports compromise over foreign quotas as Blatter backs off. *Guardian* (Sport Section), p. 3.

Taylor, T., Darcy, S., Hoye, R. and Cuskelly, G. (2006) Using psychological contract theory to explore issues in effective volunteer management. *European Sport Management Quarterly*; 6(2): 123–147.

Thelwell, R.C., Lane, A.M., Weston, N.J.V. and Greenlees, I.A. (2008) Examining relationships between emotional intelligence and coaching efficacy. *International Journal of Sport and Exercise Psychology*; 6(2): 224–235.

Thornton III, G.C. and Gibbons, A.M. (2009) Validity of assessment centers for personnel selection. *Human Resource Management Review*; 19(3): 169–187.

Todd, S. and Kent, A. (2009) A social identity perspective on the job attitudes of employees in sport. *Management Decisions*; 47(1): 173–190.

Torrington, D., Taylor, S. and Hall, L. (2005) *Human Resource Management*. London: Financial Times Press.

Torrington, D., Taylor, S. and Hall, L. (2007) *Human Resource Management*. London: Financial Times Press.

Torrington, D., Taylor, S. and Hall, L. (2008) *Human Resource Management*. London: Financial Times Press.

Trimble, L., Buraimo, B., Godefrey, C., Grecic, D. and Minten, S. (2010) *Sport in the UK*. Exeter: Learning Matters.

Tuchscherer, L. (2007, October) Jobcentre: Mixed-age workforce is important. *Health Club Management*. Online, available at: http://www.health-club.co.uk/detail1.cfm?pagetype=detail&subject=news&codeID=35973&site=HC&dom=N (accessed 16 June 2011).

Turnball, S. (2005, 16 October) Athletics: Buckner in very English row that will run and run. *Independent on Sunday*. Online, available at: http://www.independent.co.uk/sport/general/athletics-buckner-in-very-english-row-that-will-run-and-run-511102.html (accessed 4 March 2010).

Twynam, G.D., Farrell, J.M. and Johnston, M.E. (2002/3) Leisure and volunteer motivation at a special sporting event. *Journal of the Canadian Association for Leisure Studies*; 27(3/4): 363–377.

UK Commission for Employment and Skills (2009) *Ambition 2020: World Class Skills and Jobs for the UK*. London: UKCES.

Ullmen, J. (2010) A team leadership lesson from Phil Jackson: Be a leader and a half, rather than a half leader. Online, available at: http://www.motivationrules.com/2009/08/07/a-team-leadership-lesson-from-phil-jackson-be-a-leader-and-a-half-rather-than-half-a-leader (accessed 2 December 2010).

Ulrich, D.O. and Parkhouse, B.L. (1979) The application of motivation theory in management to the sport arena. *QUEST*; 31(2): 302–311.

Veal, A. and Saprestein, H. (1977) Recreation managers in Britain: A survey. Working Paper 56, CURS, Birmingham.

Vergeer, I. and Lyle, J. (2009) Coaching experience: Examining its role in coaches' decision making: Coaching experience and decision making. *International Journal of Sport and Exercise Psychology*; 7(4): 431–449.

Voskuijl, O.F. (2005) Job analysis: Current and future perspectives. In Evers, A., Anderson, N. and Smit-Voskijl, O. (eds) *Blackwell Handbook of Selection*. London: Blackwell, pp. 27–46.

Walsh, D. (2007, 23 September) He's so Ruud. *Sunday Times*, pp. 2.14–2.15.

Walters, G. and Rossi, G. (2009) Editorial. In Walters, G. and Rossi, G. (eds) Labour Market Migration in European Football: Key Issues and Challenges: Vol. 2, No. 2, Birkbeck Sport Business Centre Research Paper Series. London: Birbeck Sport Business Centre, pp. 6–8.

Wang, D.-S. and Shyu, C.-L. (2006) Will the strategic fit between business and HRM strategy influence HRM effectiveness and organizational performance? *International Journal of Manpower*; 29(2): 92–110.

Warman, M. (2010, 20 February) Tracking user data in pursuit of better returns. *Daily Telegraph*, p. 33.

Watchman, R. (2009, 28 June) A beautiful game with horrible debts. *Observer* (Business Section 5), p. 5.

Watson, J.C., Clement, D., Blom, L.C. and Grindley, E. (2009) Mentoring: Processes and perceptions of sport and exercise psychology graduate students. *Journal of Applied Sport Psychology*; 21(2): 231–246.

Weinberg, R. and McDermott, M. (2002) A comparative analysis of sport and business organizations: Factors perceived critical for organizational success. *Journal of Applied Sport Psychology*; 14(4): 282–298.

Weiss, M.R., Amorose, A.J. and Wilko, A.-M. (2009) Coaching behaviors, motivational climate and psychosocial outcomes among female adolescent athletes. *Pédiatrie Exercise Science*; 21(4): 475–492.

Welch, S. and Sigelman, L. (2007) Who's calling the shots? Women coaches in division I women's sports. *Social Science Quarterly*; 88(5): 1415–1434.

Wendell Braithwaite, T. (2004) Human resource management in sport. In Beech, J. and Chadwick, S. (eds) *The Business of Sport Management*. London: Prentice Hall, pp. 93–127.

Whetton, D.A. and Cameron, K.S. (2007) *Developing Management Skills*. Englewood Cliffs, NJ: Prentice Hall.

Whidett, S. and Hollyforde, S. (2003) *A Practical Guide to Competencies: How to Enhance Individual and Organisational Performance*. London: CIPD.

White, J. (2009, 24 October) Piggy in the middle. *Daily Telegraph Magazine*, pp. 26–33.

Whiting, S.W., Podsakoff, P.M. and Pierce, J.R. (2008) Effects of task performance, helping, voice, and organizational loyalty on performance appraisal ratings. *Journal of Applied Psychology*; 93(1): 125–139.

Whitrod Brown, H. (2010) High performance coaching in business and sport. Submitted in part fulfilment of Doctorate in Business Administration, Leeds Metropolitan University, unpublished.

Whittington, R. (1993) *What is Strategy: And Does it Matter?* London: Routledge.

Whitwoth, D. (2008, 13 September) On the waterfront. *The Times Magazine*, pp. 20–25.

Wilcockson, J. (2009, July) Why I believe in Lance. *Observer Sport Magazine*, p. 20.

Williams, R. (2008, 19 July) Out of the running: Disgraced Chambers loses court battle for a ticket to Beijing. *Guardian*, p. 11.

Wilson, D.C. (1992) *A Strategy of Change: Concepts and Controversies in the Management of Change*. London: Routledge.

Winter, H. (2011, 14 March) England manager Fabio Capello has damaged morale by giving John Terry the armband again. *Telegraph Online*. Online, available at: http://www.telegraph.co.uk/sport/football/teams/england/8382123/Henry-Winter-England-manager-Fabio-Capello-has-damaged-morale-by-giving-John-Terry-the-armband-again.html (accessed 21 March 2011).

Wolfe, R., Weick, K.E., Usher, J.M., Terborg, J.R., Poppo, L., Murrell, A.J., Duckerich, J.M., Core, D.C., Dickson, K.E. and Jourdan, J.S. (2005) Sport and organizational studies: Exploring synergy. *Journal of Management Inquiry*; 14(2): 182–210.

Wolfenden Report (1990) *Sport in the Community*. London: HMSO.

Wolsey, C. and Abrams, J. (eds) (2001) *Understanding the Leisure and Sport Industry*. London: Longman.

Wolsey, C. and Abrams, J. (2010) Managing people in sport and leisure. In Taylor, P. (ed.) *Torkildsen's Sport and Leisure Management*, 6th edn. London: Routledge, pp. 337–364.

Wolsey, C. and Whitrod Brown, H. (2003) Human resource management and the business of sport. In Trenbirth, L. (ed.) *Managing the Business of Sport*. Palmerston North, New Zealand: Dunmore Press, pp. 163–184.

Wood, G. (2010, 21 July) Does racing have the will to enter a brave new world? *Guardian* (Bibliography). Online, available at: http://www.guardian.co.uk/sport/blog/2010/jul/21/racing-television-rights-2013 (accessed 2 March 2010).

Wood, R. and Payne, T. (1998) *Competency Based Recruitment and Selection*. Chichester: John Wiley & Sons.

Wright, J. (2006) Coaching for workplace success: Crisis and opportunity: Coaching older workers in the workplace. *Work*; 26(1): 93–96.

Yates, A. (1984) *Recreation Management Training Committee*. London: HMSO.

Yee, C.C. and Chen, Y.Y. (2009) Performance appraisal system using multifactorial evaluation model. *Proceedings of World Academy of Science, Engineering and Technology*; 41: 2,070–3,740.

Young-Kil, Y. (2005) Importance of hierarchical structure of psychological factors determining football performance. *International Journal of Applied Sports Sciences*; 17(2): 72–87.

Zylberstei, J. (2010) The Olivier Bernard judgment: A significant step forward for the training of players. *European Sports Law and Policy Bulletin: The Bernard Case, Sports and Training Compensation*; 1(1): 51–68.

Index

Page numbers in *italics* denote tables, those in **bold** denote figures.